On Ancient Philosophy

John Peterman
William Paterson University

Property of
St. John Fisher College
Lavery Library
Rochester, N.Y. 14618

THOMSON
━━━━✦━━━━™
WADSWORTH

Australia • Brazil • Canada • Mexico • Singapore • Spain
United Kingdom • United States

On Ancient Philosophy
John Peterman

Acquisitions Editor: Worth Hawes
Consulting Editor: Robert Talisse
Assistant Editor: Patrick Stockstill
Technology Project Manager:
  Julie Aguilar
Marketing Manager: Christina Shea
Marketing Assistant: Mary Anne
  Payumo
Marketing Communications
  Manager: Stacey Purviance
Project Manager, Editorial
  Production: Marti Paul

Creative Director: Rob Hugel
Executive Art Director: Maria Epes
Print Buyer: Linda Hsu
Permissions Editor: Bob Kauser
Production Service: Integra Software
  Services Pvt.Ltd., India
Copy Editor: Sara Dovre Wudali
Cover Printer: Thomson West
Compositor: Integra Software
  Services Pvt.Ltd., India
Printer: Thomson West

© 2008 Thomson Wadsworth, a part of The Thomson Corporation. Thomson, the Star logo, and Wadsworth are trademarks used herein under license.

ALL RIGHTS RESERVED. No part of this work covered by the copyright hereon may be reproduced or used in any form or by any means—graphic, electronic, or mechanical, including photocopying, recording, taping, Web distribution, information storage and retrieval systems, or in any other manner—without the written permission of the publisher.

Printed in the United States of America
1 2 3 4 5 6 7 11 10 09 08 07

Thomson Higher Education
10 Davis Drive
Belmont, CA 94002-3098
USA

For more information about our products, contact us at:
**Thomson Learning Academic Resource Center
1-800-423-0563**

For permission to use material from this text or product, submit a request online at http://www.thomsonrights.com. Any additional questions about permissions can be submitted by e-mail to thomsonrights@thomson.com.

Library of Congress Control Number: 2007920377

ISBN-13: 978-0-534-59572-2
ISBN-10: 0-534-59572-3

Acknowledgments

I have been fortunate to have many sources of inspiration, support, and criticism: Angelo Juffras, the Roberts (Talisse and Tempio), Dwight Goodyear, Peter Simpson, David Roochnik, John O'Connor, Henry Johnstone, and many others. Some read and improved this book with their comments, while others helped shape for me the possibilities within these texts. William Paterson University provided teaching and research opportunities.

For their patience and support, this book is gratefully dedicated to my family: Ellen, Jeremy, and Rossie.

Contents

Preface

This book will be an experience both in watching the first recorded developments in inquiry in the Western world and in practicing such inquiry for ourselves. It will enable those interested in ancient Greek philosophy, including those motivated by academic assignments, to get more out of their reading of these early texts by providing background on Greek culture, discussions of each thinker's ideas in his context, the cumulative issues among these thinkers as the notions of philosophy and inquiry develop, and how these issues continue into our present thinking and arguments. While some books focus on the mistakes of these early thinkers, the concern here is to see what sense can be made of their ideas and how they used their reason before discussing how they may have misused it.

Two popular beliefs, present in the philosophic community as well as the general public, currently interfere with our ability to read the Greeks: that they are too unlike us to be comprehensible or relevant and that their culture has been eclipsed by progress and is now of only historical interest.

On the first belief, our culture reinforces the foreignness of the ancient Greeks in many ways. Classical languages and literature are no longer a significant part of our education. Few people know ancient Greek, and its odd-looking alphabet does not encourage learning it. Our image of the simplicity of their lives (clothes, food, housing, employment, transportation, and so on) seems like a fantasy world compared with the complexities of our own. Our stereotypical ideas that their religion was dominated by superstition, their politics by war, and their personal relations by homosexuality make it easy for us to distance ourselves.

The second belief about progress presents an even greater obstacle. We are encouraged to believe that humankind has matured in the last three thousand years and that "early" cultures like the Greeks were by comparison childlike in their beliefs and institutions. The great technological developments (we so easily say "advancements") in our culture are impressive and obscure the similarities in the social, ethical, political, and psychological dimensions of the Greeks' world. Our lives do seem more complex due to the vast choices in our daily clothes, food, housing, and so on, where the Greeks had few. Four areas in which we claim progress are especially important for our orientation to early philosophy: religion, thinking, science, and inquiry; respectively, monotheism over polytheism, logic over rhetoric, method over trial and error, and a community of informed criticism over individual speculation.

In each of these areas the claims of progress seem to be more based upon satisfaction with the present than information about the past. By 525 BC, Xenophanes had clearly described the absurdities of having anthropomorphic gods and polytheism. By 400 BC, Athens reflected similar variations in religious experience to our present society: one and many gods, atheists and agnostics, absurd stories of miracles and serious reflection on human limitations, political displays of hollow piety and private sacrifices that promote social welfare. The United States, like the Greek states, continues state-sponsored observance, as in protecting our money with "In God we trust." The human needs expressed in the religious impulse seem not much changed and remain open to the same variety of questions and possible solutions.

Just as Aristotle introduced the clarity of formal logical reasoning into Greek philosophy, so it is claimed that continued developments in logical reasoning, such as modal logic and the analytic precision that symbolic logic has given us, have exposed the causes of ancient philosophical problems and superseded their discussions. Aristotle, however, did not invent logic; he classified and named its varieties, making it easier to be discussed and applied, a service like that of his modern counterparts. Although modern notation has changed, the arguments over where, if at all, demonstrative proofs are applicable in our experience continue to be the same now as then, as has the susceptibility of our reason to be persuaded by rhetoric.

We often think that modern science is based upon better methods, such as experimentation rather than trial and error and observation rather than speculation. The impressive developments of the last four hundred years, however, did not result from new thinking but from new technologies, such as the lens and improved clocks. The strength of modern science is not new discipline but the power of its observation, the ease of sharing results with people around the world, and the numbers of educated people involved in the conduct and critique of experiments. Whatever our modern science has accomplished, it has not freed us from such superstitions as astrology, lucky numbers, and UFOs.

Modern improvements in communication and participation seem to put Greek inquiry itself at a disadvantage. We have a large and well-informed scientific community supported by democratic freedoms that promote broad participation in the acquisition and evaluation of knowledge. The Greeks, however, were also united by their culture and language, and did form a coherent community for inquiry ranging over much of the Mediterranean basin that continually developed over the two hundred fifty years from Thales to Aristotle and was further elaborated in the Greek schools for another seven hundred years until the fall of Rome. Critiques of knowledge erupted in the cracks that appeared in the authorities of religion and tradition that had ruled for centuries. The possibilities and procedures of inquiry were developed as this question-bearing space between authorities widened.

After more than twenty years of teaching this material, I welcomed the opportunity to spend the last two years reviewing, that is, seeing anew these writers for the preparation of this book. I continue to be impressed that these thinkers are more dynamic and elusive than the simple caricatures we often make for purposes of comparison, storytelling, and textbooks. Our two-dimensional versions of their ideas make great rhetorical examples of early and immature human thinking. But when these ideas are made three-dimensional, the ideas become much nearer to our own and can participate in our discussions. Thinking itself and many of the important things we think about have not changed much in twenty-five hundred years. What should I do to be successful in life, and how will I know when I have succeeded? What field should I study or pursue? Why should anyone be ethical, and how ethical does one have to be? What can one know about the universe, and what does one do with what cannot be explained? The efforts the Greeks made to address these questions, coming out of a different time and place, help illuminate our efforts, providing a fresh view of how the world can be seen and a profound view of the role of these questions in our lives.

Introduction

It is through wonder that men now begin and originally began to philosophize; wondering in the first place at obvious perplexities, and then . . . raising questions about the greater matters too, e.g., the changes of the moon and of the sun, about the stars and the origin of the universe. Now he who wonders and is perplexed feels that he is ignorant . . . therefore if it was to escape ignorance that men studied philosophy, it is obvious that they pursued science for the sake of knowledge and not for any practical utility.
—Aristotle (*Metaphysics* 982b12–22)

Philosophy is an odd business. "Busyness" occurs in the world of efficiency and popular values, while philosophy operates at the edge in a place called "leisure," where nothing has to be done. Socrates emphasized this by taking his leisure in Athens' *agora* (marketplace) and accosting those who usually had better things to do. Leisure gives us time to pursue curiosity and wonder, to examine the inexplicable ideas and events that tempt our desire to explain and know. Philosophy arises in the space that exists between what we know by the self-evidence of common sense and demonstration in science or by religious faith. We do not wonder about deep beliefs or assumed knowledge. They are the framework we habitually use to direct our daily lives. Questions only arise in the cracks, as when Socrates wonders who or what he really is.

Our society usually promotes calculation as inquiry, like comparing the cost of goods or athletic statistics, applying a ready-made formula to a predefined problem. In philosophic inquiry the problem

1

itself and what solutions might count often need as much clarifying as how to go about solving it. It arises where nothing much is at stake. The Presocratics wondered about the basic stuff that underlies the manifold universe, but this was not part of any practical debate. If it were water, we would not drink more or bleed less.

Beginning in this safe zone between religious and scientific authorities, inquiry slowly spread, in time questioning even the ideas that justified the faith of religion and certainty of common sense. The willful Olympian gods represented the apparently random events in nature, but as inquiry found nature to be more regular, the gods' behavior seemed more like temper tantrums than thunderstorms. As inquiry expanded into nature, it began to examine the divine itself and to clash with religious authorities. In most Greek cities, state-sponsored religion was fairly liberal if the political norms of public worship were met. Poets like Homer and Hesiod described the gods, but there was no centralized liturgy or creed. Early thinkers like Xenophanes questioned how superior beings could have inferior morals and showed the folly of thinking that gods resemble humans. The notion of god evolved up to Aristotle's Unmoved Mover, whose only act is thought thinking itself.

Science was similar. Four elements composed the universe (earth, water, air, and fire) and four qualities (wet/dry and hot/cold), and these explained our experience. Asking which element is most basic did not alter this framework, and self-evidence did not favor any particular answer. Inquiry was free in its speculation, spreading from basic stuffs to all aspects of experience. Soon (after a century or two) the self-evident (flat earth, small sun, random weather, and so on) became at first controversial, and then a new self-evidency corrected these false ideas among the educated. A growing technological environment supported new ideas in science (as in our last two centuries), and inquiry thrived in a liberal society willing to entertain new theories that did not disturb political peace.

The development of inquiry is the great drama of Greek philosophy, as the wonder zone slowly grows between religion and science, the known and the supernatural. Nature and human nature gradually become free of the gods' control. The nature gods lose their autonomy from human affairs, becoming reflections of human activities and personas. Aphrodite changes from a simple fertility deity to the patroness of love affairs and seductions. Nature becomes less subject to divine whim and more subject to its own rules. The common Presocratic book title is *Peri Phusis, About Nature*. Examining the gods' domain as they are vacating it is precarious, as traditionalists can claim the gods still live there and charge impiety against intruders such as Anaxagoras, Socrates, and Aristotle. Nature was so regularized by Aristotle's time that many areas of human knowledge were recognized, from astronomy and meteorology to comparative anatomy and human perception.

These early thinkers' language seems brief and strange in our era of easy publication and luxurious use of space. The Presocratics wrote in a mixed oral-literary culture, with oral techniques like Heraclitus imitating the riddling aphorisms of the Delphic Oracle or the meter and motifs of epic poetry used by Parmenides and Empedocles. Pythagoras, Socrates, and many Skeptics believed philosophy required face-to-face interaction and refused to write. Plato converted the drama of theater into that of thought, creating fictional talks between historical characters to examine the life of reason. Aristotle's fame in antiquity was for his Platolike dialogues, now all lost. In his last twelve years in Athens, he wrote amendable lecture notes for courses or talks at his school, and these perpetual works-in-progress are his writings that have survived.

As philosophy inquires into and critiques Greek cultural wisdom, it applies this criticism to itself as well. Popular belief in religion and science are dogmatic rather than dynamic. Their claims are to be accepted more than explained. Some Presocratics present themselves as sages with special wisdom, but most engage their peers and society in discussing their ideas, usually written for distribution. Philosophy examines the forms and methods of discourse to reveal its problems and address these in philosophy itself, lest it fall victim to the very dogmatism it exposes. Enabling discourse among the multiple views embodied in and promoted by Plato's dialogues and Aristotle's lectures reflects this appreciation of human fallibility.

TEXTUAL CONCERNS

This book deals with Homer and Hesiod, thirteen Presocratic thinkers, several Sophists, Socrates, Plato, Aristotle, and the schools after Aristotle. About one fourth will discuss the Presocratics, another fourth each on Plato and Aristotle, and the rest on Greek culture and the remaining thinkers. For most of the Presocratics, we only have fragments of their original writings and later testimonies about their lives and ideas that help flesh these out. We have most of Plato's writings and many of Aristotle's, but others have been lost. For nine centuries the philosophic schools continued after Aristotle. We have lost most of their Greek founders' writings but have extended works and quotations copied by later Roman followers and Christian critics. These ancient writings in a foreign language from a historically distant culture require special textual cautions. Authorship is a problem as disciples attribute their ideas to their master and use his name for their own writings. Beyond these legitimate forgeries, illegitimate ones also had ample time and motive. Rival philosophic schools caused many false attributions trying to share the glory or smear the enemy. Hand-copied and oral transmission of texts may be inaccurate, and copyists could alter texts they did not understand. Texts may also have different meanings for an inner circle (esoteric) than for the less sophisticated public. Finally, what we know of these writers (their beliefs on religion, politics, education, science, and so on) is usually skimpy, composed of centuries-old gossip in a context of polemics and self-interest.

Die Fragmente der Vorsokratiker (Berlin, 1952) first edited by Diels and later by Kranz in six editions over the first half of the twentieth century, called "Diels-Kranz" (DK), is the standard reference work for the Presocratics and Sophists. It presents the known texts with comments on their development, influences, and authenticity. Its title is slightly misleading, as some of these thinkers lived well after Socrates. Their system of notation is commonly used to identify the fragments and testimony of the early thinkers and permits comparison of texts and translations. Each is given an identifying number roughly in chronological order (Thales is 11, Heraclitus 22, Democritus 68), and each testimony (noted as "A") or fragment ("B") is numbered, so DK 22 B 1 is the first fragment of Heraclitus. There are several English editions of selections from DK. Our translations use Kirk, Raven, and Schofeld's *The Presocratic Philosophers* (KRS) unless otherwise noted, and citations will simply give the DK fragment number. The surviving fragments and testimony are the accidents of history; someone happened to quote them and in turn have his writing preserved. No original texts survive, so we depend on an extended series of copyists. As the oral-literary culture continued into the Roman Empire, sayings of the ancients often circulated in varied forms. Most early writers like Plato and Aristotle, who referred to or quoted the ancients, were concerned more with developing their own ideas than with accurately quoting others and often used them as foils. Aristotle's student Theophrastus began the doxographical tradition to preserve the ancient writings. He collected the Presocratics' *Opinions about Nature (phusis)* in sixteen books, showing Aristotle as fulfilling their efforts. Others made their own selections from his work, shaping it to fit Stoic, Epicurean, or other agendas. His collection plus material of the later schools filtered through several later compilers, especially the *Vestusta Placita* (Oldest Opinions) in the first century BC and the *Placita* by Aetius in the second century AD, and is a major source of the sources of what remains. In their books on pagan thought, church fathers such as Clement of Alexandria or Hippolytus included ancient quotes. In the sixth century AD, when Simplicius comments on Aristotle, many of the early texts were disappearing, so he preserved longer quotations than his work required. This study of fragments is detective work, trying to connect the surviving excerpts like random pieces of an incomplete jigsaw puzzle.

Testimony is similarly affected by the many layers of sources who produced it. Each philosophical school promoted its ideas at the expense of its rivals. Stories of heroic, magical, and cowardly deeds and beliefs gathered around these historical figures. Christians then added their layer of ideological interpretation and slander to show the pagans' inferiority. The few neutral collectors, like Diogenes Laertius (third century AD) seem to indiscriminately record everything or at least the most entertaining stories. His use of current research material shows much still existed and how vicious the interscholastic rivalries were, especially the forgeries confusing who actually believed what. Some biographers created organizing systems, such as Sotion arranging thinkers by successions of teacher–student relationships within schools or Apollodorus making each thinkers' *acme* or prime occur at age 40 and to coincide with a major historical event, such as a battle or the founding of a colony. He also made each student forty years younger than the teacher, making his data more regular than accurate.

Since Socrates did not write, he has no direct textual tradition. His peers, including Plato, Xenophon, and Aristophanes, wrote dialogues with "Socrates" as a character. The chapter on Socrates will show how hard it is to construct a historical person out of these dramatic characterizations. Later schools promoted Socrates as a hero of reason and used him to support their teachings against others. His own beliefs may be as elusive as Plato's in his dialogues or Shakespeare's in his plays.

For Plato, we have twenty-six dialogues generally accepted as genuine, six that are disputed, and twelve that are generally rejected as forgeries. He supposedly destroyed his early theater plays. It is unclear if any philosophic dialogues are missing. Some dialogues suggest that more were written, but this is within the story and we do not know his intentions. The modern standard edition was compiled in 1578 by Henri Estienne (Stephanus in Latin), with most texts using his pagination (Stephanus numbers) in the margin next to the text. Many stories exist about Plato's life, including some in letters he may have written. Most scholars agree some of the letters are genuine and offer some insight into his work, but they differ on the insight.

After his first dialogue, Plato never reappears as a character. It is debated if the character "Socrates" speaks for Plato or depicts an ideal philosopher. This leads to the controversy of whether Plato's own voice appears on the surface of his work or only deeper in the dialogue as a whole. Like religions with simple teachings for beginners and more complex secret (esoteric) ones for adepts, some philosophers gave public audiences simplified teachings versus their private meetings with more serious students. Pythagoras warned his pupils that his private teachings were dangerous to the ignorant general public. Plato discusses such initiations in his writings, and the possibility of a system of hidden meanings in his works has encouraged more careful reading and produced some valuable commentaries. In the last fifty years, however, more commentators have adopted a literal rather than esoteric interpretation, while the last ten years have been more even. For a critique of the literal approach, see the introduction to my book, *On Plato*.

Of Aristotle's writings, we have about forty-six of the one hundred fifty to two hundred titles mentioned by the ancient sources. Of these forty-six, thirty are considered genuine. Immanuel Bekker in nineteenth-century Berlin made the standard modern edition of Aristotle's texts. In antiquity, Aristotle was most famous for his dialogues, of which none remains, giving us access only to his later writings.

It is always difficult to relate the various moments in a thinker's career and to evaluate their differences. Often our culture prefers the most mature expression as the culmination of a career. But maturity as the full use of one's powers may happen at various ages, some fairly early with long periods of decline (for example, in old age, Darwin investigated whether earthworms caused the rocks of Stonehenge to erupt in their current positions). Also, the form and content of later writings may only make sense in the context of issues arising out of earlier ones (for example, Aristotle's early work with rhetoric shows a major interest not directly seen in the later texts and thus is often missed).

For the Hellenistic thinkers, there is no one collection like Diels-Kranz for the Presocratics. Long and Sedley's *The Hellenistic Philosophers* creates a source book like KRS with a representative selection of original texts in Greek and Latin, their translations, and some philosophical commentary. The Athenian Hellenistic schools of Epicureans, Cynics, Skeptics, and Stoics took on various identities over their nine centuries. Plato's Academy cycled between science and skepticism, the *Timaeus* and Socratic ignorance, as it still does to scholars today. Many of our sources are polemics between schools or by Christians against pagans. Though meanings may be twisted, the quotations are usually accurate, at least in terms of the prior source. As this material evolved over centuries, there is a recurring patchwork effect, with biographies bleeding into each other and adding likely material to fill bare spots.

Due to limited space, quotations may be adapted, longer quotes rarely indented, and footnotes abbreviated. To be inspired by the writings of these thinkers is easy; to be able to sort out what they actually wrote or said is difficult. The adventure of trying to understand their world and ideas may even provide us with one of those Socratic moments in which we also better understand our own world and ourselves.

1

Historical and Cultural Background

To study and understand an ancient culture like that of Greece is the work of a lifetime. Information is sketchy about the lives and ideas of most Greek thinkers before Plato and Aristotle, only fragments of their writings plus stories and gossip collected centuries later. Lacking the shared culture we use to interpret more modern thinkers, we need some general idea of the five hundred years of Greek life and culture from Homer through Aristotle. Examining three main cultural elements—politics, war, and religion—will help orient us and keep us from making the Greeks too unlike us (primitive, illiterate, illogical, god-ridden) or too like us (our science uses lenses and clocks, our world is more technological than natural, war and disease are not as imminent or mysterious, our society is global with little sense of the local or the intimacy of the city-state). See H. D. F. Kitto's *The Greeks* for a readable introduction to Greek history and culture.

THE POLIS, COLONIES, AND EMPIRES

Greece has many geographic boundaries and defenses: islands, mountain valleys, and coastal plains divided by rivers and steep, rocky hills. It is a peninsula in the Mediterranean, like Italy, with another peninsula, the Peloponnese, extending off its end. The Aegean Sea between Greece and modern Turkey was then all Greek, including the Asia Minor coastal towns. The sea was dotted with islands, making for easy sailing and commerce. Many of the coastal and mountain valleys were cultivated and developed into a *polis* (city-state) supporting a small and stable population in the temperate climate. Athens was the largest of these with 20,000 male citizens and a total population with families, resident aliens, and slaves of 350,000 in 430,[1] while many cities had less than 5,000 citizens. They shared a common language (with dialects); religious gods, beliefs, and institutions such as the oracle at Delphi; a history back to the Trojan War; and an understanding that it was better to be Greek than anything else. Foreigners (barbarians) made sounds like "bar bar"; that is, they did not speak Greek.

Each *polis* developed its own constitution and government (oligarchy in Sparta and its allies, democracy in Athens and its allies) that would include different laws and punishments, its own economy (agriculture in Sparta and commerce in Athens, which imported food from the Black Sea), and its own patron gods (Poseidon in Sparta and Athena in Athens). The cities united, with truces and safe passage guarantees, to celebrate national religious and athletic festivals such as the Olympic games. These occurred every four years and provided the structure for dating events starting from the first Olympiad in 776.[2]

There was no standard political model in these cities. The despots of Persia were a negative model that some Greek tyrants imitated, but most cities followed a written constitution. Prominent citizens, such as Draco and Solon in Athens or Lycurgus in Sparta, were sometimes asked to rewrite the city's laws when social unrest, often by the landless poor, threatened political stability. A new city or rebuilding of an old one might invite political thinkers from across the Greek world to compete in writing a new constitution. Victorious cities would impose

---

[1] All dates will be BC (before Christ was born), also known as BCE (before the common era), unless otherwise specified.

[2] The date of the first games is unknown. The traditional date of 776 is more politics than history, used in a border dispute by Elis against Pisa. The site had several owners until Elis took it for good in 572. Events were dated using the number of the preceding Olympiad and then which of the four following years was current. The games began in the second full moon after the summer solstice, starting the Greek year in late summer instead of midwinter. An Olympiad was also a convenient four-year period for approximate dating; for example, Heraclitus was in his prime (age 40) during the sixty-ninth Olympiad (504–501). For the earlier Greeks, precise birth dates were rarely known.

their form of government and laws on those defeated in war: democ-racies by Athens, oligarchies by Sparta, and despotisms by Persia.

The land available for agriculture in any city was limited. The law that citizens hold land further reduced farms, as family plots would be divided each generation among the sons, shrinking each portion. It also limited population, as the local food supply could not expand. This created excess and landless populations that early Greek cities moved to an independent daughter city or colony, tied to the mother city by blood and politics but not usually economics. After the main-land, Asia Minor, and the Aegean islands were occupied, the colonists moved west to Sicily and southern Italy, following the coast to France and founding Marseilles, Nice, Monaco, Naples, and Syracuse. These settlements in the northern Mediterranean were called Greater Greece. The Greek West shared the frontier mentality of the Amer-ican West: independent, pragmatic, experimental, yet culturally ori-ented to the mainland. Several waves of new thinking came from the West: Parmenides's monism, Pythagoras's number mysticism, and several Sophists, such as Gorgias.

WAR

The Greeks, like most peoples, defined their culture through the memories and stories from their significant wars. In the United States,for example, the Revolutionary War formed the culture, the Civil War tested its unity, and the two World Wars challenged its autonomy and led to its current global, economic, and military relationships. The Trojan War made the Greeks a unified people separate from those to the East. The wars against the Persians seven hundred years later tested their ability to fight together. This ideal unity receded into legend, as the next hundred and fifty years saw almost constant war between varying groups of Greek cities. The end of the fifth century saw Athens versus Sparta in the thirty-year Peloponnesian War, which, like our Civil War or the First World War, showed both the heroic attraction and the destructive futility of war. Shifting alliances and attacks in the fourth century, with new desires for advantage and old ones for revenge, continued until Philip of Macedon ended the independent *polis* in 338.

The Trojan War was basic to Greek education. All ages and genders heard public and private recitals of Homer's poems and more war and homecoming stories in the tragedies. Homer's own attitude toward war is complex. He celebrates the glory of the heroic deeds but also shows how good things that make fighting worthwhile—friends, family, home—get destroyed. As the hero Achilles slaughters Trojans in revenge for killing his best friend, his anger takes him over the edge, and he attacks everything in his way, including the River Skamandros. Rivers are divinities to be honored, not attacked. He shows the irrational in war, especially the anger that carries him out of and back into the battle. This is great for winning battles but can lead to excess (*hubris*) and is too dangerous for a peacetime society. In the end, Achilles fears his own rage and warns Priam, who is retrieving his son Hektor's corpse, to sleep lightly and leave early lest his emotions reignite and he kills him. The *Odyssey* also ends with the irrationality of war and its cycles of revenge that only Athena's divine reason and justice can resolve. War is a place for doing great deeds, but Homer also shows alternative contests in the athletic funeral games and rhetorical exchanges as ways to civilize these activities. Greek civil life is based on the competition for excellence that grows out of this warrior culture and into the arguments of the law courts, the marketplace and assembly, the annual theater and athletic contests that were celebrated as public holidays, the public art and architecture, and the gibes between intellectuals.

The Trojan War, for the post-Homeric Greeks, happened long ago in a mythic time, when humans and gods were so close they even talked together. The stories included monsters and larger-than-life heroes: strong Achilles and wily Odysseus. The Persian War brought the Trojan War from the mythic past into real time. It again pitted the Greeks against the East, this time with known citizens as heroes and known Greek cities, mountain passes, and plains as battlefields. The great Persian Empire tolerated the small Greek cities to the west until their independent ways and military alliances encouraged some Persian allies to leave the empire. Then Persia created a vast army to crush the Greeks and invaded their peninsula twice, with King Darius in 490 and his son Xerxes in 480. The Athenians who stopped the Persians at Marathon were the heroes of the first invasion, while the Spartans slowed the Persians at Thermopylae and then led the Greeks in ending the second invasion at Plataea. These battles proved the Greek lightly armed spearmen (*hoplites*) to be the best fighters on offense and defense.

Defeating the Persians reinforced the Greek idea that their way of life was superior. However, this fragile unity of "being Greek" lasted

11

only while there was an enemy. Soon the Greeks resumed their mutual distrust and predation, stressing the growing differences between their two most powerful cities. Athens developed its sea power during the wars and then used it to "liberate" the Asia Minor towns and islands known as Ionia. These coastal cities formed the base of her allies and soon her empire. Sparta had the strongest army, maintained with a well-developed culture and system of allies. Democratic Athens had a commercial economy, naval power, and state-sponsored cultural life encouraging innovation. Oligarchic ("rule of the few") Sparta had an agricultural and slave economy and a traditional military-based society discouraging outside visitors or influences. These cities felt as superior to each other as they did to the barbarians. The Golden Age of Athens between the Persian and Spartan wars included large civil projects, such as rebuilding the war-destroyed Acropolis; a broad flowering of the arts; open commerce in goods and ideas; and the development of a refined, democratic, and comfortable life for its citizens (Corinth was the model of overly luxurious consumption). This contrasted with the conservative culture and institutions of Sparta, where military preparedness had men and women often living in separate barracks. Amassing wealth was outlawed, and duplicating the past was the artistic standard.

These two cities each created a military empire to protect and support themselves. Financing each alliance was a privilege of membership, so smaller cities tried to get the most protection at the lowest cost. Public diplomacy still spoke of unity against the Persians, but each power revised the war's history to serve its interest, as Herodotus enhanced the Athenian role and reduced that of the Spartans at the battle of Plataea.[3] After decades of undermining each other's allies and seeking strategic advantage in small local wars, in 431 they finally began their mutual destruction in the Peloponnesian War, named after Sparta's peninsula. The war lasted almost thirty years (431–404), and like modern Europe's Thirty Years' War, it was ideological, debilitating, and ultimately self-defeating. It weakened the Greek cities for their final capture by Philip of Macedon sixty years later. Neither Greek power recovered its expenditure of human and material resources. Victorious Sparta had nominal power over other cities for thirty years and even attacked Persia again. Then Thebes defeated Sparta, and a decade later Athens defeated Thebes. In the fifty years after Persia's

---

[3] Herodotus, *The Persian Wars*, Bks. 9–46.

defeat, the mostly peaceful Greek cities developed wealth, culture, and military power previously unseen. They then spent these for the next hundred years, with each city chasing dreams of empire but finding only faithless allies or old enemies with new armies. Persian diplomacy and foreign aid also worked to keep Greece divided and nonthreatening. This worked until Macedon brought a new type of war with the unimpregnable phalanx and strategic cavalry and a new type of peace in the elimination of independent city-states that Philip of Macedon imposed on Greece in 338.

For most Greek thinkers, war was a constant companion. Socrates fought in the Peloponnesian War. For Plato's entire life Athens was either at war or planning the next one. Many of his characters were soldiers. Thales predicted an eclipse that led to a truce in one war. Pythagoras was exiled from Croton in another. Melissus was a successful admiral for Samos against Athens. Empedocles thought a basic principle of the universe was the alternation of strife and love, war and peace.

War was where heroes proved themselves. When Plato was writing in the twilight of the Athenian Empire, popular belief still revered the heroes of the Trojan and Persian Wars and debated those in the Peloponnesian War. War and conflict continued to inform the context in Plato's dialogues. He describes a new type of hero, who battles to test his godlike qualities of reason. Socrates becomes the hero and martyr in this war, fighting in the *agora* against the socially destructive forces of prejudice, sophistic rhetoric, and false knowledge.

RELIGION

The bedrock of Greek religious belief was the local shrines and cults to nature deities inhabiting bodies of water, mountaintops, trees, and so on. Greek polytheism was always syncretic, able to merge the foreign gods of new settlers into its belief system. Plato's *Republic* begins with a festival in Athens for the foreign Thracian goddess Bendis. The ecstatic worship of Dionysus entered northern Greece in the eighth century and two hundred years later had a major temple in Athens. Orthodoxy usually only arose for local political purposes, as in Socrates' trial.

Early Minoans and Myceneans believed in a female nature goddess, caring for the earth's fertility and served by a male sky-god. From these arose a divine bureaucracy with over a dozen gods and goddesses. Hesiod's tale of generational fights among the gods may reflect this process of assimilation. For those used to the Judeo-Christian eternal God creating out of nothing, it is strange that Greek gods can be born while the universe remains eternal. Gods are immortal and bring order to the previously chaotic universe. This order is not forever fixed, as new gods can change it. This idea affects philosophy, where seeking the divine order in the external world reveals the ordering power in the human mind, which then becomes its own object of inquiry.

The original gods are Gaia (earth) and Ouranos (sky). Their son Chronos (time) castrates his father to take over his power. His son Zeus does the same to him. This third generation of Zeus and the Olympian gods and goddesses is described in Homer and Hesiod and in the heroic adventures of Heracles, Jason, and Theseus. These oral stories were handed down for centuries, some with alternate versions, as when Zeus frees his older siblings (whom their father ate and kept in his stomach). Does he force them to be regurgitated or cut them out with his sword? Both stories exist, showing the religious system is more inclusive and pluralistic than orthodox and exclusive. Greek orthodoxy is usually a political concern.

The Greek thinkers develop their ideas in a context of popular religious beliefs. As they examine the traditionally divine nature world, they increasingly describe regularity rather than divine caprice. Necessity or a thing's nature rather than divine choice determines what it is and how it acts. The nature gods as players are moved to the sidelines, shifting the focus to the rules they play by. The gods of right thinking and behavior still attracted followers, if only to use their imagery. Parmenides' poem begins with a religious scene but ends with no room for gods or any other things. Pythagoras depicts a divine force in the afterlife judging our behavior and fittingly rein-carnating our souls. Empedocles considers himself (and likely us too) a semidivine being with better reincarnations if he does not eat meat. Socrates calls himself a follower of Apollo, Zeus, or Eros, depending on whether the situation requires healing for the soul, justice, or love. He swears by the Dog, an Egyptian god. Most writers do not state clear religious views. Some, like Pythagoras, obscure their powerful divine knowledge so it does not fall into irresponsible hands. As Plato does not speak directly in his writings, he has been interpreted as either a religious mystic or an atheist. Aristotle rarely mentions gods but describes god in his *Metaphysics* as thought thinking itself, again linking the divine and the order of reason.

Religious language and beliefs were a part of daily experience with church and state united. Each house had a shrine with divine statues, and the political calendar had festivals for many gods and temples, such as the Dionysian theater festival in Athens. (Politics always enlists religious support. Even the secular United States has political holidays at Christmas and Easter, and its money reassures that "In God we trust.") A citizen's duty included respecting its gods. Such laws were mostly enforced in times of political stress, such as the impiety charges against Socrates by the reinstalled Athenian democracy, or Anaxagoras by those opposed to Pericles, or Aristotle by the anti-Macedonian revolt when Alexander died. More typical of Greek religious tolerance is the acceptance of a figure like Euthyphro, a religious zealot who admits he is not taken seriously. By the year 400 Athenian religious belief resembled the variety of belief and nonbelief in the United States today. Some held traditional beliefs in the temples, oracles, and stories of Homer's Olympian gods. Some reformers made these less superstitious and more rational and moral. Some followed newer, often imported religious movements such as the Orphic, Eleusinian, and other mystery cults. And some denied gods exist, at least any gods known by humans.

Traditional beliefs were both national and local. Each city had its own local ancient nature deities (rivers, trees, caves) and hero cults. Phaedrus in his Platonic dialogue parodies this in selecting a nearby tree to secure his oath (236d). Each city had its own patrons among the gods. Athena in Athens, Poseidon in Sparta, and Hera in Argos were special protectors of these cities but had their normal functions elsewhere. All Greeks shared the national holy sites, such as the divine colony on Mount Olympus, Apollo's oracle at Delphi, and Zeus's oak at Dodona. The gods were worshipped separately for each of their several qualities: Aphrodite as goddess of both physical fertility and high-minded love of virtue[4] or Zeus as human savior and king of the gods.

New religious beliefs mostly came from the East, gradually assimilating through the eastern and northern Greek cities. One important belief was the enthusiastic ("divinely possessed") and orgiastic ("merging of self into group") worship of Dionysus, an uncivilized god of intoxication and reincarnation. Reincarnation was not part of usual Olympian belief, as it was in Egypt and India.

---

[4] Plato's Pausanias uses this in his *Symposium* speech. Athens had two Aphrodite temples, a
local cult possibly tied to the city's courtesans (Uranian) and an older tradition
(Pandemos), possibly from Syria.

However, it was an early and persistent presence in Greek religious thinking, from the Dionysians and Orphics to the Pythagoreans and Plato. The Orphics developed from Dionysus worship and affected Pythagorean reincarnation beliefs and Plato's dialogues. They believed humans are of mixed divine and earthly origin, created with the blood of the slain Dionysus, who was resurrected by mixing with the ashes of the previous gods, the Titans. Our bodies imprison our divine souls, which can be freed after several reincarnations of the ascetic Orphic life and then initiation into the Dionysian orgies. Our life here is a test of our fate in the next. The similar beliefs in Christianity led many Greeks to see it as just another such mystery cult.

The Eleusinian Mysteries created an optimistic view of Hades and how humans can gain a better life there. Demeter and Persephone got new roles preparing humans for death. These Mysteries had a two-step initiation leading to the final revelation of the life-renewing seeds of a wheat stalk, imaging the soul's renewed life in the next world. The Mysteries required only purification through initiation with no need for ongoing ritual. *Once life is understood correctly, it will be lived correctly.* This idea that to know the good is to do the good will echo through philosophy. Mystery initiates swore to (and did) keep secret their rituals, which would be unintelligible and dangerous for outsiders.

Orphism built upon these earlier Eleusinian Mysteries, preparing for a better next life. Orphism influenced Pythagoras, whose religious beliefs influenced his community, mathematics, and astronomy. He also believed in the denial of bodily desires and purifying the soul in a series of reincarnations. From the Mysteries, Pythagoras took a centralized priestly authority, secret initiation, super-rational revelation, and the promise of a better life for the soul in the next world.

Among those with some learning, scientific inquiry reduced the arena of divine activity and drove it from most daily affairs. As Aristotle said, rocks fall down due to their downward nature, not from divine whim. While the religious sought divine help in times of need, most cultured Athenians knew arguments for the earth being round, the apparent motion of the sun across the sky, and natural events like rainbows or lightning not requiring divine involvement.

Xenophanes wrote many of the first arguments against multiple humanlike gods and supernatural explanations, setting up the basis for later atheism and agnosticism. He attacked the Olympian gods on several fronts. If we use the gods to explain natural phenomena, we will never be able to understand and use nature to improve our lives.

Divine intervention interferes with our efforts to care for ourselves. The gods' sexual and social amorality is fitting for forces of nature, but as they became more human, they became our role models. Divine beings know and do the good, so either the stories need to be corrected or these gods need to be rejected. Finally, the religious effects of cultural relativism showed that when we make our gods in our own image, each culture makes their gods resemble themselves. He even pushed this further: "But if cattle and horses or lions had hands . . . horses would draw the forms of the gods like horses, and cattle like cattle, and they would make their bodies such as they each had themselves" (KRS 169).

The gods we imagine are idealized projections of ourselves. If there are gods, why should they have a human or any shape at all? Do they offer us direction or confusion in guiding our behavior? Are they ordering principles in nature or obstructions? Such questions were part of fifth-century religious discussions. The culture that prosecuted Socrates was closer to the minority opportunistic McCarthy era witch-hunts than to a rigid orthodox majority, as in Puritan Massachusetts.

FROM RELIGION TO PHILOSOPHY

We often use religious language to express our sense of wonder ("Jesus Christ"), even in profane situations. Our early experiences of wonder or awe are given religious accounts: the tooth fairy, Santa Claus, fate, and so on. We keep using this language that pulls in two ways, back into the tradition beyond our control but also into language that can give an account of this. Such religious language at first is a Band-Aid, enough of a grasp to begin connecting it to the rest of our knowledge. When sensitivity wakes us from our habits, we see new connections and seek to account for them. Religion gives the security and stability for inquiry to proceed, even when this inquiry might undermine the religion itself.[5]

Socrates' religious posing in Plato (swearing "by the Dog," a god in Egypt, or claiming to follow Zeus or Apollo, or repeating religious

---

[5] In the 1950s, Sidney Hook saw religious myths as dangerously antirational, a fascist and communist tool, while Ernest Van Den Haag held religious myths less vicious than secular ones and needed to explain the inexplicable. Their debate over the value of this mythic penumbra of reason is in Hook's *The Quest for Being* (New York: St. Martin's Press, 1961).

myths) shows this tension, whether he actually has some faith or these are the ironic gestures of an agnostic or atheist. In the *Meno*, he links a religious story to his faith in inquiry, "We will be better men, braver and less idle, if we believe that we must search . . . rather than believe that it is not possible to find out what we do not know" (86 b–c). The Myth of the Metals and other "noble lies" in the *Republic* are religious stories to fill our brains, like Santa Claus and the tooth fairy, until we can understand better ones.

As inquiry proceeds, aided by religious language and myths, it may affect these religious ideas as well. In *The Firmament of Time*, Loren Eiseley shows this in the generations of scientists from 1650 to 1850 who explored the earth's age in a series of issues from fossil formation and mountain building to ice ages and evolution.[6] Each informed his inquiry with current religious ideas, seeking to better appreciate God's handiwork in his Creation. But each found this handiwork took more time than current belief provided. Each limited his explanations by his beliefs but suggested a new compromise to the next thinker to include new data. In 1600, Christians counted the generations in the Bible to see that the creation was 5,361 years ago. But for species to disappear and leave fossils or mountains to thrust up and erode needed thousands upon thousands of years. One way to find this time is with the analogical approach, described by St. Augustine in his *Confessions*, finding a symbolic meaning in the Bible's account. The "six days" of creation symbolized a series of geological epochs, providing the millennia needed to form mountains and evolve species. Radioactive dating now puts the present earth at 4.5 billion years old. Perhaps God's creation is a series of Big Bang expansions followed by black-hole contractions.

What determines when religion or science opens or closes to new inquiry and viewpoints? For Eiseley's European Enlightenment, the exploration voyages of the 1500s expanded the scope and mission of science. New lands, cultures, and species required a larger, more universal organization of facts. Concurrently, the religious authority upholding the traditional Catholic beliefs was splintered by the Reformation. Religion became a matter of choice, not inheritance. Thus, in both science and religion new beliefs and facts were in the air. Philosophy, like Lucretius's gods, exists in the interstices between the known beliefs of religion and the believed knowledge of science.

---

[6] Loren Eiseley, *The Firmament of Time* (New York: Atheneum, 1965).

These spaces grew, welcoming inquiry and the multiple perspectives of modernity.

The Greeks also had a cultural renaissance after a dark age of reduced commerce and communication. Renewed contact with a larger world brought new religious options and experiences to be incorporated into the cultural base. Herodotus in his fifth-century travelogue describes the odd customs of many barbarian ("Greekless") peoples with an openness of observation and curiosity not found in a culture that has all the answers. This inquiry-friendly climate informed the speculations and experiments of the early Greek thinkers, resulting in the grand enlightenment projects of the tragic poets, Thucydides historical dialogues, and Plato and Aristotle's explorations of systematic thinking.[7]

Religious language and imagery were common in Greek communication. Everyone knew the stories of the gods from Homer, Hesiod, Pindar, and the tragedians and used them to illustrate their ideas or justify their actions. This set of images also helps in discussing the metaphysical realm, another larger-than-usual view of reality, which also tries to depict the intangible basic nature of the universe and human beings. Nonbelievers like Parmenides appropriated this religious language and imagery for secular purposes to expand our vision beyond the limits of our physical world. We can think in a religious way without being religious, think about gods and goddesses without believing in them, and use their divine qualities for other purposes.

This review of ancient Greek culture provides some feeling for Greek life so that we may be less misled by false similarities or differences. Politics and war played a bigger role in their lives, while religion played about the same in both. We can afford more leisure than they, but we occupy it with more work or mindless television, just as most were too busy to speak with Socrates in the *agora*. The leisured mental space where philosophy occurs is as difficult to find today as it was then. What follows will describe experiences in exploring this space. The Greeks found these to be as strange and provocative as we do. Not all Greeks were philosophers, but anyone then—as now—could be. We have looked at a few areas of Greek culture that inform any inquiry into ancient Greek texts and thinkers, to which we will now turn.

---

[7] cf. Solmsen, *Intellectual Experiments of the Greek Enlightenment* (Princeton, NJ: Princeton University Press, 1975).

2

The Presocratics

Inquiry, as we have seen, exists in the precarious space between the assumed knowledge of religion and science. The investigations of the first Greek philosophers in this space concerned the foundations of the world and our experience of it. Their work regularized inquiry and extended its application to ever-greater areas of experience. The recent development of the social sciences similarly shows inquiry bringing new areas of our behavior and environment under scientific examination and explanation. For example, language was seen as a given aspect of human nature, its variations supported by cultural myths, such as the tower of Babel. There was nothing to inquire about. Now linguistics studies the common roots, structures, and evolution of languages, creating an area where problems can be pursued rather than explained away. The Presocratic thinkers began this orderly and expanding application of reason to the wonders of the world.

IONIA

Homer and Hesiod

As Greece was reviving from its dark ages in the eighth century, Homer and Hesiod composed poems summarizing their cultural legacy, as poets had been doing for at least the four hundred years since the Trojan War. As Dante stood between the closed medieval religious system and the renaissance opening of inquiry into self, society, and the universe, so these poets began to shift the focus of such stories from scripture (exact repetition) and chronology to narration and inquiry. Hesiod's complaints against his brother stealing his inheritance begin to express the individual's desire to understand the nature of justice and the gods' role in it, while Homer desires to understand why events happen as they do and the place of human control and responsibility in them. They create some space for humans to examine both the gods and themselves.

Homer's version of the Trojan War and its heroes' homecomings presented a new rational and dramatic ordering that became the most popular and the standard for the rest of Greek history.[1] The creative freedom of the Homeric poet existed in a delicate balance between divine and human inspiration. The basic plots were well known, but the poet controlled which episodes to include and how to connect them, as well as choice of words and poetic devices. The audience's expectations controlled the stability of these stories, as in our acceptance of a new translation of a standard text like the Bible or the movie version of a popular book. Innovations of plot or diction were accepted if they kept enough of the traditional substance while providing a more pleasing sense or style. Homer's version set the standard in the oral culture until the texts were written down and stabilized in the next century.

A central concept Homer used to rationalize his material is the notion of *crisis,* the moment of judgment, a test or trial that reveals the character or basic nature of a person and determines his or her fate. The poet selected which critical events best revealed the rational order in the otherwise merely time-ordered series of episodes, finding the logic of a narrative in the events of a chronology.[2] The tragic poets later push this further by shrinking time into one critical twenty-four hour period, when the meaning of the action and the fate of the characters is revealed. Four hundred years later, Thucydides tells his history of the Peloponnesian War using critical discussions between its combatants to reveal the ideas and motivations that caused the events in the war to happen.

---

[1] We lack any historical evidence for the identity of the poet "Homer." Did one poet write both poems? If there were two, was one a woman? Was Homer an honorific name attached to a poem as it continued to be altered by later poets? Was Homer a name for a school or style that continued after he died? We do not know.

[2] Note the striking difference from the episodically ordered *Epic of Gilgamesh,* where there is no center of gravity or defining moment.

Homer similarly compresses time. Out of ten years of battle, his *Iliad* describes only the several weeks that determine its outcome. He omits the well-known events—the judgment of Paris, the flight of Helen, Agamemnon sacrificing his daughter for the Greek fleet's sailing, the deceit of the Trojan horse, the killing of King Priam and enslaving of Queen Hekabe—all are left out and heighten the tension because of their absence. The audience knows the general plot but not how this poet will reveal the meaning of these events.[3] The Greek army suffered from divided leadership. Agamemnon was the most powerful general, but Achilles the best fighter and Odysseus the most clever at strategy. Homer finds the key to resolve this tension in the anger of Achilles. After Agamemnon slights him, he angrily withdraws from battle to watch the Trojans push the Greeks back to their ships and kill his best friend Patroclus. Achilles then turns his rage against the killer, the main Trojan hero Hektor, whose death is also that of Troy. The book closes with the doomed King Priam reclaiming his son Hektor's body from the doomed Achilles. Anger clearly wins the war, but at what cost?

The *Odyssey* similarly selects the critical weeks in a ten-year sequence of events. Homer inherited a series of episodes variable in number and length and created a tight dramatic structure in a limited time frame. He determined the *cosmos* (order), explaining why things occurred as they did, creating a human ordering of time rather than vice versa. Ten years after the war, Odysseus is the only hero who has not returned, and hope for his return officially ends when his son Telemachus becomes an adult and is able to rule on his 20th birthday. In Odysseus's absence, Ithaka has no ruler. Many suitors are vying to marry his presumed widow Penelope and assume the throne. Now that Telemachus might inherit the throne, they plan to kill him, and this crisis motivates the plot. At the same critical moment, Odysseus is released by the goddess Kalypso and begins his trip home. Both go on a journey to test their mettle, Telemachus crossing Greece while Odysseus crosses the Mediterranean. The two stories are told in parallel time sequences until they meet in the swineherd's tent on

---

[3] Children love to hear the same story repeatedly, as adults repeatedly see the same movie. The movie dialogue never changes, and a knowing audience can repeat all the lines. But there is tension in a live story over whether the text will change. If an adult skips some of a bedtime story, the child invariably knows. But additions and elaborations are often greeted with delight, making both listening and telling more interesting. It is pleasurable to bring the world into a new focus.

their farm and together face the final heroic test by killing the 108 suitors. Homer sets the enforcing of justice as his dramatic center first by Odysseus killing the suitors and then by Athena ending the wars of vengeance, just as in the *Iliad* Zeus's justice is fulfilled when Achilles kills Hektor, with himself to die soon after. Homer moves Odysseus' travel adventures, likely the best-known part of the book, out of the center by having Odysseus relate these to his hosts in Phaeakia.

Homer gives both traditional and more modern explanations. He relates the divine stories of heroes and gods from the Greek dark ages but also begins the renaissance of reason by explaining the affairs of humans, gods, and the universe, since they are all rationally ordered. He describes human choice more than divine intervention. Odysseus repeatedly succeeds with his Athena-like reasoning instead of relying on the gods for aid. Homer makes Zeus describe how humans blame the gods to avoid taking responsibility:

> Oh for shame, how the mortals put the blame upon us gods,
> for they say evils come from us, but it is they, rather, who
> being reckless win sorrow beyond what is given, as now
> lately, beyond what was given, Aigisthos married the wife
> of Atreus' son, and murdered him on his homecoming,
> knowing he would also die, for we ourselves had told him.[4]

Although the gods sometimes help, the humans accomplish most deeds by themselves. Athena, in disguise, encourages Telemachus to visit Menelaus, but the boy makes the trip by himself. While the gods intervene more in the *Iliad,* it is not their capricious desires that decide human fate but the rule of a more basic force called Necessity. When Zeus tries saving his half-mortal son Sarpedon from death, the other gods remind him that mortals by Necessity die. The Presocratic inquiries will pursue the understanding of this divine Necessity.

Homer's world is not a god-benighted one of superstition and fate. Humans think and then act upon their reasoning. Justice, divine and human, is a matter of order, not whim. Humans come to realize that they share the rational ability that formulates the organizing principles of universal order. Rather than simply using the gods to explain why events take place, thus prohibiting further human

---

[4] Homer, *Odyssey*, trans. R. Lattimore (New York: Harper & Row, 1967), Bk. I, lines 32–37. Adapted.

inquiry, here the actions as rational can be explained and inquired into, opening rather than closing further human reasoning.

Hesiod's view is both more human and mundane and more supernatural and superstitious. His *Works and Days* is a self-help book addressed to his estranged brother, advising what to expect from life and how to attain it. His approach is to work hard, worry, and not take chances. "Observe measures. Timeliness is best in all matters" (694). The brother, evidently, knew a different way to success and bribed officials to get the greater share of the family inheritance. His book details the proper daily activities in a world where gods are hard to know or please. He explains five historic ages of man (gold, silver, bronze, heroic, and the present iron) in a degenerating pattern of growing estrangement from the gods and social disorder.

Justice, both divine and human, keeps Hesiod's iron generation from completely dissolving. Gods grant prosperity to the just and punish evildoers. If not for this, Hesiod says he would follow his brother's easier evil path. This justice concerns proper proportion in human thinking and action and is reflected in the balance of nature itself. Determining this proportion is a key motivation for the Presocratic thinkers. Yet alongside this growing sense of the power of reason, Hesiod remains quite superstitious. Daily activities are ritualized to show respect for the gods, with prohibitions against making water while facing the sun or trimming fingernails at a religious festival. Hesiod fluctuates between rationally explaining a rational world and superstitious accounts of the supernatural. He is still hemmed in by the precariousness of life, threatening an end not only to us but to our entire Iron Age.

Large pieces remain of Hesiod's other two works, the genealogy of the gods in his *Theogony* and the description of the shield Heracles used to defeat Ares' son Kyknos. This divinely-made shield, like that of Achilles described in the *Iliad,* depicts the universe of gods and mortals at peace and in war with figures so lifelike they appear to move. The elaboration of its scenes makes its recitation a tour de force. The gods' begettings in the *Theogony* are reminiscent of the biblical human begettings in the Old Testament and emphasize their being in nature, unlike the Judaic God outside of it. Thus, Greeks can inquire into aspects of nature without being sacrilegious. The basic stuff of the universe, as predating the gods, is fair game for the early thinkers.

As the renaissance of Greek culture and commerce gathered steam in the seventh century, a gap of intellectual uncertainty arose between the more fixed certainties of religion and science. Religion claims a divine order accessible to faith and prayer but not reason. Science claims an order explained by the most reasonable theory based on common experience or facts. Hesiod presents a pregap stable worldview accounted for by facts and prayer. His listing of the proper days of the month for each farming activity, how to purchase and train the right animals, and how to raise the best family are all simple reports of facts for him. However, when he discusses the gods' whims controlling the winds or a person's fortune, then reverence and moderation are the rule; human reason has no access to the big picture of divine reason. Philosophy arises where the gods leave humans room to think and science shows that it does not have all the answers. In seventh-century Greece, the expanding worlds of commerce, literacy, colonization, political pluralism, craft production, and so on were finding ever more experiences not determined by either past facts or divine rituals and dogma.

THE MILESIANS

We do not know how many thinkers after Homer and Hesiod participated in this developing inquiry into the ways of gods and men, but our first records come from the cities of Ionian Greece (now the Aegean coast of Turkey), especially the independent and peaceful town of Miletus. Between the seventh and sixth centuries, three related thinkers here speculated on the basic stuff of the universe. Thales thought it was water, his pupil Anaximander thought it was the Unlimited, and his pupil Anaximenes thought it was air. As we have seen, for the Greeks the universe came before the gods. There was something out of which came the gods themselves (thereafter immortal), who then organized this stuff into a *cosmos* (order). This basic stuff was fair game for inquiry.

Determining the basic stuff of the universe introduces the world to the problems of metaphysics. This term was first used by a later Aristotle editor to name the work that appeared after ("meta") his book on natural science ("physics"). It also means "beyond physics," as this inquiry examines the rules and structures underlying the world and science as we know them. As these principles cannot be directly experienced by us, it requires thinking beyond the limitations of our physical experience to contemplate the stuff and its organization that makes this world possible. In Greek atomic theory, for example, no one could see these invisible particles that explained the organization of things in nature. Today's Big Bang theory is similarly beyond observation, being at the beginning of time. It also has unanswerable problems: What went bang, and why and when? The Big Bang might be as far back as we can coherently imagine, but it is not a self-explanatory and absolute beginning. To speculate what was the situation before this is to seek a more satisfactory order of things, though not yet directly verifiable.[5]

Metaphysical inquiry is always in danger of falling into extremes of either the occult or hyperrationalism. One claims a disconnect between being and human reason, seeking explanations in the supernatural. The other forces experience to fit rational structures, as Voltaire's *Candide* or Parmenides' "One." There are dangers of superstition and fantasies of reason when human thought ventures beyond the confines of ordinary experience, but there also are opportunities for thinking outside the limits of current prejudice, cultural authorities, and the accidents of experience. Metaphysics provides an open space for inquiry and reason, where ideas gain somewhat of a life of their own.

Inquiry arises only where a hole appears in the coverage of explanations. No practical concerns were affected by the search for the basic stuff. It made no difference to our behavior. It was a problem neither the gods nor the facts gave any account of or had any interest in doing so. Neither religion nor science supported or condemned it. Later thinkers did see implications for these theories; for example, if there were just one kind of stuff and it could somehow be experienced directly, then the multiplicity of experience would disappear. But the Milesians were just wondering which stuff is more basic than the others.

The Milesians became curious that while the gods who ordered the universe were well explained, the material stuff they ordered was not. A unified theory with a single source of all things is the most mentally satisfying but difficult to sustain when explaining how this

---

[5] As the nature of God is outside our experience, discussions about it resemble metaphysical speculation and are worth practicing. If God is unlimited, does She/He/It exist outside or in all of time and space? How can we conceive of either since we are always limited to one time and place? Can we conceive any form of infinity (God's power, knowledge, substance)? If the universe was created, what was God doing before this? As God is perfect and unchanging, can God really "do" (create) anything without changing? If motion always has a cause, what caused the first motion? For a lighter look at these issues, read Italo Calvino's *Cosmicomics* (New York: Harcourt Brace, 1965), about life in a black hole.

one came to be a *many*. What causes the original one to diversify? If these differences are real, then was not the initial unity only apparent and merely covered up the more basic plurality of original stuffs? Once the basic stuff becomes a many, then the limiting of this many to some definite number also becomes problematic. Take the periodic table of elements. In 1996, there were 112 elements: 29 discovered since 1900, and 14 in the last fifty years. Our ability to see such elements depends on the technology of observation. The recently discovered elements have extremely short life spans and are observable only with the recent apparatus of subatomic particle research, which also shows that the elements in the periodic table have elements. The possibility of an indivisible smallest division of matter, the *atom* (uncuttable), resists any resolution. Our periodic table of the elements is useful to explain how basic substances combine and separate. But there is no proof that we have determined all of these substances, and it is clear these are composed of more elementary particles. The way of pluralism with many basic stuffs can reach relative closure defined for a particular purpose, such as the periodic table, but cannot attain any final resolution. On the other hand, the unified approach with a single stuff as the root of all things has difficulty explaining how the multiplicity in the universe is real. The many things keep reducing into some form of the original stuff from which they came, and then they are no longer many things. The Greeks, as we will see, took both approaches and worked through the problematic consequences of each.

Thales

Most of the Presocratic inquiries into the stuff of the universe took the unified approach. Thales opens the story of recorded Greek philosophy with the claim that there is only one stuff and that it is water. We have no actual fragments of his writings. We have comments on his activities by Herodotus and about his beliefs by Aristotle. Thales had an enduring reputation, making most of the Seven Wise Men lists of the sixth-century Greek world. Stories about his wisdom were widely circulated. He predicted an eclipse of the sun in 585 that affected a battle between the Medes and the Lydians. He observed one year that the climate was unusually favorable for a large olive crop, so he bought up all the olive oil presses and made a fortune renting them out. He calculated the height of a pyramid by measuring its shadow when his own shadow was just as long as he was tall. He temporarily altered the course of a river so that an army could ford it without having to build a bridge. He proved his reasoning could solve everyday problems, but he seemed to prefer more abstract inquiries where it is not even clear what formula to use, much less how to perform the calculations. He experimented with applying his reason at the boundaries of experience or, in the case of water, at the very foundation that makes experience itself possible.

Water is an impressive prime-stuff candidate. The Greeks had four main types of stuff: earth (all solid matter), air, fire, and water. Water comes out of the air as rain and out of the earth as springs, dew, and mists, and even fire creates water vapor and steam given off by hot foods. A cold rock in the morning sun appears to give off steam from within. When cut, solid animal bodies reveal watery blood inside, just as fruits and vegetables contain juices. New life comes from watery semen. The shields of both Achilles in Homer and Herakles in Hesiod are bounded by the Ocean River, the surrounding water that limits the land. Most objects in the right conditions reveal that they contain water, and our not seeing it only shows our physical limitations. The gods, who see all things, swear their oaths upon water as the holiest of things.

We do not know the arguments or observations Thales used to support his primacy of water nor his claims that the earth rests upon it. Aristotle claims he meant the earth floats like a piece of wood in water, but Thales knew the earth is made of stone and sinks in water, so this would have to be special water or earth. One possibility is the Egyptian idea that the earth floats because it is bowl shaped. KRS discusses several ancient near eastern stories agreeing that the earth in some way rests on the water beneath.[6] In either case, water is the stuff surrounding the universe, just as the River Ocean surrounds the earth. We see a blue substance when we look at the sky, and it might as well be water.

Aristotle also mentions Thales' ideas on motion, particularly the presence of souls in inanimate (Lat. "soulless") things. He claimed that the magnetic stone (and amber) had a soul because it could cause other things (iron) to move, and that all things are full of gods, as the principle of motion is divine and present through the soul. The Greek *psyche* (soul) originally meant the life force in things permitting them to move, especially humans. If life is the cause of motion, then were it

---

[6] Kirk, Raven, and Schofield (KRS), pp. 91–94.

destroyed, all motion and the known universe would also cease. It must go on living, as even disembodied souls do in Homer's Hades. The Egyptians developed this idea into a system of reincarnation, which was never a mainstream Greek belief but had some significant later proponents. The early Greeks cared for the soul by appeasing the gods and ensuring the continuity of life, while Aristotle pursues the physics problem within the religious one, seeking the origin of motion, the Unmoved Mover. Thales' comments on gods dwelling in all things and the magnet's soul causing other things to move show the use of religious language to further his nature inquiry beyond usually accepted religious belief. If the presence of souls or gods provides a framework to examine how and why things move, then religion becomes the unexpected partner of inquiry.

Using religious language does not preclude philosophic activity any more than scientific language does. Philosophy lives in the quest for certainty and ceases at either of the extremes of natural or supernatural certainty. Religious or scientific language and ideas provide an essential framework for pursuing our wonder and desire for completeness and security. Thales seeing gods in all things gave him hope, perhaps, that in time he could understand these things, as they were endowed with order instead of chaos. That the magnet had a soul both created and made problematic the relation between that soul and his own. It also made possible that he could discover what this relation was.

Anaximander

Anaximander was a younger fellow-citizen of Thales and probably his student. They shared interests in astronomy, the geometry of land surfaces and navigation, and the orderly system of natural changes, as in meteorology. He was also involved in practical projects like constructing the first Greek sundial, drawing a map of the known world and possibly one of the heavens, perhaps leading a colonizing expedition to the Black Sea, and predicting an earthquake in Sparta. His legacy, however, is much more rich and complex than that of Thales. He was known for a book called *On Nature,* a descriptive title perhaps attached later. For Thales we only have a guide to navigating by the stars. Thus, more of Anaximander's ideas have been preserved, but we do not know which may have come from his mentor.

Anaximander and Thales differ on what the basic stuff is, how all things come to be from it, and how the earth is held in place. He believed the earth does not move, as it is in equilibrium at the center of the universe, with no reason to go in any one direction more than another. This idea of natural balance is the basic principle in his general theory of natural change. His basic stuff of the universe is the *apeiron*, the unlimited or undifferentiated, pure divine-like (immortal) being, out of which come to be all things that we can differentiate by qualities and names. It is a level of being more fundamental than the usual four elements and not subject to their limitations. As the limited things come out of it, there is a balance among them to which they must adhere: cycles such as change of seasons; opposites such as night and day, youth and age, hot and cold, wet and dry. To be a thing is to be in balance with other things. Nature is the supporting web of these balanced relations. Anaximander's one remaining fragment, later quoted by Simplicius, describes this balance among the limited beings in terms of divine justice. He says that it is neither water nor any other of the so-called elements but some other *apeiron* nature from which come into being all the heavens and the worlds in them. And the source of coming-to-be for existing things is that into which destruction, too, happens, "according to necessity; for they pay penalty and retribution to each other for their injustice according to the assessment of Time."[7]

Simplicius wrote a thousand years after Anaximander. As ancient Greeks did not use quotation marks (KRS put them in), it is debated exactly which terms belong to Anaximander, but it is clear that he models his notion of natural law and enforcement on divine law and enforcement. The existence of the *apeiron* and the balance of things that issue from it are as necessary and permanent as the fate and justice enforced by Zeus himself. Greek justice is concerned with measurement and calculation, proper portion and proportion, and evolves from a material concern to one of ideas. Assessment determines what adjustment, if any, needs to be made. Here, time itself does the assessing. With enough time and at the proper time, natural balance will be restored, often through the work of natural cycles. (Greece had clearly separated rainy and dry seasons, as well as summer and winter. There were also cycles on a much larger time scale, such as the earth slowly drying out and then flooding. Religious stories of a flood covering the earth came from the East, suggesting that the earth was more watery in the past.)

---

[7] From *Simplicius* (DK12A9), quoted in KRS, pp. 107–108.

All the basic stuff accounts faced the problem of why and how any one could become a many and why this particular many. The original chaos of the universe was amenable to reason and ratios and thus could be ordered by division into more or less stable kinds. The Milesians seemed to take these as givens to answer the "why." Thales seemed interested only in the what and not the how. Anaximander addresses the how by making a parallel with divine justice. Anaximenes next will take on the how directly, as more of the given becomes matter for inquiry. Some later commentators give Anaximander a principle of motion to organize the Unlimited, such as a vortex to push heavier elements (earth and water) into the center and pull lighter ones (air and fire) out to the edges, but there is no reliable evidence for this. The origin of motion needs no more explanation than the origin of the universe. His primal stuff just is, the ancestor of both Parmenides' One and Aristotle's Unmoved Mover, while the limited stuff moves and must move to maintain the balance.

Anaximander also explained a variety of natural phenomena. The earth was a flat circular disk with a 1:3 height-to-diameter ratio and landmasses on the top surface. When the earth was created, there was a husk of flame around its atmosphere. This eventually broke up into a number of circles or wheels, becoming the sun, moon, planets, and stars. These lights are seen through holes in the air as the wheels carry them around the earth. The clogging of these holes explains alterations in the moon's light and eclipses, but an explanation for what covers the holes and why it is in such a regular pattern has not come down to us. Some justice in the balance of light and dark could be at work here as well.

Ancient writers also described his interest in the development of human beings from other animals, especially fish. This fits with his cycle theory that the world used to be more watery, with perhaps only water animals to start. As more land emerged, some of the fish became land animals. This is not a general notion of evolution or survival of the fittest, but it has the rudiments of mutation and adaptation. Conditions on the earth were once far different, and the ensuing changes have brought about different forms of life. Although traditionally gods control such changes, Anaximander neither mentions them nor discounts them. The gods are totally absent from his accounts.

Anaximenes

Of the three Milesians, we know the least about Anaximenes. He is not known for interests in geometry or astronomy nor practical applications of his learning. His main contribution is the theory of condensation and rarefaction to explain how all things are produced out of his basic stuff: air. This is more observable than Anaximander's natural balancing or Thales' presence of gods as the source of motion and change.

As air condenses, it successively changes into wind, cloud, water, earth, and stones. When rarified, it becomes aether (the visible sky) and then fire. He agrees with Anaximander that the elements arise out of the primal stuff and in turn make all things. Thales' water, as it becomes more dense or rare, changes into ice or steam, which are not other elements but just forms of water. Since air is invisible, it can contact all things without being seen and thus claim to be present in every change. Things become more or less dense by changes in temperature, but what causes this is not explained. Air seems to be always in motion, as airborne dust is always drifting about. Nothing seems to be required to make it move; its being is to be moving. But if everything is made of air, then everything is also self-moving, which is not explained. Also, dense things such as earth and stone can become very hot without changing into another element, although a volcano does turn stone into liquid but not into water. A corollary of his condensation theory is a radical instability of all elements; any could change into another at any moment, as air turns into lightning with little warning. The denser elements seem more stable, as stones rarely change into anything. Over time these enduring elements would accumulate, locking up the air in them, so the proportion of stony elements would become irreversibly greater.

From what we know, Anaximenes neither asked nor answered such questions. His condensation theory was the most concrete mechanism for natural change of the Milesians. He grouped all things into categories or elements that could change into each other, all according to the same cause. Thus, changes in our experiential world have the same explanations as the events that formed the elements in the universe. Nature acts everywhere and always just as we see it act here and now. Since the basic stuff is invisible, this mechanism can only be extended in theory to account for the derivation of fire or water out of air. Applying the same principle everywhere with continuity in time and space is good science; that this principle cannot be directly experienced leaves the road to further inquiry open—and increasingly traveled.

Diogenes Laertius says Anaximenes used "simple and economical Ionic speech," suggesting that he wrote a book, but we have no other record of it.[8] His one surviving fragment says, "As our soul being air holds us together and controls us, so does wind (breath) and air enclose the whole world" (Fr. 2). For him all things—including gods and souls—come from air, so the life force that animates us (whose sign is breath) is of the same stuff as the winds that connect and animate the universe. Air is everywhere and the moving principle in all things, including the soul, the traditional principle of being and motion.

Anaximenes' air-centered idea of nature had several other consequences. Like Anaximander, he saw the earth as a squat cylinder, flat on the bottom but now covering the air beneath it like a lid. This trapped air thickens as it is weighed down and supports the earth. Why the condensed air is not changed into another element is not discussed. Stars were created by "exhalations" of the earth, which rarify as they ascend until they change into fire. Stars move due to different densities of the air and travel around the edge of the cylindrical earth instead of going under and around it. Finally, he thought earthquakes happened when the earth violently cracked open due to too much or too little moisture. Most of these ideas did not lead very far, although the earth maintaining its position by resting on air was taken up by later thinkers.

Xenophanes

Xenophanes was a contemporary Ionian from up the Aegean coast in Colophon who examined the nature of religion instead of the nature described by religion. He was not interested in the stuff of the universe but in the stuff of god, simple or plural, created or eternal, humanlike or pure being. Greek inquiry began with those aspects of nature not explicitly determined by the gods, such as the nature of the original stuff that predated them. As these speculations (efforts to reason beyond direct perception) were more widely discussed, it seemed inevitable that this attention would turn to the stories about the gods themselves and inquire into both the nature of the divine and how humans can come to understand this. Xenophanes applies the Ionian basic stuff inquiries to the basic nature of the divine and prepares the way for Parmenides to apply it to the basic nature of all beings, divine or other.

---

[8] Diogenes Laertius, *Lives of the Philosophers,* II, 3, in KRS, p. 143,

Xenophanes noticed that each culture pictured their gods as resembling themselves and said that if animals had gods, horse gods would resemble horses, and cattle gods, cattle (Fr. 15–16). He wanted to determine the nature of God that must be the same beyond the various cultural images. Just as Descartes' idea of God later turns on the quality of perfection, so Xenophanes found the divine distinguished by its superlative nature; God is the supreme. "One god, greatest among gods and men, in no way similar to mortals either in body or in thought" (Fr. 23). Homer and Hesiod erred in picturing a variety of gods doing a variety of human things (Fr. 11). "But mortals consider that the gods were born, and that they have clothes and speech and bodies like their own" (Fr. 14). As god's qualities are beyond compare, Xenophanes removes all physical humanlike traits. God is not born; does not have a body like we know; does not move; acts only through thinking; and thinks, sees, and hears with his whole being (Fr. 24, 25, 26). As Descartes prepared the idea of God for coexistence with science by pruning any interactions with humans (miracles), so Xenophanes prepared the divine for Parmenides' reduction to Oneness by excising all physical acts (such as raping) and including only qualities beyond compare.

Xenophanes had this one touchstone of incomparability for determining what was divine, but this leaves God beyond any clear human conception or description. He readily accepted this limit and challenged any who claimed to overcome it. "No man knows, or will ever know, the truth about the gods and about everything I speak of; for even if one chanced to say the complete truth, yet oneself knows it not; but seeming is wrought over all things. . . . Yet the gods have not revealed all things to men from the beginning; but by seeking men find out better in time" (Fr. 34, 18). This introduces into the Ionian discussions the problems of how we know what we think we know (epistemology) and how we distinguish knowledge from illusion (appearance). These concerns will build for the next two centuries up to Socrates' paradoxical claim that all he knows is that he does not know. Like Socrates, Xenophanes also claims that seeking knowledge is a better way to live, even though he believes no knowledge is ever fully trustworthy.

He saw such problems as how finite humans can comprehend completeness. As we are limited in time and space, how do we understand an unlimited or at least undetermined universe? He saw we were created not as knowing but as able to learn. As we experience that we do learn, a tension arises about how far we can expand our knowledge. Descartes' meditation on similar problems of skepticism and doubt two thousand years later repeats this Xenophanic line, wondering how much of the divine completeness humans share. As we see development in the method and content of our reason, what if we were to complete our potential—could we ever become truly knowing and divine?

> Possibly I am something more than I suppose myself to be. Perhaps all the perfections which I attribute to the nature of God are somehow potentially in me.... Experience shows... that my knowledge increases and improves little by little, and I see nothing to prevent its increasing... to infinity; nor even why, my knowledge having thus been augmented and perfected, I could not thereby acquire all the other perfections of divinity.... But even if my knowledge increased, ... I am still unable to conceive how it could ever become actually infinite, since it would never arrive at such a high point of perfection that it would no longer be capable of acquiring some still greater increase.[9]

Skepticism is not opposed to inquiry but wants to temper its conclusions. Modern science does this through experimentation. Knowledge gained through experiment is only as good as the *next* experimental results and never finally proven. We can use this knowledge in practice and further inquiry but always open to correction. Xenophanes appreciated the second-best nature of such knowledge when he said, "Let these things be opined as resembling the truth," or, as our next thinker Heraclitus stated, "Nature loves to hide."

Responding to our limited ability to know, Xenophanes supported his skepticism with a naïve Humean empiricism. He ignored the basic stuff controversy, as such speculations exceeded the evidence of direct experience. He shared the Milesians' interests in astronomy, meteorology, and geology. He said the sun and other heavenly lights were collections of fiery particles reformed every day, since there was no evidence of the sun's permanence but there was of embers growing into a fire. The sea was the source of weather as "the begetter of clouds and winds and rivers" (Fr. 30). Material objects were fluctuating combinations of earth and water. The land on the earth has arisen from the sea (he saw fossils on mountains) and is now in a cycle of

---

[9] Descartes, *Philosophical Essays*, trans. Lafleur (New York: Macmillan, 1964), p. 103.

eroding until only mud and no people remain. Then a new cycle of earth drying and humanity will begin. His naïve empiricism was consistent, even ironic, as in saying that the earth under his feet continued downward indefinitely.

This introduction of irony as a writing strategy is a significant development for inquiry. Poets made use of linguistic expressions that could have multiple meanings, but Milesian rational explanation tried to use direct univocal language. Xenophanes realized that qualities of language as media are too easily attributed to what it describes. His skepticism required a type of language that was descriptive yet also open to further revision and understanding. Irony works by suggesting one level of simple or common understanding and a second more difficult level that is more satisfying to comprehend. Fear of differing interpretations is changed into a strength. This suggestion of continuing levels of understanding, perhaps even beyond the author's intentions, helps keep inquiry open. Such irony leads beyond itself without closing down the meaning of this "beyond." How to inquire and talk about what cannot be fully known will dominate the expression of the ideas of two of the next philosophers, Heraclitus and Parmenides.

Heraclitus

Heraclitus summarized his thoughts in his observation on the philosophic nature of dogs (Gk. *kunos*, the name adopted by the Kuniks, or Lat. cynics). "Dogs bark at a person whom they do not know" (Fr. 97, W 90).[10] Dogs bark at what they know that they do not know. Thus, they are superior to humans who—at best—like Socrates, can claim that he knows only that (not what) he does not know. Heraclitus is one of Socrates' models for both skepticism and inquiry. He is the first Presocratic with substantial surviving writings, some 120 fragments. He continues Xenophanes' concerns with the role of the inquirer and the conduct of inquiry. His skepticism is based on two observations: that all things we experience are involved in some process of change, as in his famous claim that one cannot step into the same river twice (Fr. 12); and that things are not necessarily how we experience them, for "nature loves to hide" (Fr. 123, W 17). If the world is unstable and our access to it is uncertain, then what is the

---

[10] While KRS has 50 fragments, Philip Wheelwright's commentary on Heraclitus lists 124, arranged by topic with his own numbering system. When I use his translation, I will give both the DK and the W numbers. *Heraclitus* (New York: Atheneum, 1968).

purpose of inquiry? How can something changing be known? As our bodies mature (or change due to disease or emotion), does the information from our senses also change? As our minds mature and change, are the same mental formulas still compelling? Such reflections on the process of inquiry give his writings a modern or even postmodern feel, and he did influence Nietzsche and his followers. Recent inquiries into the basic structures and possibilities of specific inquiries, such as meta-ethics or meta-logic, are the progeny of Heraclitus. He revises the earlier role of wise men (*sophoi*) as experts in worldly affairs. The Milesians had sought the gods' knowledge of weather cycles, celestial motions, or geometry. Heraclitus sympathized with this but saw its futility, as we become caught in the wishful knowledge claims of either religious superstition or scientific hubris.

Heraclitus shifted the model and problems of knowing from measurement (geometry and astronomy) to the stable definition of what is to be measured. He developed a new language of change, imitating the epigrams of the religious oracles. Greeks wanting to know the truth of a situation or what action to take asked a religious oracle, usually at Delphi. Heraclitus wanted a way of answering questions that did not close the inquiry but promoted further reflection, and he found it in the oracle's irony and riddles. "The lord whose oracle is in Delphi neither speaks nor conceals, but gives a sign" (Fr. 93). The oracle showed that saying the truth created a problem for human interpretation rather than a solution. Traditional stories show how the direct perception of truth or gods was overwhelming and blinding. In *Oedipus the King,* the blind seer Tiresius lost his sight upon seeing Athena naked, and Oedipus blinds himself when he sees the horror of his fate in the naked body of his dead mother and wife.[11] We cannot comprehend when we *see* divine things (whether physical or mental vision) and so experience blindness. Oracular sayings allow us to view truth through the relative safety but also the ineluctable ambiguity of language.

---

[11] Teiresias's blind wisdom is also credited to his unusual experience as both man and woman. A taboo sight (snakes coupling?) turned him back into a woman as punishment. Seven years later the same sight turned him back into a man. Hera then drew him into a dispute with Zeus over which gender enjoys sex more, each claiming the other does. He admits it is women, and Hera blinds him for revealing secrets. We cannot see the divine directly, as the biblical God appears as a whirlwind or burning bush, or even name this God, only the placeholder "I am who I am."

An oracle's surface meaning often caught the unreflective in the effects of their shortsightedness, as prejudices, superstitions, and other ill-founded beliefs trap us. King Croesus, an infamous example, asked if he should invade his neighbor's kingdom. When told that "a great kingdom would fall," he invades, only to have the falling kingdom be his own. The Greeks recognized the human desire to do or know what the gods do or know as overreaching our place in the order of things. They called this disdain for natural limits *hubris,* the excessive behavior arising from the blinding belief that one is absolutely right. Making pride the greatest sin is similar in Christianity, isolating humans from the presence and knowledge of God. Philosophy always straddles the boundary of *hubris,* making the strongest knowledge claims possible without closing off further evidence and argument. Pride becomes *hubris* when one cannot entertain any critical stance toward his or her knowledge. *Hubris,* then, is the inability to inquire. "To extinguish *hubris* is more needful than to extinguish a fire" (Fr. 43, W 88).

The oracles tested the petitioner's character in his construal of the divine riddle. Greek culture had a rich tradition of proving oneself through a contest or trial.[12] Homer's heroes eagerly measure each other's worth in public displays and rewards, especially in the multi-day athletic contests. The epics of Heracles and Jason describe the repeated tests they surmount, like the weekly episodes of a televised superhero. The Olympic games, ancient and modern, exhibit personal and national superiority. The oracles were also such a test. One of the mottoes at Delphi was "Know thyself," and the oracle offered this opportunity in its sayings. Oedipus answers the Sphinx's riddle, as he knows human beings in general, but fails with Delphi's oracle because he does not know his own parents or himself. When the oracle informs Socrates that "no one was wiser than he," he took this as a test to find out how wise he was. Every participant in Plato's dialogues has such a chance to test the worth of his ideas. At his trial, Socrates thanks Athens for this chance to prove the worth of his ideas and to help him not be misled. Heraclitus, following this tradition, says, "I have searched myself" (Fr. 101), linking himself to the Delphic goal of self-knowing.

Heraclitus knows the contest, like the experiment, must be repeated indefinitely. There is no final contest, and our past success

---

[12] Nietzsche saw the contest or trial to show one's worth as central to Greek and any other healthy culture. See his "Homer's Contest."

can distort our future vision. His aphorisms are short and memorable challenges, available in our daily trials to encourage criticism and avoid *hubris*. Socrates and Plato later expand this Delphic role by testing friends with easy but false arguments and then revealing their unacceptable conclusions. Heraclitus uses the Delphic sense of paradox and inaccessible authority to show the limits of human reason, as the oracle's priestess did not comprehend her own divine words. He presents his ideas, like Nietzsche, as truths that will not be easily understood, but this does not put them beyond evaluation. His severe criticisms of the ideas of other thinkers also apply to his own sayings. "Learning of many things does not teach intelligence; if so it would have taught Hesiod and Pythagoras, and again Xenophanes and Hecataeus" (Fr. 40).

We want language in practical affairs to be transparent, to lead from thing to thing with as little upset as possible. For philosophy, language is at best translucent, with the awareness of using a medium always present and open to inquiry. "If one does not expect the unexpected one will not find it out, since it is not to be searched out, and difficult to compass" (Fr. 18). Formalizing this further, Plato presents his ideas as a dialogue among characters, making us examine both how and what they are saying, to question the surface coherence we give to words and push them into new patterns of meaning. Today Jacques Derrida similarly uses a method of partial erasure or crossing out to display both the written word and its "trace," the cultural, historical, and psychological contexts that limit our possibilities of meaning.[13]

Heraclitus' inquiry is motivated by *logos*. This word covers a rich variety of meanings connecting language, its use in reasoning (explanation, proportion, and analogy) and reason itself.[14] It opens the Gospel of John, "In the beginning was the *Logos* (Word), and the *Logos* was with God and the *Logos* was God." This biblical god's creating is represented as speech ("Let there be light"), but its Being is greater than any appearance of its rational order. *Logos* mediates between the thought of God, the order of the world, and its description for us. Medieval alchemists later tried to capture the creative power of God's spoken formulas. "Abra ca dabra, efra ga hafra,"

---

[13] Jacques Derrida, *Of Grammatology* (Baltimore: Johns Hopkins University Press, 1974).

[14] See *logos* in the *Greek–English Lexicon* by Liddell and Scott (Oxford: Clarendon Press, 1996).

sought power in the alphabet. Mickey Mouse in Disney's *Fantasia* stole the magic words for the broomstick to carry the water and Big Anthony in one of Tomie de Paola's stories used Strega Nona's words for the cooking pot to make spaghetti.[15] Like us, the apprentices mistake a piece of knowledge for the whole, initiating a process and disaster they cannot control.

For Heraclitus, the universe has a coherent rational order but, as always, that order is difficult to comprehend and more difficult to express.

> Of the *Logos* which is as I describe it men always prove to be uncomprehending, both before they have heard it and when once they have heard it. For although all things happen according to this *Logos,* men are like people of no experience, ... I distinguish each thing according to its constitution and declare how it is; but the rest of men fail to notice what they do after they wake up, just as they forget what they do when asleep. (Fr. 1)

For the basic stuff debate to continue, it needs to resolve the *logos* problems: right thinking, speaking, and experiencing. Heraclitus chose ever-changing fire as his stuff, but was this as a symbol of ceaseless motion and change or as the real source of all other things? In one place he describes fire as the origin of water, which became earth, and then the reverse, earth to water to fire (Fr. 31). Elsewhere he changes the order and includes air: water to earth to fire to air to water (Fr. 34). He does not explain how water and fire, which seem mutually exclusive, change into each other. A later account claims he said that evaporation fed the heavenly fire that in turn, through rain, fed the sea. His fire informed and controlled the whole process, being orderly and indefinitely mutable. "All things are an equal exchange for fire and fire for all things, as goods are for gold and gold for goods" (Fr. 90). "Thunderbolt (divine fire) steers all things" (Fr. 64). "This world order did none of the gods or men make, but it always was and is and shall be: an everlasting fire, kindling in measures and going out in measures" (Fr. 30).

This last fragment shows Heraclitus' belief, like Anaximander's, in an overall balance sustained through opposite processes. Fire is a Zeus-like ruler or manager, maintaining the just and necessary

---

[15] de Paola, T., *Strega Nona* (Englewood Cliffs, NJ: Prentice-Hall, 1975).

proportion among things to keep the world as it is. "Fire in its advance will catch all things by surprise and judge them" (Fr. 66, W 72). "Wisdom is one—to know the intelligence by which all things are steered through all things" (Fr. 41, W 120). "One thing, the only truly wise, does and does not consent to be called by the name of Zeus" (Fr. 32). The governing reason in the universe can be equally called (and not) Zeus, fire, or *logos*, each useful as a symbol rather than a full explanation.

The many things can exist with stability only if they are in balance, which a system of opposites provides. "When earth has melted into sea, the resultant amount is the same as there had been before the sea became hardened into earth" (Fr. 31, W 33). The opposing forces must be in harmony; the bowstring is pulled back to make the arrow go forward and the tension on the lyre string released to sound the note. "Opposition brings concord. Out of discord comes the fairest harmony" (Fr. 8, W 98). "People do not understand how that which is at variance with itself agrees with itself. There is a harmony in the bending back, as in the cases of the bow and the lyre" (Fr. 51). "It is by disease that health is pleasant, by evil that good is pleasant, by hunger satiety, by weariness rest" (Fr. 111, W 99).

These opposites must be in active opposition, a state of strife or war. "Homer was wrong in saying, 'Would that all strife might disappear from amongst gods and men.' For if that were to occur, then all things would cease to exist" (no DK, W 27). "It should be understood that war is the common condition, that strife is justice, and that all things come to pass through the compulsion of strife" (Fr. 80, W 26). The many can only exist in an active relation to each other. This supports Heraclitus' interest in fire as dynamic and always moving. It does not exist and then move but exists as moving. If things fell out of opposition, they would fall apart completely, and the original chaos would return. Chaos is not a group of things without order but a condition where the unrelated things lose their identity as things. He uses the image of a drink that must be stirred to keep its components blended and drinkable. "Even the sacred barley drink separates when it is not stirred" (no DK, W 125). Constant motion of the related parts (heavy–light, bitter–sweet, solid–liquid) creates a dynamic stability to maintain the whole. Empedocles will later further develop this role of strife.

Heraclitus believes the world gives signs instead of truth, yet he still embraces the richness of our sense experience. "Things of which there can be sight, hearing, and learning—these are what I especially prize" (Fr. 55, W 11). "Men who love wisdom should acquaint themselves with a great many particulars" (Fr. 35, W 3). He realizes the senses do not provide direct understanding but require interpretation. Sensory illusions deceive us, such as "The sun is the breadth of a man's foot" (Fr. 3, W 37).[16] "Eyes and ears are bad witnesses to men having barbarous souls" (Fr. 107, W 13). As a barbarian does not speak Greek, most people do not speak the language of reality. "Although immediately connected with the *Logos,* men keep setting themselves against it" (Fr. 72, W 64). Since the *Logos* is the same for all humans, its language is available to all. "Thinking is common to all," and "we should let ourselves be guided by what is common to all. Yet, although the *Logos* is common to all, most men live as if each of them had a private intelligence of his own" (Fr. 113 and 2, W 80 and 2). Using the *Logos,* our souls can appreciate, if not totally comprehend, the universe. "You could not discover the limits of soul, even if you traveled by every path in order to do so; such is the depth of its meaning" (Fr. 45). Thus, the *Logos* that can be explained is not the true *Logos,* just as any explanation of how the soul understands the *Logos* cannot be wholly true.

Our soul is able to see but does not; it is able to perceive and conceive but not often understand. "Fools, although they hear, are like the deaf: to them the adage applies that when present they are absent" (Fr. 34). In sleeping dreams or waking delusions the soul creates fantasies in a sleeplike state. "The waking have one world in common, whereas each sleeper turns away to a private world of his own" (Fr. 89, W 15). As fatigue causes a bodily sleep state, so a moist soul, intoxicated by drink or desire, becomes dopey and dormant. "It is hard to fight against impulsive desire; whatever it wants it will buy at the cost of the soul" (Fr. 85, W 51). It creates its own *logos* rather than participating in the reason of reality. "Souls take pleasure in becoming moist" (Fr. 77, W 47). A moist soul loses its affinity with the dry heat of fire, the Zeus-like element that can assume all shapes and think all things. Deceived by the surface stability of things, it becomes attached rather than opposed. "Soul is the vaporization out of which everything else is composed; moreover it is the least corporeal of things and is in ceaseless flux, for the moving world can only be known by what is in motion" (no DK, W 43). Like Zeus trying to

---

[16] Heraclitus' choice of the foot instead of the hand gives the self-consciously humorous picture of the thinker at work flat on his back.

save his mortal son Sarpedon,[17] we try to stop the flux of necessity and justice, thinking our advantage lies in the exception rather than the rule. We think we deserve to stop moving and keep things as they are. Moisture gathers in puddles—until it dries up.

How to avoid or overcome soul moisture is difficult. There is no automatic sign whether what we think we have learned is what is to be learned. "Most people do not take heed of the things they encounter, nor do they grasp them even when they have learned about them, although they think they do" (Fr. 17). Human reason is developmental but lacks any measure of proper functioning. Civil law is a source of guidance that supports the "thinking [that] is common to all" (Fr. 113, W 80). "Men should speak with rational awareness and thereby hold on strongly to that which is shared in common—as a city holds on to its law, and even more strongly. For all human laws are nourished by the one divine law that prevails as far as it wishes, suffices for all things, and yet is something more than they" (Fr. 114, W 81).

That civil reason embodied in civil law prepares us for grasping and obeying the laws of logic and nature is developed more in Pythagoras, Plato, and Aristotle. Heraclitus has no political inquiry but does see its educational role. Linking the development of soul and civil reason is a common idea from Confucius to the Enlightenment, which our current era of economic and moral individualism often overlooks.

ITALY

The conflicting results of the Milesian nature inquiries led to questions about their methods of reasoning. The limited capacity of our minds, our limited experience in space and time, and the ambiguous information from our perceptions, all influenced Heraclitus to be skeptical about the potential of human thinking. Yet he never gave up on the enterprise of inquiry. Although the world was problematic to know, this was no reason to give up on inquiring into its nature. As Aristotle will say, inquiry is not a choice, since the desire to know is intrinsic to our nature. We must inquire; the only question is how we will go about it.

Heraclitus' criticism and skepticism brought Ionian speculation to a halt. New thinking arose in the Italian frontier colonies. The margins of a culture often permit more radical reconstructions, as happened with

---

[17] *Iliad*, Book XVI.

Pythagoras and Parmenides. Slightly older than Heraclitus, Pythagoras also responded to the failure of the Milesians' plurality of candidates and arguments to reach agreement. Like mythical Daedalus, he revised the problem in a new direction. Instead of traversing the horizontal Labyrinth that imprisoned him, Daedalus decided to fly out of it vertically. Instead of asking which element is primary, Pythagoras went up one level to find what ordered the elements: numbers. These make the proportions and harmonies that constitute the true reality of all things. Obtaining this higher view required a prescribed program of studies, reinforced by a dedicated community of inquirers living together and consciously following it. Thus, he developed gymnastics for both mind and body. Discipline quieted the disruptive desires of the body and, using mathematics and geometry, trained the mind to see the world as numbers. This required a way of life whose commitment and practice could only occur in a small authoritarian community, guided by the immortal divine intelligence in our soul and its reincarnation throughout time. If properly trained, we can have such consummatory experiences as hearing the music of the spheres, recovering knowledge of past reincarnations, and attaining a harmonious soul able to prosper both in this life and beyond. These reveal the universal order in the union of opposites (limited–unlimited, mental–physical, human–divine), resolving the Milesians' problems that led to their unsolvable arguments and Heraclitus to his skepticism.

Parmenides' solution also required a new mental discipline, using Cartesian-like experiments to rid us of false hopes of finding truth, as experience entails only doubt and the logical demons of nonexistence. Our mental lives and the universe are only connected by the sheer existence of each, which turns out to be the same, the existence of existence itself. He overcomes skepticism by finding a truth ("isness is") of universal power and application. Like a black hole, it absorbs into itself all distinctions, such as time, place, and motion. Only isness is. To save truth, Parmenides transports it beyond the mistaken distinctions of human experience and then explains these faulty distinctions by offering a secondary logic of seeming. We will examine Pythagoras' worldly discipline first and then Parmenides' antiworldly one.

Pythagoras

Along with the ceaseless flux of Heraclitus and the unitary stability of Parmenides, the Pythagorean belief that proper thinking required an ordered way of life was the third main influence on future Greek philosophy. This proper thinking enabled one to see the organizational and at times magical powers of numbers. This power informs human inquiry from the nuptial number controlling reproduction in Plato's *Republic* through the creative power of the One in Neoplatonism and numerical formulae in medieval alchemy to modern applications in atonal music and digitalized information. Pythagoras limited his teachings to his community of initiated followers. The unprepared general population could not safely understand the teachings that only disciplined thought could produce. So he wrote nothing, leaving his followers to differ as to what he really said. Among the Presocratics, he is the most shrouded in legend, false attribution, and controversy.

Although much has been written, little is reliably known about Pythagoras' life or ideas. He was born in Ionia around 570, is said to have toured the eastern Mediterranean and studied with various religious masters (both often attributed to wise men), was unsatisfied with the life and politics in his native Samos, and moved to the Italian Greek colony Croton in 530. He there founded a community of inquiry and religious practice that lasted over thirty years, until other citizens, tired of its ascetic and authoritarian excesses, drove it out. He died shortly after this purge, and disciples continued teaching his ideas for the next two centuries. This was the first Greek school of thought, and it continually influenced later developments in philosophy and religion. Defining his ideas is difficult because he left no writings, he successfully swore students to secrecy, and his later disciples attributed their own teachings to his name. As true reason is the same in all and the disciple owes the development of his reason to the Master, so all of one's true ideas are attributable to his teacher.[18] Thus, many ideas called "Pythagorean" owe more to developments in his school than to him.

The broad content of these beliefs is generally agreed upon. Human souls are immortal and reincarnated and can improve their well-being between and even beyond incarnations. Numbers are the basic stuff of the universe, compose the harmonies that give value to both mental and physical things, and provide the best discipline to think properly. Naïve experience of the world is one of opposition, division, and discord, while the initiated can see the union that numbers (like the Heraclitean *logos*) bring to all things and the harmonies by which due proportion rationalizes the apparent distinctions between opposites. Proper experience results from training one's ideas and actions with an enlightened Master, living a simple

---

[18] The all-knowing Master (*sophos*) contrasts with the skeptic concerns of Heraclitus, Socrates, and others. Whether the teacher is the authority or provocateur becomes central in the development of inquiry.

life in community with other seekers, and experiencing the universal order by practicing the numerical disciplines such as mathematics and geometry. The Milesians used reason as it was given to them, while Pythagoras saw that human reason could be trained over time. How one learns to think affects what one can think.

How these beliefs in the existence and power of numbers, the soul's reincarnation, and the disciplined development of reason fit together and to what end is today much debated, for example, if his religious and philosophical ideas and initiatives are mutually supportive or exclusive. For the Ionians, new approaches to religious thinking opened new areas of experience and thought to philosophical inquiry. Pythagoras saw numbers as divine objects of veneration and ritual that built the ordered universe and our experience. His followers pursuing these religious objects began more organized inquiry into their formal qualities and relations. What began as mysticism evolved into mathematical inquiry.

Pythagoras pursued both religious superstition and philosophic inquiry. He spoke and acted more like a traditional shaman than a Milesian nature philosopher. Many of his prescriptions for living, such as not to eat beans or urinate facing the sun, seem to be superstitions and are dismissed as contrary to philosophy. While Pythagorean communities were infamous for their intolerance in enforcing these rules, the philosophical possibilities in these prescriptions should not be overlooked. As our ability to reason becomes more complex, we understand more complex explanations. But the initiate's immature mind needs simpler and more authoritative explanations, like these prescriptions. Here religious-like indoctrination (for example, literal interpretation of texts and memorization of "facts" or beliefs) might actually promote the development of abilities to later question these facts. The conscious manipulation and secularization of this developmental process continues into the self-correcting aspects of Plato's "noble lie" and Aristotle's mean.

Pythagoras borrowed the Mystery religions' central priestly authority, a moral code, secret initiations and superrational revelations, the promise of a better life for the soul in the next world, and reincarnation from the Orphics.[19] The final Eleusinian revelation was

---

[19] After Homer, the Eleusinian Mysteries create a more optimistic view of Hades and how we can live better there. Persephone and Demeter were given new roles to help us prepare for death. Orphics later use Dionysian and Mystery elements in a ritual practice, while the Mysteries demanded only purification and revelation. There was no ongoing ritual, for once life is understood correctly, it will be lived correctly. This idea that to know the good is to do the good will keep recurring.

the life-renewing seeds on a grain stalk, promising the soul's continuing life in the next world. Perhaps the Pythagorean final revelation was the square root of two, equal to the irrational number 1.41421.... Simple integers were his foundation for all thinking and being, and the failure of this useful but irrational number to be definable presented a serious challenge. The response was to elevate the inexplicable into a Mystery, a sign of the even more powerful divine reason that can define this. Plato later in his *Meno* compares the mystery of this irrational number to that of defining virtue; both can be seen but not explained.

Pythagoras realized that true (adequate, mature, perfected) reasoning required care and education, so he was the first Presocratic to create a school and treat rational development and pedagogy systematically. Education makes experiences more conscious and accountable. It balances religious or scientific indoctrination (external authority) with developing the tools of philosophic inquiry (self-authority). Math and logic reasoning can be attained at an early age, but reasoning about the world's content and its inhabitants' behavior requires much experience. Aristotle connects ethics (right behavior) and politics (right social order) to emphasize that our social and intellectual context makes our experiences coherent. Both our ability to reason and our faith in its efficacy develop as we are conscious that our experiences are reasonable.

Pythagoras raised this consciousness by purifying experience to its most constant and rational aspect, numbers. The ambiguity and equivocation of language promoted the confusions of Heraclitean flux and Milesian variation rather than restraining it as univocal and stable numbers could do. Pythagoras, like the Mystery religions, demanded secrecy to limit the profusion of undisciplined language that encourages undisciplined thinking. Language should be used sparingly, intentionally, and questioningly. It must be nurtured in a right-thinking community, informed by mathematics and practiced in a context of purified experiences guided by an all-wise Master to help find the truth.

The Master's authority rests upon his ability to develop reason to its highest level. Like the religious shaman or oracle, his will was connected with the universal truth, and he was no longer an independent agent. Sharing a common truth leads to sharing a common life. Our differences recede as we move toward becoming the same thinker, agent, and person. In his community, members awakened in silence to remember the prior day's experiences and thoughts and organize these with the ones from previous days, years, and ultimately lives. Reincarnation permitted them to gather knowledge from previous lives, beyond the limits of an individual's space–time experiences. Reincarnation thus grounded his metaphysics. The members' knowledge expanded both horizontally, uniting the community and Master as one mind, and vertically, with incarnations going back indefinitely into the heart of being.

His followers split into two camps over how to use this knowledge, the Mathematikoi (*mathema* = things learned) and the Akousmatikoi (*akousma* = things heard). The Akousmatikoi derive from his earliest followers, emphasizing ascetic preparations for a better next life. They systematically shunned the body (minimal clothing, food, and hygiene), avoided hurting other souls (vegetarianism), and followed the *akousmata,* epigrammatic definitions and rules for a good life attributed to Pythagoras. Aristotle's book on the Pythagoreans (quoted by Iamblichus 650 years later) divided the *akousmata* by the type of question each answers: what is it, what is the highest degree of a quality, and what must be done. Walter Burkert, in trying to separate Pythagoras' own ideas from those of his followers, gave the following four types (the fourth includes Aristotle's three types) with some examples:[20]

> Some reveal the hidden order not apparent within certain things:
> The rainbow is the reflected splendor of the sun.
> The ring of bronze when struck is a demon's voice trapped
>   in it.
> What is the Oracle at Delphi? The tetractys, which is the
> harmony in which the Sirens sing.
> An earthquake is a mass meeting of the dead.
>
> Some explain the heavens as both divine and the next life's realm:
> What are the Isles of the Blest? Sun and Moon.
> The Great Bear and the Little Bear are the hands of Rhea.
> The Pleiades are the lyre of the Muses.
> The planets are Persephone's dogs [they wander about].
>
> Some offer direction for ritual and sacrifice:
> One should not sacrifice a white cock.
> One should sacrifice and enter the temple barefoot.

---

[20] Walter Burkert, *Lore and Science in Ancient Pythagoreanism* (Cambridge, MA: Harvard University Press, 1972), pp. 167–168.

Eat only the flesh of animals that may be sacrificed.

Abstain from beans.

Do not break bread [it needs to be cut in the proper ritual].

Some offer general guidance and understanding:

Pythagoras is the Hyperborean Apollo [mythic Mystery leader].

Friendship is harmonious equality.

Old age is decrease, and youth is increase; health is retention of form, disease its destruction.

The most just thing is to sacrifice.

The most wise is number.

The most beautiful is harmony.

The most true is that men are wicked.

The most beautiful shapes are the circle and the sphere.

One ought to beget children, for it is our duty to leave behind people to worship the gods.

One ought to put on the right shoe first.

One should not travel by the main roads.

One should not help a person to unload but only to load.[21]

Such directives resemble the religious conformity given by an all-wise shaman more than philosophical inquiry. As Pythagoreans became more sophisticated, they reinterpreted them as riddles with deeper, hidden meanings. Burkert says they were "a lofty wisdom in language unintelligible to the uninitiated.... Allegorical interpretation, here as elsewhere, was the necessary means of adapting ancient lore to new ways of thinking, and thus preserving its authority."[22]

Pythagoras was also shaman-like with many stories of his supernatural acts, as the following examples from Burkert illustrate:

At the same time he was seen in Croton and in Metapontum.

When Pythagoras stood up among the spectators at Olympia, people saw that one of his thighs was of gold.

As Pythagoras was crossing the Casas River, the river hailed him in an audible voice, "Greetings, Pythagoras!"

---

[21] Burkert, pp. 170–173. Explanations in brackets are added.

[22] Burkert, pp. 174–175.

Pythagoras took from Abaris, the Hyperborean priest of Apollo, the arrow with which he traveled, and thus established himself as the Hyperborean Apollo.[23]

Stories of bilocation and aerial transportation using magic arrows were an embarrassment to later philosophers but during Pythagoras' life gave evidence of his authority as a seer and wise man. The shadow of this absolute authority, the shaman Master who must be obeyed, overcast future generations of his followers. All later developments continued this authority by claiming to have come originally from him, and the disciple learned by uncritically accepting the truth from the Master.[24] The Akousmatikoi prescribed this narrow way of life, limiting inquiry to the health of the soul here and hereafter.

The Mathematikoi, who were dominant by Socrates' time, followed Pythagoras' vision of numbers as the universal basic stuff and inquired into how they worked. They recognized the Akousmatikoi as legitimate but inferior brethren, arrested at the early religious stage of thinking, believing in reincarnation, the *akousma*, rigid asceticism and the miraculous shaman stories. The Mathematikoi used Pythagoras' teachings to develop their reason to better understand this life in this world. They followed the words of the *akousma*, but gave them symbolic meanings offering direction in the life of inquiry more than asceticism. They investigated numbers at work, such as proving the Pythagorean Theorem and determining more carefully due proportions such as the harmonic intervals and planetary motions and distances.

While Pythagoras did little scientific work with numbers himself, he helped develop the capacity for abstraction in Greek thought by seeing the world as made of numbers. The Heraclitean flux depends upon the changes brought by the future, to which Pythagoras countered with stability continuing from the past, both in the continuity of reincarnated souls and in the numerical identity of things. Parmenides tried to destroy the flux by eliminating time and space, while Pythagoras tried to slow it down by simplifying experience and language and then numerically regularizing it. Hidden behind the Milesians' basic elements, Pythagoras found that numbers run through the flux and reveal the timeless harmonies by which all things are described. In the words of

---

[23] Burkert, pp. 141–143.

[24] The Pythagoreans' Simmias and Cebes in Plato's *Phaedo* want the Master Socrates to tell them the truth, while he wants them to find it.

the fifth-century Pythagorean teacher Philolaus, "Number is the ruling and self-creating bond which maintains the everlasting stability of the things that compose the universe" (Fr. 23, W16).[25]

Milesian basic stuff theories failed to prove that one element was more basic than another. Qualities seemed to divide the universe, while numbers were able to run through all things. Pythagoras thought direct experiences of the organizing power of numbers, as in musical or geometric harmony, should help us understand the less direct experience of how they organize the universe itself and our souls. Such numerology can easily sound silly (justice is four), but its fascination continues in our attachment to lucky and unlucky numbers. He would readily understand our cultural fear of the number thirteen. Gambling, whether stock market or poker, shows a belief in the power of numbers and our ability to control it.[26] Pythagorean belief informs Dante's medieval use of numbers to reveal God's power in *The Divine Comedy*. The three-in-one mystery of the Trinity provides his basic plan. From his use of *terza rima* (three rhyming lines spread over three lined stanzas) to his inclusion of one hundred cantos ($3 \times 3 + 1 = 10 \times 10 = 100$), his numbers reveal the presence of God in all things. Dante's final image of God in Paradise harmonizes the three primary colors resolved by a prism into a single pure white light, the prism revealing the numerical order and unity usually beyond our experience. Pythagoras would have loved it.

Pythagoras' idea of a world ordered by numbers had both supernatural and sophisticated developments. It is tempting to see him bringing mathematical rigor into Milesian nature inquiry, but this potential was only developed after his death. For early Pythagoreans, numbers resembled Olympian nature gods, with human traits (male and female) and human relations, such as justice is four, marriage is five, and the moment of opportunity (*kairos*) is seven. He may have discovered the theorem relating the three sides of a right triangle and the numerical basis of musical harmonics but likely did not formally prove the former or experiment with the latter. For him the numerical basis of reality was a divine revelation, inviting veneration not investigation.

---

[25] "W" means translation from P. Wheelwright, *The Presocratics* (Upper Saddle River, NJ: Prentice-Hall, 1966).

[26] *Pi* (Artisan Entertainment, 1998) is a good movie on the power of numbers in our lives. Computers fill the hero's apartment as he seeks meaning in the endless calculations of pi. Others want these patterns to corner the stock market or interpret ancient scriptures. It is obsessively uncomfortable to watch.

The most interesting and powerful numbers were the simplest: the first four whole integers. These four numbers were responsible for generating and defining the rest of the number system, geometry, and the harmonics of music. However, as rational principles, numbers were even more invisible than the Milesian elements and difficult to verify.

Pythagoreans primarily saw numbers through the spatial relations of geometry. The square of a number is the geometric idea of a square erected upon a certain length of line, and a cube is the solid figure constructed upon the square. This spatial approach was limited to three dimensions and downplayed the significance of motion, except when it described a geometric figure, as in the circular orbits of heavenly bodies. The dependence of motion on time leads beyond the simple geometry of points at rest and into the fourth dimension. Desiring to neutralize the Heraclitean flux, Pythagoreans chose the stability of three-dimensional, spatially regular motion over irregular motion varying with time. Their practice valued rest and immortality over motion and so limited the value of time to cycles. Daily meditation on past acts and incarnations unified one's self over time. Pythagoras tried to save a limited time and motion before Parmenides decided both had to go.

Greeks, like many early cultures, used physical devices, such as pebbles or dots, in addition to ten fingers and toes to help with counting or geometry. The pebbles could be arranged in various ways to represent a number, some of which have become standard on dominoes, playing cards, and dice. If the first four numbers are each represented by the appropriate number of pebbles juxtaposed on a line (. .. ..) and these four groups are then arranged vertically to form an equilateral triangle with a base of four units, a tetractys is formed.

This basic Pythagorean symbol shows the power of numbers to unite the universe. Their greatest oath was to swear by "Him (Pythagoras) who gave us the tetractys, which contains the fount and root of ever-flowing nature."[27] Out of these four numbers comes the world. Together they equal ten, whose divinity is seen everywhere: fingers,

---

[27] Sextus Empiricus, as quoted in KRS, p. 233.

toes, the decimal number system, and the number of heavenly objects orbiting around the universe's central fire (the sun, moon, five planets, fixed stars, earth, and counterearth—a never-seen body needed to equal ten). In geometry, these numbers depict respectively the point, line, plane, and solid. Their progression expressed as a series of ratios (1:2, 2:3, 3:4) gives the musical harmonies of octave, fifth, and fourth. They describe human qualities and relations: one is soul, two female, three male,[28] and four justice. Five, the sum of male and female, is marriage, while the moment of opportunity (*kairos*) is seven, The tetractys also shows how numbers are generated: adjacent lines combined create a masculine number (odd and even equals odd), every other line combined makes an even feminine one (two odds or evens equals even).

The perfection and maleness of odd numbers is shown by their successive sums and pebbles always equaling a square.

$$1 = 1 \times 1$$
$$1 + 3 = 4 = 2 \times 2$$
$$1 + 3 + 5 = 9 = 3 \times 3$$
$$1 + 3 + 5 + 7 = 16 = 4 \times 4, \text{ and so on}$$

Even numbers progress in a lopsided way, creating a rectangle with ever-shifting (imperfect and thus feminine) proportions.

$$2 = 1 \times 2$$
$$2 + 4 = 6 = 2 \times 3$$
$$2 + 4 + 6 = 12 = 3 \times 4$$
$$2 + 4 + 6 + 8 = 20 = 4 \times 5, \text{ and so on}$$

As the multiplicands each increase by one, the rectangle they describe shifts the ratio of its sides. Later Pythagoreans developed the *gnomon,* a device to picture and generate these number series. The masculine one was an equilateral right angle forming two sides of the square that expands as the sum of odd numbers increases. The series of even numbers is encompassed by an oblong right angle, with each arm increasing one unit for each additional even number.

$$1 \qquad\qquad = 1 \times 1 \text{ square} \qquad 2 \qquad\qquad = 2 \times 1 \text{ oblong}$$
$$3 + 1 = 4 = 2 \times 2 \text{ square} \qquad 4 + 2 = 6 = 3 \times 2 \text{ oblong}$$
$$5 + 4 = 9 = 3 \times 3 \text{ square, etc.} \qquad 6 + 6 = 12 = 4 \times 3 \text{ oblong,}$$
etc.

---

[28] The number one was considered both odd and even as the unity and origin of all numbers. Thus, three was the first odd number.

This way of representing numbers emphasizes certain character-istics over others. The two gnomoi stress the qualities of odd and even, while others, such as being divisible by three or five or being prime or irrational, are not. As Pythagoreanism developed, a list of the opposing qualities based upon the differences between the gnomoi was gener-ated. Ten qualities were enumerated, following the organizational power of the divine tetractys. Aristotle gives us the following list:

limit and unlimited

odd and even

one and plurality

right and left

male and female

resting and moving

straight and curved

light and darkness

good and bad

square and oblong[29]

The left column members have positive values, while the right column members have negative ones. (Note that "right" is on the left, as coming first in a series is also positive.) Six of these pairs arise from qualities pictured in the gnomoi, the first three and the sixth, seventh, and tenth. Greek culture saw male as regular (square) and female as irregular (oblong), and similar cultural values explain the fourth, eighth, and ninth pairs. The first pair, limited and unlimited, reflects the organizing role of numbers.

Pythagoras grasped the abstraction of number as a presence in all existing things, bringing order and understanding. His early inquiry venerated the power and presence of number more than explained it but set the stage for a less religious inquiry into how their proportions inform our experience. As Pythagoras' "basic stuff" speculations tended to think of numbers as things,[30] so our next figure posited the thing-hood of the most famous abstraction in all philosophy: being itself.

---

[29] Aristotle, *Metaphysics*, 986a22.

[30] A sublime Pythagorean moment is when the hero of *The Matrix* (Warner Brothers, 1999) finally sees the matrix, streaming series of numbers on a monitor screen green field that are the reality of the various things we experience.

Parmenides

After the rich and multifaceted world of Pythagorean political activity, spiritual exercises, and number mysticism, Parmenides seems to inhabit the uniform and inert environment of the North Pole. His answer to the Milesian confusions was likewise even more radical. Not only was the world not as we perceive it to be, as when Pythagoras said that things are really numbers, but now the very multiplicity of things is an illusion. Parmenides finally reduced the basic stuff of the universe to just one thing that simply existed, complete and inert, with no means of creating any multiplicity out of itself. The basic stuff was existence itself, and his writings concern why this must be true and what follows from it. Like the Heraclitean Flux, the Parmenidean One caused a crisis in thinking that had to be resolved before inquiry could continue.

Little is known about Parmenides. He is a man of few qualities, befitting one who believed the only quality is existence. He lived in the colony of Elea in Italy. Evidence from Plato's *Parmenides* suggests he was born around 515, while Apollodorus later suggests 540. Neither is compelling.[31] When he died or when he wrote is not known.

He is known to have written just one poem and used the epic style of Homer and Hesiod. We have some twenty fragments of this, totaling 160 lines, perhaps half the original. He is not much of a poet and may have chosen this familiar form to help his audience deal with his unorthodox ideas. The poem uses traditional religious imagery: a goddess leads an initiate beyond the everyday world into a hidden realm where true reality is revealed. He uses these images to examine questions that finally push one beyond them, for the revelation is the total oneness of all existence. This negates the journey as well as the poet, the goddess, and all sequential thinking. How are we to respond to such a story? If this reasoning puts an end to all reasoning, how does this affect our lives? His simple idea quickly has large consequences for which he seems to offer the traditional advice of mystery

---

[31] Neither is reporting our idea of history. Plato's priorities are philosophic and dramatic; it could be ironic to give an exact age to a man who denies qualities. Apollodorus creates order in his material, arranging all thinkers in teacher–pupil successions with a forty-year age difference. Xenophanes was 40 in 540, so then his future pupil Parmenides must have been born. Forty years later, his pupil Zeno conveniently was born. These dates seem made to fit a pattern; birth dates are soft data.

religions, that the nature of the revelation itself will change and reorganize one's life.

The poem opens with a traditional god-assisted journey to find knowledge. The hero's horse-pulled chariot[32] follows the sun's handmaidens into the light, where the road is broad and easy to follow beyond the everyday world defined by opposites like day and night. Here he meets the goddess who speaks for the rest of the poem. She explains two methods of understanding the world, the divine way of truth and the mortal way of opinion. The first reveals there really is no journey because there is no motion, nor is there a hero because there are no individual beings, only being itself. The quasi-being goddess then goes on to describe the opinions on which we mistakenly base our understanding of the world. We organize these opinions so well that, like the Milesians, we think they are true. How uninitiated human beings experience multiplicity or initiated ones, each a piece of the indivisible whole, can experience anything is not explained. The Heraclitean Flux renders the world incoherent, which the Parmenidean logic corrects. If we reason carefully, the only sensible account of our experience is that only one existence exists, period. Rational argument has to take priority over and give guidance to experience, as parodied later in *Candide*.

His religious imagery may be primarily stylistic, yet it provokes traditional monotheistic issues such as how can all things ultimately be the same single being and what could be the experience or thought of such an only being. These lead later historians to link Parmenides with Xenocrates. How pure being (unlimited and thus undefined by space, time, and so on) could think or do anything at all has always been a problem, and Parmenides raises the specter, not for the last time in philosophy, of reason destroying itself in its own completion. The realization that all is one with no qualities other than existence puts an end to the movement of language and ideas and thus to thinking itself. The being of being is mute. He never says what we gain by dissolving all of the world's distinctions. Perhaps like Wittgenstein at the end of the Tractatus, he envisioned a silence beyond language as the way to address life's basic questions.[33] This creates a surreal context, as the goddess can only speak in the world of opinion, addressing the hero as a separate being and using multiple words and

---

[32] Compare Plato's use of the same imagery in his *Phaedrus* .

[33] L. Wittgenstein, *Tractatus Logico-Philosophicus* (London: Routledge, 1971), p. 151.

ideas to prove that this world of multiplicity is incoherent and cannot be thought at all, which leaves us as fish out of water. The thought process that disproves our thought processes must itself be a disproved process. This gives us the feel of Parmenides' universe, preparing us for the goddess's inquiry.

She claims there are only two possible ways of thought: that a thing is and cannot not be or that a thing is not and must necessarily not be. The first is the way of persuasion and truth, while the second cannot truly be followed, "for you could not know what is not—that cannot be done—nor indicate it" (Fr. 2). Not being is a way of thinking we use, to our sorrow, all of the time. We think and say that unicorns do not exist or Superman is not human. Parmenides' point is the same for all of the ten ways Aristotle later finds in which we speak of being. All claims of not being are based on claims of being. We think we know what unicorns, Superman, and humans are before we say what they are not, and so they all *are* in some sense, if only in my imagination and the stories I tell from it. The impossibility of thinking or saying something is not in an absolute sense, that it *is* in no way, is his first point.

After this first limit to human reason, he turns to his main task, examining our reasoning about change. If the change is absolute, where something comes into being that was not in any way there before, then we run afoul of his first prohibition. Absolute novelty makes no sense; it could not be recognized. Change has to connect with prior language, experience and stuff to be understood. This is his second limit upon reasoning. Just as something cannot absolutely not be, so something cannot come into being from absolute not being. The need for faith to believe the Judeo-Christian God's creation of the universe out of nothing emphasizes this point. Our reasoning cannot grasp this in any way, and unless we jump to faith, we must agree with his second point.

Since we cannot conceive of absolute nonbeing nor absolute change, Parmenides now goes on to show that all cases of nonbeing and change are in actuality absolute ones, and thus impossible.

> On this way [that it is] there are very many signs, that being uncreated and imperishable it is, whole and of a single kind and unshaken and perfect. It never was nor will be, since it is now, all together, one, continuous. For what birth will you seek for it? How and whence did it grow? I shall not allow you to say nor to think from not being; for it is not to be said

or thought that it is not; and what need would have driven it later rather than earlier, beginning from the nothing, to grow? Thus it must either be completely or not at all. (Fr. 8)

How can something change if it is what it is? How can we understand something being what it is and also being different? The differences must somehow be made trivial, with the thing itself being what is understood. This issue of how a one could also be a many, how I can be the same person as before I learned Greek or became a father, endures in philosophy. The most famous Greek solutions are Plato's notion of abiding form and Aristotle's idea of unfolding potential to explain enduring being and experienced change. Plato's Form[34] is the essential definition present in all instances of a thing. A bicycle must have two connected wheels but could be any color, size, materials, and so on. The Form is not solely present in any example of a thing; there is always some nonessential element whose variations account for change. Aristotle changes the Form into the actualized and describes change as potential developing in the preactualized thing, as an acorn into an oak tree. A natural being (tree) expresses itself in different ways at different times (seed, sapling, full canopy, stump, and so on) Such change is orderly as it follows a natural sequence. This orderliness in fixed kinds is questioned by evolutionary mutation, as fish evolving over generations into birds. In fact every living thing seems to have this potential to change beyond its current identity, as stem cells seem to do. Unless some higher being or rule maintains the integrity of species and limits the expressions of potential (more Aquinas's God than Aristotle), potential here might merely increase the Flux. We will revisit these ideas later.

For Parmenides, such solutions miss the point. Introducing enduring things or types that can persist through change merely delays realizing the irrationality of change to a higher level of thought. Their change-resistant beings are all in some way distinguishable, with our idea of being changing as our minds move from one to another. But the Parmenidean nemesis arises when we claim this Form or actualization is not the same as that one. Differences among Forms or actualizations are as illusory as those between their individual manifestations. We temporarily feel secure in these stipulated definitions of

---

[34] We often capitalize technical terms in philosophy, such as "Form." Greek used either all upper- or lowercase letters, so Plato would not have set off this word by using the capital.

the things around us, but this is only a framework we impose on the world. Dividing the world into kinds of things seems like such a practical idea, but we cannot deny the Justice of the Goddess, the due proportion between ideas and things. Our shortsighted pragmatic use of "is not" blinds us to the proper role of "is," and we are punished by accepting incoherent reasoning as valid and finally reducing our ability to think.

> Therefore Justice has never loosed her fetters to allow it to come to be or to perish, but holds it fast.... And how could what is be in the future? How could it come to be? For if it came into being, it is not: nor is it if it is ever going to be in the future. Thus coming to be is extinguished and perishing unheard of. Nor is it divided, since it all exists alike; nor is it more here and less there, which would prevent it from holding together, but it is all full of being.... Remaining the same and in the same place, it lies on its own and thus fixed it will remain. For strong Necessity holds it within the bonds of a limit, which keeps it on every side. (Fr. 8)

Being is now fully defined. It is totally separated from nonbeing and thus from change, as its only change could be into nonbeing, which is impossible. Its existence is the same everywhere, making everywhere the same. Occupying all everywhere, there is nowhere to move, so being remains fixed in place and time, which is all place and all time. He says it is like always being in the center of a ball.

> But since there is a furthest limit [it occupies all there is], it is perfected, like the bulk of a ball well-rounded on every side, equally balanced in every direction from the center. For it needs must not be somewhat more or somewhat less here or there. For neither is it non-existent, which would stop it from reaching its like, nor is it existent in a way that there would be more being here, less there, since it is all inviolate: for being equal to itself on every side, it lies uniformly within its limits. (Fr. 8)[35]

This being-in-a-ball image ends the goddess's "trustworthy discourse," and she turns to "the beliefs of mortal men [and] the deceitful ordering of words" (Fr. 8). Why Parmenides adds this is debated, as Schofield observes, "Why that elaborate account [of

---

[35] Compare Leibniz's monads.

CHAPTER 2

opinion] was included in the poem remains a mystery: the goddess seeks to save the phenomena so far as is possible, but she knows and tells us that the project is impossible" (KRS, p. 262). The goddess began telling us, "It is proper that you should learn all things, both the unshaken heart of well-rounded truth and the opinions of mortals in which there is no true reliance" (Fr. 1). We can conceive the One but cannot help perceiving the Many.

Comparing Parmenides' oneness of being with Buddhism's similar claim may help us see the need for this second way. Attaining enlightenment (Parmenides' higher state is also light) is usually achieved only briefly and at irregular intervals. We keep falling back into the world of separation, desires, and suffering. The Buddhist writer Jack Kornfield's title *After the Ecstasy, the Laundry*[36] reflects this persistence of the illusory in our lives. To live well, we need to know both the illusions of the perceived world where we spend most of our time and how to manage them. Success here seems to be satisfying the demands of reason so far as this is possible. Socrates' lament in Plato's *Phaedo* that he had to take a second best way (a "second sailing") in his intellectual pursuits[37] echoes this concern about the propriety of examining the realm of illusions. A true and necessary foundation for our reasoning whose certainty grounded the understanding of all of our experiences would be nice. Lacking this, Socrates creates his own contingent explanations by making his best guess and then seeking to verify each. This is the way of opinion, and as he says in Plato's *Meno,* true opinion tells you how to get somewhere just as well as knowing the way.[38] Though perhaps difficult to find, both Socrates and Aristotle believed opinion always contains some truth. The goddess says we need these studies so that we are "not surpassed" by the thoughts of others. Being able to understand and critique apparently reasonable opinions can save us from following them further than is warranted or healthy.

The goddess uses light (fire) and dark (earth) dualism as the foundation of the daily world, reentering the gates of day and night. Dualisms

---

[36] Jack Kornfield, *After the Ecstasy, the Laundry* (New York: Bantam, 2000).

[37] "Unless someone should make that journey safer and less risky upon a firmer vessel of some divine doctrine.... However, since I was deprived and could neither discover it myself nor learn it from another, do you wish me to give you an explanation of how, as a second sailing [alternative to the best], I busied myself with the search for cause.... I started in this manner, taking as my hypothesis in each case the theory that seemed to me most compelling...." (*Phaedo,* 85D and 99D–100A).

[38] Meno, 97B.

promise stability but need a third force to maintain their separation and balance. The Christian Trinity's genius is its ability to be one and many at the same time. Humans like this idea of a blending and balancing of elements, and the goddess gives such an account of the heavens with concentric rings alternating light and dark or mixed, with the earth compressed into dense matter, the sun an exhalation of fire, and the moon a mixture illuminated by reflected light. An incomprehensible divine force initiates and maintains heavenly movement, following Justice and Necessity as in the way of truth. This divine force "governs the hateful birth and the mingling of all things, sending female to mix with male and again conversely male with female" (Fr. 12). She harmonizes the opposing basic powers, perhaps mirroring the medical idea of health as a proper blending of opposites. Schofield thinks Parmenides could have known Alcmaeon in Italy, who wrote, "Illness comes about directly through excess of heat or cold. . . . Health on the other hand is the proportionate admixture of the qualities."[39]

Finally, he explains the origin of thought in bodily changes between hot and cold. As Theophrastus later commented, "He regards perception and thought as the same." When the body in death becomes cold, it loses its ability to perceive (think) heat or light but still can sense cold and dark. As even corpses can still think, so everything that exists (as a balance of hot and cold) had some mental activity (KRS, p. 261). As planets moving at similar intervals as strings on a musical instrument will produce similar music, so if hot and cold explain reasoning in humans, they must produce reasoning in other similar circumstances. Reason here tries to explain itself as a quality of the material stuff but ends up being absorbed into this stuff and disappearing.

Parmenides' arguments should help us get over the habit of viewing the world and our experience as multiformed and occupying time and space. Yet each argument as a movement of reason itself re-encourages our beliefs in motion, change, and time. We can never fully escape these illusions but with effort and discipline can recognize their irrationality. Unlike the Mystery religions, Parmenides' revelation of the Oneness of being does not lead to any new way of living, -less it is a certain quietism. He does not organize a community, diet, o~ ~~ does write a poem and evidently had some students, showing he did be~ ~e need for communication. He is willing to pass along his wisdom _ ~~ ~ach person to his or

---

[39] KRS, p. 260.

her personal experience of the One. Bare isness does not lend itself to the founding of a school.

Later Parmenideans: Zeno and Melissus

Zeno was Parmenides' pupil and fellow citizen. He wrote a book (now lost) of arguments to support Parmenides' criticisms of our common-sense ideas about our experience of the world. Rather than developing positions, he is known for his method of reducing to absurdity his opponent's claim about the nature of reality. He is most famous for the four paradoxes of motion reported in Aristotle's *Physics* and his appearance in Plato's *Parmenides,* where he supports Parmenides' claim that all is one by defeating all claims that the many exist.[40]

Aristotle claims Zeno was the first to discover dialectic, the careful analysis of the consistency in a person's language and beliefs.[41] Starting from a commonsense premise, such as things move, are many, or have size, he used Parmenides' logic of being to reduce the claims to absurdity, usually a pair of contradictory conclusions. His negative method is critical rather than constructive, identifying problems rather than solutions. Zeno's paradoxes are like Parmenidean *akousmata,* meditations to keep us on the right track. However, such arguing can also be seen as merely destructive and serving only competitive urges. "Zeno" in Plato's *Parmenides* is apologetic that his youthful book exhibited this love of victory, or what Plato calls *eristic,* arguing only for the thrill of winning, not inquiry. His way of arguing influenced later developments in rhetoric by the Sophists and speechwriters. His paradoxes have fascinated logicians for centuries and continue to confound. "Of all the Presocratics, Zeno has the most life in him today" (KRS, p. 279). Simplicius preserved the actual words in one of his typical arguments, showing belief in the existence of many things is paradoxical.

> If there are many things, the things that are are unlimited; for there are always others between the things that are, and again others between those. And thus the things that are are unlimited.

---

[40] Plato writes philosophical inquiry, not history. Information about philosophers or their ideas serves the purpose of the particular dialogue and could be invented, ironic, or provocative but need not be true. Zeno probably resembled "Zeno," but may not have said what "Zeno" says.

[41] As reported by Diogenes Laertius, KRS p. 278.

> If there are many things, it is necessary that they are just as many as they are, and neither more nor less than that. But if they are as many as they are, they will be limited. (DK Fr. 3)

Since space is infinitely divisible, there is this multiplication of "others between the things that are." Boundaries are difficult things to describe. If too thin, they fail to divide, and if too thick, they take on a life of their own, increasing the number of things that are. But the same argument can be used against the reality of the One. "The One, as all that is, is limited. The One, as not being bounded by anything else, is unlimited. So we cannot understand the One as it is both limited and unlimited." Parmenides could accept both solutions as denying understanding the world through oppositions, for the One cannot really enter into a pluralistic argument with premises moving to a conclusion. The ultimate goal of Zeno's Parmenidean logic is to go beyond logic.

Aristotle discusses Zeno's four most famous paradoxes of motion. Infinity makes these paradoxes work. Any length of space or time contains the same infinite number of points. And a geometric point or a moment in time has no dimensions yet composes lines and periods that do. The first describes a runner in a stadium who must run half of a distance before he can run all of it, but first must run half of this half and again half of this new half, and so on. Because the distance is infinitely divisible, he must pass through an infinite number of halves in a finite time, which is impossible. The second is similar, with Achilles trying to pass the tortoise, who has been given a head start. As Achilles reaches the tortoise's starting place, it has crawled to a new spot. This process is infinitely repeatable, as the space between the two is infinitely divisible. So Achilles can never pass the tortoise. The third uses the infinitely divisible moment in time to prove that a flying arrow cannot move. At any point in time, the arrow must be in a particular space, so there is no time at which it could be moving. It is always (at every moment) stationary. The fourth is the most complicated and modern. Three bodies of equal length are placed end to end in a straight line and then two are moved on to two other parallel lines. Thus, each has a parallel straight line upon which it could move. While the middle body remains still, the two outer bodies move at a constant speed toward each other. They begin passing each other at one space unit per time unit, but pass the stationary body at half this speed. Thus, at the same speed, they are moving at two different speeds. Aristotle puts it in terms of time (one body is passed in half the time it takes to pass the other) and thinks it is patently false. Measuring motion requires a fixed frame. Each body has its own framework (moving or not) in relation to the others, and any motion outside (even apparent) makes one feel that one was moving in the opposite direction.

Melissus of Samos was a younger defender of Parmenides, best known for saving his island in a naval victory over Athens. It is unknown if he ever knew Parmenides or how he came to support him. He seems to know some of Anaxagoras and Empedocles. It is unknown when he wrote or where he fits in the lineage of ideas.

Instead of exposing language and logic as self-destructive like Zeno, Melissus is more accepting of language and concepts like space and time as he examines the nature of isness. Unlike Parmenides, he thinks there is a perspective from which one can see or think about the one that is not within the one itself. His isness has duration (past and future) and extension (here and there) but not a beginning or end. This unlimited one seems to contradict Parmenides that the one limits itself by its own nature, being what it was and only this, but Melissus claims that it cannot be limited by anything *external* since there is nothing external to it. His goal is to show that if existence has the qualities Parmenides gives to it, then it must necessarily have a singular nature.

> "For if it were [infinite], it would be one; for if it were two, the two would not be infinite, but would be limited by one another."
> "Being one is alike in every way; for if it were unalike, being plural it would no longer be one but many." (Fr. 6 and DK 30a5)

He argues against motion because it would require a void to move into. Being must be full, as any emptiness would involve not being. Since being is the fullness of all that is, it thus cannot move. This echoes Parmenides' rejection of plural and changing sense data, since whatever is real can only be what it is and thus it cannot change, "for nothing is stronger than true reality" (Fr. 8). Later the Atomists will rehabilitate the void to explain their way to have both plurality and being.

REINTERPRETING PARMENIDES:
THE RETURN OF THE MANY

Any fifth-century Greek philosopher had to address Parmenides' logic about existence and illusion. His arguments that being is one and unmoving so contradicted our daily experience that they demanded some new view that could "save the phenomena." Without an overwhelming reason to reject daily experience (such as Pythagorean salvation of our immortal soul), it is most difficult to take all sense data as illusory and accept an abstract idea of inert unity as the true reality. Unlike Pythagoras, Parmenides had no religious future to compensate for the loss of the sense world. The ascetic purity of his reason is already succumbing to human desires in Zeno's multiple supporting arguments. Using so many arguments obscures the intended goal of unity and might reflect his desire to display his ingenuity more than Parmenides' doctrines. Melissus goes further by accepting Parmenides' core teaching, the inert unity of existence, but discarding his rejection of time and space, those aspects most contrary to our experience. Multiplicity proved fun for Zeno, while no time and place was too much for Melissus to conceive.

Without a religious agenda or a secular ethical one as in Plato and Aristotle, the life of pure reason is too difficult, and we seek other more illusion-friendly explanations. Four thinkers after Parmenides tried to follow his notion of unchanging reality yet also explain how this reality provides for the changing world of our experience. They all developed some notion of a plurality of basic stuffs, unchanging elements that mix and separate to form the various things of the world. Empedocles accepted the traditional four elements: earth, air, fire, and water, mixed by two forces, union (Love) and dissolution (Strife), that were set in motion by an eternal whirling vortex. Anaxagoras' elements were all things that were not mixtures of other things. Gold and iron, blood and bone were among the basic stuffs minutely present in all things but in great concentration would appear as the element itself. The Atomists Leucippus and Democritus return to one main indivisible stuff, called the "atom." They posited an infinite number of infinitely small particles varying in size and shape but all of the same matter. Clumping together in endless variations, they form all visible things.

All follow the requirement that reality cannot change, always being what it is. But each figures out a way to overcome Parmenides' prohibitions on plurality, relative change, and motion and to turn unchanging reality into our experienced world of ever-varying things.

EMPEDOCLES

Empedocles, from the Sicilian town of Akragas, is the last Presocratic from the West. He is also the last with active religious beliefs and the last to write in poetry. He is a transitional figure with echoes of Pythagorean mysticism alongside the new cosmological materialism. He was known for strong democratic beliefs and founding a school of medicine, but he may not have practiced medicine himself. He was a careful observer of the types and qualities of plants and animals. He developed his philosophy early and influenced the slightly older Anaxagoras.

He wrote two books: *On Nature* and *Purifications*. Books were referred to by their subject matter, so most nature inquiries were called *On Nature*. Although only 10 percent of his work, the 450 lines we have are the most of any Presocratic. He wrote in the epic poetry of his major influences, Hesiod and Parmenides, but unlike them was known for an effective style. Aristotle called him the inventor of rhetoric. His two books respond to the two main philosophies in the Italian colonies, Parmenides' ontology, and Pythagoras' religious mysticism.

Unlike Parmenides, he follows ordinary reason with only hints of the supernatural. Like Hesiod, his poem is friendly advice without divine logic or revelation. He begins with two Heraclitean views: skepticism about people's ability to understand and the possibility of some knowledge with proper use of one's senses and mind. He hints that such knowledge brings special powers, as controlling the weather, curing ills, and raising the dead, but here does not discuss these further.[42]

He revises the means and rules by which nature (Necessity) organizes the four elements (earth, air, fire, and water) to make the ever-changing things we experience. He explains *why* change happens but not *how* to control it, as we are also just phenomena in a larger cycle of unending natural processes. He symbolically describes each element through an Olympian god, but only to illustrate their natural ordering and the regularity of their interactions. Two natural forces, not gods, cause the elements to move: Love brings all things together and Strife pulls them apart. They alternate being dominant in an eternal cycle. Extreme unity is an undifferentiated uniform sphere, like Parmenides' being-in-the-ball but made of the four elements. In extreme separation the four elements are entirely differentiated into their cosmic layers, with fire and air above and earth and water below. The eternal vortex (which we see in the celestial rotation) keeps all things moving and brings Love or Strife back into the mix after the

---

[42] DK Fr. 111. This material seems more appropriate to Empedocles' second book but has traditionally been placed in the first.

opposite completion. This apparatus keeps all things from mixing or disintegrating until the extremes of the cycle; thus, it permits both identity and change. The vortex is always circling, so the system never "dies." The small-scale organizations of matter that we call mortal creatures are not actually new beings but only new mixtures, so that in Empedocles' healthy way of speaking, they neither are born nor die. They merely move in and out of being an organized mixture. These material mixtures seem at odds with his belief in souls subject to divine justice and reincarnation.

Empedocles does not specify the duration of this cycle. We are now in the increasing Love and mixing phase, which gives birth to all mortal things. Stable species develop in a manner resembling Darwin's "survival of the adaptable." The mixtures are random, often unviable pieces of things that gradually became more united and organized. "Here sprang up many faces without necks, arms wandered without shoulders, unattached, and eyes strayed alone, in need of foreheads" (DK Fr. 57). Some of these collected into functioning structures that in time were refined into coherent plants and animals.[43] When fully developed, they reproduce by themselves. The proliferation of mortal things out of just four elements is similar to the palette of a painter where a few colors create an infinite variety of shades. Divine beings are only symbols in his materialistic account of elements and forces.

> And earth chanced in about equal quantity upon these, Hephaestus [that is, fire], rain, and gleaming air [lit. *aither*], anchored in the perfect harbors of Cypris [that is, Love], either a little more of it or less of it among more of them. From these arose blood and various forms of flesh. (Fr. 98)
>
> And kindly earth received in its broad melting-pots two parts of the glitter of Nestis [that is, water] out of eight, and four of Hephaestus; and they became white bones, marvelously joined by the gluing of Harmonia. (Fr. 96)

His book ends with several biological inquiries. Since plants and animals are mixtures of mixtures of mixtures of the elements, a similar

---

[43] Aristotle gives a good account of the randomness of this process. "Wherever, then, everything turned out as it would have if it were happening for a purpose, there the creatures survived, being accidentally compounded in a suitable way; but where this did not happen, the creatures perished and are perishing still, as Empedocles says of his 'man-faced ox-progeny.'" He felt a theory of natural kinds explained natural stability better than these random mixings of complex pieces.

level of mixture (arm, wing, fin) appears across seemingly different kinds. This relation of all creatures began comparative anatomy. "The same things are hair and leaves and the close-packed feathers of birds and the scales which come into being on sturdy limbs" (Fr. 82). In his theory of sensation, various-sized particles flow off the surfaces of things and into the different-sized openings of our sense organs. The right-sized particle activates the sensation, while the too-small pass through and the too-big cannot enter. Once activated, various sensations combine in the blood and gather in the heart, initiating thought. The blood is where "above all other parts the elements are blended" (DK 31 A 86). Thinking most occurs in the heart, "dwelling in the sea of blood which surges back and forth, where especially is what is called thought by men; for the blood around men's hearts is their thought" (Fr. 105).

Empedocles explains the world as materialistic and god-free in conformity with Parmenides' logic. Knowledge of the gods is beyond any explanation. Thought arises from matter processed in our senses, while the immaterial gods provide no sense data. He elusively defines God as "mind alone, holy and beyond description, darting through the whole cosmos with swift thoughts" (Fr. 134).

Empedocles' second book *Purifications* deals with more religious and Pythagorean issues. He calls himself a *daimon,* a semidivine spiritual being moving in and out of mortality, divine being, and reincarnation into various life forms. As incarnation is a punishment for intentionally shedding blood either by sacrificing or eating an animal, he supports Pythagoras' vegetarianism. Our souls pass into different forms, so any killing of animals could involve a former family member. "The father lifts up his own son changed in form and slaughters him with a prayer, blind fool, as he shrieks piteously, beseeching as he sacrifices. But he, deaf to his cries, slaughters him and makes ready in his halls an evil feast. In the same way son seizes father and children their mother, and tearing out the life they eat the flesh of those they love" (Fr. 137).

This shows his high rhetorical style that impressed Aristotle. One escapes punishment by avoiding bloodshed for thirty thousand years of reincarnations. If good, one attains more suitable mortal forms, approaching their original divine status. "At the end they come among men on earth as prophets, bards, doctors and princes; and thence they arise as gods highest in honor, sharing with the other immortals their hearth and their table, without part in human sorrows or weariness" (Fr. 146–147). Plato revisits these images and issues in the *Phaedrus.*

The immaterial *daimon* can respond to ethical teaching as the materialist mixings of the "four elements, two forces, and a whirlwind" cannot. Empedocles opposed Parmenides with a pluralistic cosmology and the *daimon* to make possible an ethical-spiritual life. Parmenides' helpful goddess is a bloodless image of necessity, dissolving with the other illusions. Knowing her leads nowhere. Empedocles' gods, Love and Strife, do explain change. Love properly mixes all things, even uniting thinking with its proper objects. Being pure mind, it does not act materially but has material results, like its modern analogy, gravity. Love's thinking moves the entire universe. Empedocles' daimonic thinking shares in this divine thinking, mixing the colors on the divine palette. Thus, he sees how all things are connected, understands reincarnation, and rejects bloodshed, fulfilling Parmenides' quietism. His materialism is compatible with committing to a better life through higher stages of reincarnation. He described an ethics beyond Parmenides, not totally coherent but enough to inspire later thinkers such as Plato.

Anaxagoras

Anaxagoras first brought philosophy to Athens, starting its fame as the philosophical center of Greece. He came from Clazomenae in Ionia as a young man after the second Persian War and was exiled back to Lampsacus in Ionia before the Peloponnesian War. He was a friend and public associate of Pericles, active in the intellectual ferment of Athens' Golden Age. Political rivals wanting to damage Pericles tried, convicted, and exiled Anaxagoras for impiety (heavenly bodies are hot rocks, not divine beings). He died in exile as a revered elder.

His philosophy is similar to Empedocles, and it is uncertain which influenced the other. Both agreed with Parmenides that the real is eternal and unchanging but rejected that it must thus be one and undifferentiated. What is real exists through, instead of beyond, time and space. Both developed systems with multiple elemental basic stuffs, each stuff remaining what it is while mixing with others to produce the things we experience. Empedocles does this with four elements, two opposed forces, and a whirlwind. Anaxagoras uses an infinite number of elements, each infinitely divisible in size and mixed so that each contains miniscule particles of all the others. He also has an immaterial initiating force called "Mind," which creates a rotation in the universe, causing the elements to begin separating out, like joining with like. Both systems use a motion, a godless mechanical procedure that, once begun, continues forever making the mortal things of experience, thus causing both permanence and variety in the world. Anaxagoras used a commonsense simplicity, in contrast to Empedocles' vivid imagery, florid rhetoric, and divine topics.

Anaxagoras' universe is eternal and contains everything that ever was or will be as an infinite number of infinitesimally small things that are too small for our eyes to experience directly. Thus, all of reality is present all of the time. Time began after a primal state when air and aither (his fire) held all things, including Mind, in suspension. Mind is an infinite being, "the finest of all things and the purest" (Fr. 12), not material like the elements or in contact with them. It thinks and knows, thus ruling itself and all other things. "Mind controlled also the whole rotation, so that it began to rotate in the beginning" (Fr. 12). Why it began and why in a rotation are not discussed. He presents many claims and descriptions but few arguments or evidence. In accord with Parmenides, he maintains the separation of being and motion. Mind does not move materially. It has mental motion, but how this affects physical movement is not addressed. The Cosmic Mind is like the human mind, which also initiates physical activities while not sharing their matter.

Both Anaxagoras and Empedocles find something more than Parmenides' matter. Anaxagoras needs immaterial Mind to move resting matter. As the rotation it creates begins to mechanically organize (laws of nature) the things of the world, Mind retreats from these areas yet still somehow remains in touch with all things (Frs. 13 and 14). His Mind is only a momentary player, establishing the rules for informing the things of nature but not forming them. It inspired further work on the form–matter problem, giving Socrates hope that Anaxagoras could provide reasons both for what was chosen and why this was for the best. But his Mind does not explain, and Socrates was broken-hearted.[44]

Greeks liked the vortex idea (the rotation, whirlpool, whirlwind) because it was circular (stable continuous motion) and also sorted its contents, the lighter and faster on the outside and the heavier in the middle. Thus, it both mixes and separates and keeps separated the things of our experience as they formed out of the primal undifferentiated mix. To imagine the rotation of the sky as the constant movement of the

---

[44] Plato, *Phaedo*, 97c–99d.

vortex that creates and maintains the order of all things (or for Empe-docles, the motion of all things) is an amazing idea that unites our observations with the greater mechanics of the universe. Anaxagoras, again, offers no proof for this claim other than its reasonableness.

But more is required beyond separating light and heavy to form the things we experience. The difference between flesh and stone or hot and cold is locked in the infinitesimal particles and lacks the density to be centrifuged. Anaxagoras' solution is seeds, particles with an unexplained greater portion of one element, which attract more of it and eventually become identifiable, while retaining infinitesimal particles of all others. There seem to be seeds both for things and for qualities (opposites such as hot and cold, dry and wet, light and dark, and so on). The vortex sorts the elements in stages, first separating fire (up) and air (down) and with them respective qualities (hot, dry, and light with fire) and things (stars and lightning with fire, but steam or lava?). The vortex sorts things by weight, but how does it sort qualities, and would they then be in only certain areas of the vortex? Anaxagoras never explains the vortexing of qualities or how seeds arise and attract in a uniform mix. They are promising ideas and apparently satisfactory enough.

Anaxagoras was an acute observer, realizing that the moon's light was reflected (and cut off in an eclipse) and that rainbows were reflected sunlight on the clouds. He understood the cycle of water evaporation and condensation, that the stars are glowing hot rocks and that the moon is made of earth with hills and valleys. He thought the earth was flat but also that the heavens revolved completely around it (KRS 502, DK 59a42). Finally, unlike Empedocles, he felt sensation resulted from the meeting of unlike things. We do not sense a temperature that is the same as ours but only those that differ. As Theophrastus explains, "Every perception is accompanied by pain, a consequence that would seem to follow from his hypothesis; for everything unlike produces pain by its contact, and the presence of this pain becomes clear either from the too long duration or from an excess of sensation" (KRS 511, DK 59a92). The understanding that nerves react because they are irritated is still centuries away, and to suggest that perceptions arise from being poked is typical of him, provocative but not provable for him.

Leucippus and Democritus

Atomism is the third response to Parmenides, developed by Leucip-pus and elaborated by Democritus. We know little about either, and the stories we have may have been amended by later Epicureans who adopted atomism as their physics. Leucippus responds to Melissus' version of Parmenides and is thus taken to be younger, perhaps born around 470. Democritus is usually taken to be his pupil, but only ten instead of the standard forty years younger. Leucippus probably came from Ionia and Democritus from Abdera in Thrace. Perhaps Leucippus had a school in Abdera where they met, and Democritus then took over. Both spent some time in Athens. The older Sophist Protagoras also came from Abdera and is reported to have taken lessons from him.

Leucippus wrote at least one book, called *Great World System* (a change from *On Nature*), explaining how atomism works in the universe. One fragment survives. Democritus was the most prolific Presocratic, writing over sixty books with several hundred fragments still existing. His many topics included the *Small World System* (atomism on the human level, "Man is a small ordered world" (Fr. 34, W), the planets, the senses, reason, logic, the soul, flesh, colors, flavors, images, Pythagoras, dispositions of the wise, tranquility, and so on.[45] His fragments testify to the accidents of survival, as over 80 percent are due to the ethical interests of a fifth-century-AD anthologist, John of Stobi. Leucippus shares Empedocles' Heraclitean skepticism toward naïve human knowledge and his speculation on the materialist basis of reality but rejects all religious imagery and creates a totally materialist cosmology.

They agree with Parmenides that the real must be eternal and unchanging but see that multiplicity and motion are also real. Empedocles and Anaxagoras overcome Parmenides' reduction to the One by equating the one and the many, since sensible things are only temporary compounds of an invisible basic substance and eventually dissolve back into it. Our sensible experience of the world is an accident of our poor vision and short life. The real particles are invisible to us, and the ephemeral constructs around us only happen to last longer than we do. Atomist materialism removes Mind, Strife, and Love to see how far matter alone can explain all things. Our experienced world is just mixtures of atoms passing in and out of connections. Our perceptions and thinking are just atoms. There are only atoms—and the Void.

Atoms are indivisible (Gk. *atomon*), invisible, hard particles, infinite in number. They vary in size, shape, direction of turning (like quarks), and interface or contacting surface, but all are the same

---

[45] Diogenes Laertius IX 46–49, in Wheelwright (W), p. 195–196.

unchanging substance. This can manifest itself in many ways, but these differences do not make any difference; none alters its basic being. As the atoms collide, they may stick together or bounce off. Certain features encourage sticking, as an atom with a hook meeting one with a loop. Convex fits into concave, corrugated into corrugated, and so on. The stronger the connection, the longer lasting the bond.

Atoms have to move and collide to construct our visible world, and so their nature is to do so. Democritus did not explain why atoms initially move. In *On Democritus* Aristotle gives this report: "They struggle and move in the void because of the dissimilarities between them and the other differences already mentioned [shape and size]; and as they move they collide and become entangled" (DK 68 A 37). Motion also requires an unoccupied space through which to move, which they called the Void. This makes two basic stuffs, one of things and another of no things. Each needs the other to make our world, straining the monistic simplicity of just atoms. Melissus had already argued against a Void. "And nothing of it is empty. For what is empty is nothing. Well, what is nothing could not very well exist. Nor does it move. For it cannot give way at any point, but is full. For if there were such a thing as empty it would give way into what was empty; but since there is no such thing as empty, it has nowhere to give way" (Fr. 7).

Melissus denies an actual infinity of space can exist, and the atomists do not explain. They reply, "You have what is necessary"; motion needs space, so there is space, an infinite space. With an infinity of atoms in infinite space, the density of atoms in the Void looks constant, like gas dispersed in a vacuum, to maximize motion and collisions.

Democritus did see the need for a local container to maintain local stability. He thought groups of atoms would break off from the rest, (a random momentary density), begin to whirl (another vortex), and as a result form a spherical membrane (gravity?) around the group, as the dense moves to the center and the rare to the edges.[46] Our heavenly dome displays the lighter objects, caught and dried in the membrane, burning in the rare air out there. The membrane creates this

---

[46] Gas uniformly disperses in a vacuum unless there is a current. Thus, the whirls must precede the separating off of groups of atoms, and the initiating atoms must have a whirling tendency.

atmosphere of air within the Void. Clumps and whirls can appear and disappear at any moment, making other worlds large and small.

> Democritus spoke as if the things that are were in constant motion in the void; and there are innumerable worlds, which differ in size.... The intervals between the worlds are unequal; in some parts there are more worlds, in others fewer; some are increasing, some at their height, some decreasing; in some parts they are arising, in others failing. They are destroyed by collision one with another. There are some worlds devoid of living creatures or plants or any moisture. (Hippolyus, DK 68 A 40)

The only principle for generating these worlds is random collisions in the void. With an infinite number of atoms, it seems an infinite variety of worlds could be created. The kinds of things in our world are an accident of the kinds of atoms in the clump that divided off. However, if the atoms were randomly ordered, the contents among clumps and the worlds arising from them would not differ much except in size. Concentrations of different kinds of seeds could also explain variation. Leucippus' fragment then provides an ironic motto. "Nothing occurs at random, but everything for a reason and by necessity" (DK Fr. 2).

The atomic stability of things is relative, as with time all dissolve. Collisions finally break all bonds yet are not so strong as to prevent any bonds from forming. There are no natural kinds, only temporary repeated patterns. Atoms do have certain connecting patterns (for example, hooks) but might never come in contact. The collisions and connections resemble Empedocles' Strife and Love with an idea of cosmic balance but are not ordered or cyclic. That atoms naturally move also resembles the life force in the soul. Such ideas likely informed his thinking. Issues such as why one vortex does not engulf the rest like a black hole are not explained. He grasps the big picture, saying, "My account gets us here."

The strict materialism of atomism says thinking arises from images striking the mind (heart) through the senses. Like Empedocles believed, sensations arise when an atomic film (effluence or image) emitted by the sense object hits the sensory organ, but he thought the eye projected its own effluent that meets the incoming effluent from the object. The moist part of this datum then passes into the moist inner eye. Thinking occurs with spherical nonsticky soul (mind) atoms that move easily and are dispersed all through the body. Atoms all act the same, so thinking is only a temporary byproduct of a mixture. The values given to certain sense data are as bogus as humanlike gods for Xenophanes. "Democritus sometimes does away with what appears to the senses, and says that none of these appears according to truth but only according to opinion: the truth in real things is that there are atoms and the void. 'By convention sweet,' he says, 'by convention bitter, by convention hot, by convention cold, by convention colour: but in reality atoms and void'" (Sextus, KRS 410, DK Fr. 9).

He does not explain how mind developed, remains stable, or manipulates ideas. The passing phenomenal mixes of the world (including mind) are another Parmenidean Way of Seeming, a procession of things inviting inquiry but lacking any real structure or order. Random collisions can describe a causal sequence but not an organization of such causes. Inquiry is ultimately fruitless. Since mind is created by sense data, a theory going beyond sense data is problematic. He wrote a dialogue where the senses express this, "Wretched mind, do you take your assurances from us and then overthrow us? Our overthrow is your downfall" (Fr. 125). But there really is no mind to fall down, just as Zeno's mental exercises serve a mindless cause.

The goal of atomist inquiry is emotional well-being. After he explains being as the necessary mechanics of atoms, Democritus, unlike Parmenides, still discusses ethics. "Choice" is also determined by how the atoms collide and stick. His interest in ethics is only to be comfortable. His attitude toward the world is as cold as Parmenides' toward the one and finally as inert. He expresses Parmenides' quietism, advising to do only what is clearly in our power and not more.

> The man who is going to be in good spirits must not do too much, neither in private nor public, nor, whatever he does, must he aspire beyond his natural power. But rather he must be so much on his guard that, even when chance comes his way and points to more, in his judgement [sic] he can lay it aside and not put his hand to more than what lies in his power. The right load is a safer thing than a large load. (DK Fr. 3)

He advises a life without investments. The temporary universe beguiles us with illusions of order and stability to hope and plan, but we must not. The risk of conceiving a child, for example, without knowing the qualities of the outcome, would be foolish. "He who wishes to have children...would do better to adopt them from families with which he is on friendly terms. Thereby, being able to select, he can get the kind of child he wants. . . . For if he begets a child of his own, the risks are many and he is bound to accept whatever comes" (Fr. 277, W).

Mental hygiene is to remove "untimely pleasures" and "immoderate desires" from our consciousness, just as we removed the illusions of the world of opinion and convention. "Virtue consists not in avoiding wrong-doing but in being without any wish for it" (Fr. 62, W). The soul does more harm through its pursuits than if it were to just accept life as it comes. Democritus goes almost so far as to prefer that there not be a soul, as when he puts the soul on trial for abuse. "[The body] would take pleasure in finding the soul guilty, on the ground that she had gravely injured the body by her heedlessness, had dissolved it with drunken revels, and corrupted and torn it apart by her lust for pleasure—in the same way that I would blame one who handled carelessly some valuable but fragile instrument" (Fr. 159, W).

But the body's value is also illusory. Like any compound, it falls apart. "Old age is scattered mutilation: it still has all of its parts, but each of them is somehow lacking" (Fr. 296, W). In the end, the soul has its own pleasures that at least make life interesting. "I would rather discover one cause than to possess the kingdom of Persia" (Fr. 118, W).

3

The Sophists

The Sophists offer a different reply to Parmenides than did the Pluralists and Atomists. If individuals can take liberties with logic to save the multiplicity of experience, individuals and not logic are the arbiters of truth. "Man is the measure," whether as privilege or curse. Ignoring the basic stuff wars, the Sophists secularize inquiry as nonreligious and nonphilosophical. They moved the metaphysical debates from the unseen structure of the universe to the unseen nature of human beings, from the understanding of nature to the nature of understanding. To appreciate their role in the development of Greek reason and inquiry, a review of the ideas we have discussed will clarify the influences they were responding to and help focus their contribution.

The Milesians used their reason as they experienced it. They made relations they saw among things into theories about the nature of all things, including those beyond their experience, and felt confident in these applications of reason. Xenophanes began the vertigo by emphasizing the difference between the mind of god and that of humans. Perhaps our reasoning is not the pure reasoning of the gods but a deficient form of it. Then Heraclitus sees the world is in flux, making knowledge a problem since everything is always changing, including the knower, thus denying any shared context. Parmenides further limits reason, as it cannot be applied in a world without time, space, or any distinctions. If only one thing is and its only quality is being, then there is nowhere to go in either the physical or mental world. Reason ceases in the speechless awareness of unitary being. But his follower Zeno finds pleasure in the illicit play (motion) of reason as he multiplies its paradoxes, and Melissus finds he cannot live without seeing the one in time and space.

Our experiences of time, space, motion, and multiplicity are too powerful to easily let them go. If we accept Heraclitus' Flux or Parmenides' Unity, we are still confronted with the "illusion" that experience is diverse, relatively stable, and contributes to our feeling happy, successful, knowing, or their opposites. We are stuck in a world of experience we did not make and not totally subject to our reasoning. The bald assumptions in the Pluralist and Atomist responses to Parmenides reflect their idea of human reason as limited, guessing at the invisible because our eyes cannot see it. As finite beings, we will never know the infinite universe: why atoms always move, how matter can be infinitely divided, or why Strife and Love alternate in the universe. Human reason here takes whatever clarity it can find, accepting there are things beyond both our physical and mental ability to grasp. Thus, Democritus claims his atomic theory applies universally, determining our actions, yet he also promotes a life of quietism. Our *logos* no longer directly joins us to the universal *logos*. Our imperfect sense data help verify our constructions of how things are but give no certainty or revelation everyone must accept. The arguments are suggestive but do not attain the level of assent-compelling demonstration.

Thus, the Heraclitean–Parmenidean loss of Reason left a power vacuum. With traditional customs and beliefs compromised by Xenophanian monotheism, Pythagorean number mysticism, Herodotean comparative anthropology, and Anaxagorean heavenly hot rocks, and reason no more able to guide people's lives than the amoral gods, the field is open for the imitators of reason to make their claim. Natural necessity is found only on the microscopic level of unseen particles, leaving macroscopic human affairs free to develop their own truth. This truth frees people from logical constraints, including the Flux and the One, and leaves them able to believe whatever they want (the upside of democracy). However, the beliefs that are most attractive may not lead to a good life (the downside of democracy). This was the time bomb Parmenides left us in the plausible arguments of his Way of Opinion.

Interest in Zeno's arguments showed this was a product that people wanted and a market to develop. Any physical view of reality revealed paradoxes, showing the power of reason to unsettle the mind. "If anything is moving, it must be moving either in the place in which it is or in a place in which it is not. However, it cannot move in the place in which it is [for the place in which it is at any moment is of the same size as itself and hence allows it no room to move in], and it cannot move in the place in which it is not. Thus movement is impossible."[1]

The Sophists applied this technique to truth. Both sides of an issue (smoking does or does not cause cancer) could be developed to have equal strength and plausibility and thus both be true. These are the two-sided arguments, the *dissoi logoi,* a primary exercise for the Sophists' students. The goal was to convince someone on either side of an issue that the opposite of what she initially believed was true. This was done for display and in jest, as when Gorgias proves Helen was not to blame for starting the Trojan War, or for work, as when he convinced his brother's medical patients to permit some painful procedure.

The itinerant Sophists marketed this skill in the later fifth century. They serviced the ambitious citizens' and youths' desire for success[2] in the social, political, and juridical debates in the market-places, assemblies, and law courts, especially in the democratic cities. In deciding which of the two sides is true, it all depends on the debate you are trying to win. "Man is the measure of all things: of things that are, that they are; of things that are not, that they are not" (Fr. 1, W).[3] These words were Protagoras' sword to split the Gordian Knot of Being and legitimize Parmenides' Way of Opinion for the market-place of discourse. It was the defining moment in the Sophistic movement. I can only judge the reality of experience or truth of an argument limited by whatever methods and data I have collected to date. How you do your judging is irrelevant unless I choose to acknowledge it. New evidence may later arise, but at this moment neither of us can think differently than we do. I am the master of my fate, but as I can only follow what I happen to believe at any moment, my fate becomes the master of me.

To be human is to measure and judge. With this commonsense statement a new, yet familiar, kind of necessity has appeared, that of being at this moment in time and space with a unique viewpoint. Truth becomes a constant companion; whatever I think is happening is truly what is happening for me. I cannot think anything else is

---

[1] Wheelwright, *The Presocratics,* Fr. 3, p. 108. Quotation from Epiphanius, *Against Heresies.*

[2] The Greek term *arete* unites virtue, success, and excellence, but the culture questioned the relation. Which one is the measure of the others?

[3] No Sophists are found in KRS. "W" is Wheelwright's *The Presocratics.*

happening until the next moment, which is a new moment with a new truth for me, and so on. The events flowing by on "reality television" show this notion of truth. "From moment to moment" defines one dimension of our lives, and whether any more enduring qualities exist requires more inquiry. Protagoras discounts the past and future, as they exist only through the current moment. He makes both change and stability irrelevant by his emphasis on the moment. He tames Heraclitus' Flux by knowing what anything is at every moment, and Parmenides' Unity is benign in each moment, for whatever is, is exactly what it is, necessary and complete. He humanized the bogeymen, so long as we stay in the moment.

The Sophists became the wise men of the Moment, changing the ancient name for a skilled or wise man, *sophos,* to *sophistes,* practitioners of wisdom. As visiting teachers, the early Sophists' received support and even respect in many Greek cities. Gorgias was asked to give commemorative speeches at Delphi, Olympia, and Athens and to serve his city of Leontini on diplomatic missions. But as with traveling salesmen of "life-enhancing" aids in all eras—from elixirs to encyclopedias—locals are wary of strangers giving advice, especially to their children. Even before the Peloponnesian War, Sophists' students realized their teachers' ill repute. In Plato's *Protagoras,* young Hippocrates blushes when asked, "Would you not be ashamed to present yourself to the Greeks in the character of a sophist?" (*Prot.* 312a). As the War went on, the standing of the Sophists sank further. Aristophanes' *The Clouds* in 423 satirized Sophists as greedy, fast-talking quacks, preying on the rich and the dim and manipulating already shaky social values.[4] Wartime scandals, as those of the Sophist-trained Alcibiades, led Anytus in Plato's *Meno* to know all Sophists are evil, though he never met one. "May no one of my household or friends, whether citizen or stranger, be mad enough to go to these [Sophists] and be harmed by them, for they clearly cause the ruin and corruption of their followers" (*Meno* 91c). But interest in the skill of persuasion continued.

Fifty years later, Plato still so fears the Wisdom of the Moment that rhetoric and the Sophists remain a major focus. The reputations of the Sophists and Plato usually move in opposition. At the end of the nineteenth century, Plato was tied to traditional Victorian values, so that

---

[4] Aristophanes uses Socrates as his model Sophist, though he never taught outside Athens or for pay. The play's farmer-hero seeks rhetoric to avoid paying bills but finds its corruption threatens to destroy his culture, so he destroys Socrates' school. Only choking stops the force of rhetoric, as the burning school's smoke finally ends all speaking.

humanism, democracy, liberalism, enlightenment, reform, progress, and empiricism were lined up with the Sophists and against him.[5] They were heroes against the "platonic" reactionary, dogmatic, and totalitarian forces. Following World War II, the outcry against Plato as the Muse of fascism's perverse idealism was as fervent (and wrong) as that against Nietzsche. Now the cycle is reversing, with Plato even linked with liberal democracy against the anarchist liberalities of the nihilist Sophists. The swings of popular opinion continue, as terms like *liberal* and *conservative* change meaning at least once every Olympiad.

Plato gives us the most complete portraits for several Sophists. Some say these are too one-sided to serve as better foils for Socrates, yet the characters must fit their popular image for the audience to accept the story. I think Protagoras was as self-promoting, Gorgias as self-confident, and Hippias as self-sufficient as Plato represents them. Protagoras, Gorgias, Hippias, and Euthydemus each have their own dialogue, and Thrasymachus has a major role in the *Republic*.[6] The first three are good businessmen, offering a quality, if not always appreciated, product to a broad and lucrative market. They hold conventional ethical beliefs (as good for business) and are generally decent fellows. Euthydemus and his brother are charlatans who enter the word-wrestling business because it is easier at their age than their prior body-wrestling one. Thrasymachus, like Kallikles, is a second-generation Sophist freed of his elders' conventional ethical beliefs and ready to maximize his business potential. To acquire and use power is now explicitly his trade, manipulating language as well as beliefs in this pursuit. With "words meaning what I want them to mean,"[7] this "moment-to-moment" imitation of reason is unstable and not viable. The dissolution of the political state into tyranny in Plato's *Republic* is a metaphor for that of the linguistic community into ad baculum (force of the fist) arguments, "My definition is true because I can make you believe it—at the risk of your life." Plato critiques rhetoric to deal with these corrosive effects.

---

[5] W. T. Stace in 1920 gives the traditional anti-Sophist case. "They laid the emphasis on . . . my impulses, feelings, and sensations, and made these the source of truth and morality, instead of emphasizing as the source of truth and right the universal part of me, my reason." *A Critical History of Greek Philosophy* (New York: St. Martins Press, 1962), pp. 122–126.

[6] Plato also wrote the *Critias,* about his uncle who did not teach but helped develop rhetoric. Prodicus is also mentioned but not featured.

[7] Remember the Red Queen in *Alice in Wonderland.*

In Plato's *Phaedrus,* Socrates says a science of rhetoric requires a large (perhaps impossibly large) amount of learning. "A man who sets out to mislead without being misled himself must have an exact knowledge of the likenesses and unlikenesses between things" (*Phaedrus* 262a). He must know enough to convince his ever-changing audience, which may always include experts in the moment's topic. His appearance of knowing must be supported by actually knowing whatever information could be known. He also must know all the types of people so that he can tailor his persuasion to their individual desires and beliefs. He needs to be a psychologist of extraordinary breadth.[8] In fact, the ultimate rhetorician looks much like Socrates, with his daily inquiries into the knowledge and personalities of his fellow citizens and his capacity for rhetoric in these pursuits. He vitiates the manipulative dangers of rhetoric by showing that to avoid mistakes, personal success requires communal validation instead of preying upon such communities. Persuasion is a necessary part of education and public discourse. The patient will not take the medicine or the citizen change a habit unless persuaded. The problem is how to safely domesticate rhetoric.

The understanding, application, and teaching of rhetoric requires knowledge of many disciplines. The usual preparation to be a speaker, politician, or lawyer required one to learn logic, grammar, history for the cultural context of stories and examples, and literature for the allusions and models of style. The Sophists' lasting influence was the social impact of their teaching, yet they studied and contributed in all of these areas. They made detailed studies of the history, composition, and use of language. Prodicus differentiated similarly defined terms. Cratylus studied the history and development of words. Pericles chose Protagoras to create the laws for the colony at Thurii. Gorgias, Prodicus, and Hippias served their cities on diplomatic missions. Hippias was a polymath and walking encyclopedia, teaching a profusion of courses: astronomy, geometry, math, grammar, rhythm and harmony, and ancient history (favored by the Spartans). He made his own clothes, poems, and skillful commentaries on others such as Homer.[9] Plato's Protagoras, however, says his way avoids all this liberal learning.

---

[8] Athens produced at least three outstanding psychologists at the end of the fifth century: Socrates, Thucydides, and Euripides.

[9] "You are the wisest of people in the greatest number of crafts, as I once heard you boasting" (Lesser Hippias 368b–e).

(My students) will not experience the sort of drudgery with which other Sophists are in the habit of insulting their pupils who, when they have just escaped from the arts, are taken and driven back into them ... and made to learn calculation, and astronomy, and geometry, and music. ... But if he comes to me he will learn only that which he comes to learn. And this is prudence in affairs private as well as public, ... to speak and act most powerfully in the affairs of the state. (*Prot.* 318d–e)

Protagoras describes a modern academic major with its career technical training as opposed to a broader general education that applies and tests this. Most sophists (and universities) agreed that technique always trumps context, that is, defines its own success. Only Sparta asked Hippias to recite history and saw rhetoric training as subversive. The Sophistic Being in the Moment shrinks the culture to whatever beliefs the audience happen to share at that moment. Technique for dealing with the moment overcomes knowing what it might mean.

Many *Art of Rhetoric* handbooks tried to systematically explain this technique. In the *Phaedrus,* Socrates mentions works by Tisias, Corax, Protagoras, Theodorus, and Polus. In his *Rhetoric,* Aristotle says these emphasize too much manipulation of the emotions and beliefs of jurors in the law courts and too little examination of the logical basis of arguments. Like Plato, Aristotle studied rhetoric as the necessary persuasion in civil discourse and to control those who abuse it.[10]

As itinerant teachers, the Sophists brought a generic education to Greece. Instead of teaching the traditions, customs, or gods of any one city, they had a secularizing and homogenizing effect. Their teaching claimed to be neutral on value issues and thus suitable for all value systems. Traditional education was either practical tasks learned as an apprentice or civil tasks learned as an observer at the law courts, temples, and festivals. Society, however, was becoming less cohesive and coherent. Greece lost its isolation after the Persian Wars. Commerce brought new ideas and influences. Plato's *Republic* opens with a new religious festival challenging old beliefs, and Thucydides shows Athenian morality changing as they enforce their new imperial power. They ignore the tradition against Greeks killing

---

[10] Plato's *Euthydemus* displays the tricks. R. K. Sprague's *Plato's Use of Fallacy* shows Socrates uses fallacy, like a Sophist, to advance his arguments but also to challenge and teach his listeners. The Sophists are in *The Older Sophists* (Columbia: University of South Carolina Press, 1972).

Greeks in their destruction of the Melians. Teaching how society works and how to work in it is replaced by how to gain individual *arete* (virtue, success), or at least its reputation. Reflecting the loss of a shared necessary truth, success also shifted from a communal recognition of achievement to an individual display of power.[11] For example, in Plato's dialogue Meno is going to Persia as a soldier to show his *arete,* the power to get life's goods (*Meno* 78b). His army is betrayed deep inside Persia, and all its leaders are killed, with Meno's death the most gruesome. Power never by itself creates truth, as Plato's sad stories of friendless and unvalidated tyrants remind us. Socrates stays in his native city all his life. He can only become virtuous among people who will criticize him—in the stable language by which they live their lives and not just manipulate those of others.

The Sophists' students sound like convincing experts on any topic. "(Gorgias) accustomed you to give a bold and grand answer to any question you may be asked, as experts are likely to do. Indeed, he himself was ready to answer any Greek who wished to question him, and every question was answered"[12] (*Meno* 70b–c). This claim to answer any question was common. Plato's Gorgias boasts, "I just now made that claim and I say that no one has asked me anything new in many a year" (*Gorgias* 448a). All differences are reduced to displays of style. When asked if his answers are good, Gorgias' student Polus replies, "What does it matter, as long as they are good enough for you?" (*Gorgias* 448b). Truth is what we each make of it. This may be flattering and empowering but also upsetting in light of our individual limitations. Gorgias convinces patients to accept treatments better than his medical brother does; he makes the medicine sound appealing (*Gorgias* 456b). If "experts" are teaching or advising, we are at their mercy as long as their speech is believable and presented with style.[13] Ignorance of content means reliance on style, for example, in forensic testimony, where citizens decide which competing esoteric expert is telling the truth.

---

[11] The *Iliad's* Hektor hopes to do a last grand deed before dying. "Let me at least not die without a struggle, inglorious, but do some big thing first, that men to come shall know of it" (XXII 304–305). Traditional *arete* was a community–based value; it had to be recognized by another.

[12] Some professors reword students' questions, making them sound impressive while shifting them to what the professors wish to discuss. This flattery distracts from realizing the question was not answered.

[13] Information is not all true, which makes the Internet so precarious. Lacking knowledge, we often evaluate it based on style and familiarity.

The Sophists promoted modernity in the social and intellectual debates: skepticism vs. religious belief, technique vs. tradition, nature vs. convention, and virtue (*arete*) as power. Protagoras's religious ideas got him exiled from Athens. "As for the gods, I have no way of knowing either that they exist or that they do not exist; nor, if they exist, of what form they are. For the obstacles to that sort of knowledge are many, including the obscurity of the matter and the brevity of human life" (Fr. 4, W). "Common sense" was used against obscure and superstitious beliefs but also gave an anti-intellectual message. Complexity was considered obscurity, so experts do not really know what they are talking about. Anyone should be able to understand anything of importance. The "lowest common denominator" best persuades a crowd. Their interest was more in political popularity than reform. In Plato's *Symposium,* Pausanias sounds like a social scientist, but this veneer is only to promote his interest in seducing boys.

After "man is the measure," the Sophists are best known for a natural standard in ethics, dismissing traditional values as arbitrary and local. Antiphon's argument is typical.[14]

> A person would make most advantage of justice for himself if he treated the laws as important in the presence of witnesses, and treated the decrees of nature as important when alone and with no witnesses present. For the decrees of nature are necessary; those of the laws are the products of agreement.... If those who made the agreement do not notice a person transgressing the prescriptions of the laws, he is free from both disgrace and penalty.... Most of the things that are just according to law are ... hostile to nature. (DK 87 B 44, CCR Fr. 16)[15]

Antiphon thinks the law restricts our natural satisfactions. As Thrasymachus says in the *Republic,* the law is created by the strong to control the weak, often the many weaklings against the few naturally strong. Happiness is doing as you wish, not what society's

---

[14] cf. Plato's "Ring of Gyges" (*Rep.* 359d). Glaucon imagines a ring that makes one invisible and not subject to society's rules. Why would such a person not follow his desires to get goods and harm others? Desire is often unaware of all its consequences. The soul needs justice to educate and direct it in more fruitful desiring, beyond the Moment.

[15] "CCR" is Cohen, Curd, and Reeve, Readings in Ancient Greek Philosophy (Indianapolis, IN: Hackett, 2000).

rules say. Our animal nature is a better guide to happiness than our artificial social nature. Happiness is getting your way every moment. This is part of our nature, but as Aristotle shows, feeling regret is another. After the Sophistic Moment, we wish we had done things differently. Unlike Nature, we live in the past and future as well. The naturally strong men like Kallikles or Thrasymachus try to use the satisfaction of desires to remain in the Moment, beyond regret and guilt, but their engaging in dialogue pulls them back into history and mutual agreement. Plato's Socrates agrees that only individuals can measure their own lives but shows this must occur in a viable community. Plato and Aristotle agree.

Gorgias created the most famous stylistic effects, adapting poetic techniques into prose. Rhetoric studies now enshrine six of these as the "Gorgianic figures": *homoioteleuton* (repeat words with similar endings), *anadiplosis* (repeat word that ends one phrase at the beginning of the next), *parechesis* (repeat similarity of sounds, as in alliteration and assonance), *paronomasia* (word play with similar sound or etymology), *isocolon* (same structure and length of phrases), and *antithesis* (opposed ideas in a balanced, parallel construction). He employed all sorts of repetitions, including *polyptoton* (repeat word with changed form or cognates) and *pleonasm* (amassing of similar, apparently redundant terms).[16] The effect was a flood of sounds, hypnotically repeated phrases and ideas, and emotional appeals to popular culture ideals. It was an overwhelming performance, similar to rap music today. The intricate wordsmithing, rhythm, and social commentary make rap lyrics startling, engaging, and memorable. But after awhile these qualities become exhausting, then predictable, and finally boring. Gorgias' assaulting style ran the same course. His most famous display pieces defend Helen against charges of causing the Trojan War and, in "Concerning Not-Being," argue that nothing exists, but if it did, it could not be known, but if it could, it could not be communicated.

His Helen speech is a typical legal defense ("I wish to free the accused of blame"), easily adaptable to his audiences' legal needs. He lists four possible causes of her going to Troy: divine will, human abduction, human seduction, and erotic (Aphrodite) possession. In each, he finds her the victim of overwhelming force and thus innocent. Even her response to seduction is not her free choice. Persuasion (his

---

[16] The final flourish in Agathon's *Symposium* speech (197c–e) reflects Gorgias. Piles of sound overwhelm reason. Style becomes meaning.

own trade) is just as compelling as divine possession, physical force, and Fate. Listeners mindlessly respond; they do not judge.

> Speech is a powerful lord, which by means of the finest and most invisible body effects the divinest works: it can stop fear and banish grief and create joy and nurture pity... Helen similarly, against her will, might have come under the influence of speech, just as if ravished by the force of might.... The effect of speech upon the condition of the soul [mind] is comparable to the power of drugs over the nature of bodies... some distress, others delight, some cause fear, others make the hearers bold, and some drug and bewitch the soul with a kind of evil persuasion. It has been explained that if she was persuaded by speech she did not do wrong but was unfortunate.[17]

His "Concerning Not-Being" parodies Parmenides to the opposite conclusion that not anything is, nor is knowable, nor communicable. It is a tour de force with intricate principles of organization, division and negation. He begins like Parmenides, claiming either *what is* is or *what is not* is or both *what is* is and *what is not* is but concludes that they are both not-being. He quickly proves that *what is not* is not. Then he offers two proofs that *what is* is not. First, *what is* is neither eternal nor generated nor both contrary to what all things must be. "If eternal, it has no beginning, is unlimited and thus nowhere." If generated, everything either is or is not (no becoming) and so no generation. And being opposites, they cannot both be true (a false option). His second proof claims everything is either one or many. If one, it must have some size or other divisible quantity and thus is a many. And since a many is made out of ones and *what is* is not a one, it cannot be a many either. Next he proves that even if *what is* is, it is not knowable. We can think about things-that-are-not, such as a world at peace. If we think of things-that-are-not, then even if things-that-are exist, we do not think of them. His equivocation of "all of X are _" and "some of X are _" is a typical Sophist move.[18] Last, if able to think of things-that-are, we cannot express them to anyone else. If they are perceivable, how can these be communicated except by means of perception? "Words are not the objects" (84). We

---

[17] Rosamund Kent Sprague, ed., *The Older Sophists*, pp. 52–53.

[18] Agathon in the *Symposium* uses fallacies of whole and part (196d).

develop a *logos* due to the external object impacting on our senses. "*Logos* does not make manifest the external object, but it is the external object that comes to be communicative of the *Logos*" (85), for Gorgias's *logos* and mind only process sense data without any work of their own. The self that could do such work, as creating Gorgias' speech, is again only an artificial construction of the Moment.

The Sophists were more parasitic of popular culture than contributory in the development of ideas and inquiry. Inquiry was not their concern and was pursued only for practical answers. They encouraged anticommunity politics and anti-individual ethics, as no community or self lasted long enough to be taken seriously. Their arena was the Moment. They sought no fame beyond the earning power of their lifetimes.

And yet, their presence and problems push the ethical and political developments in Socrates, Plato, and Aristotle, especially the search for a method of using language and reason that could live with rhetoric and not destroy itself. Heraclitus retreated from public life, and Parmenides passed over in silence what Thrasymachus flaunted, that unless a good reason appears, the strongest at the moment will exert his power and rule. Socrates, Plato, and Aristotle spent their lives defining this "good reason" and who is strongest beyond the Moment. Their techniques grow out of all the Presocratic thinkers, while they are motivated by the later Sophists' claim that the good life can ignore thinking and civility. As lying undermines languages and friendships, so rhetoric finally destroys itself; the self requires more substance than the Moment. Gorgias realized the connection: "Those who do not care for philosophy, but engage in ordinary studies are like the Suitors, who wanted Penelope but slept with her handmaids" (DK 82 B 29, CCR 10).

4

Socrates

The Presocratics' ideas multiplied as they tried to understand the world, while the Sophists shifted these variations inward as a part of our psychology. By the time of the Peloponnesian War, philosophy had been torn apart between those who reduced the world and our experience to nature (all is atoms) and those who see only power (all is rhetoric). Socrates recreated the space where inquiry can occur: rescuing language from rhetoric; applying reason to ethics, politics, and psychology; connecting mental and moral health; and maintaining a critical community.[1] His famous paradox, "All that I know is that I know nothing," moves from knowing as a theory or definition to knowing about how to inquire into knowing. He never wrote of these concerns, as he felt philosophy was too easily misunderstood to survive except in direct conversation. The experiments by his

---

[1] Socrates' therapeutic ignorance, like a psychoanalyst's emotional neutrality, offers a screen on which the rational relationships of the one analyzed can be projected (objectified) and observed. As the analyst's emotions could interfere with the one analyzed expressing his, so Socrates' knowledge could interfere with his partner's free expression of ideas. As the expressed emotions are made more stable and less menacing, the analyzand sees the analyst as the source of these healthier emotions (cf. the *Phaedrus*'s myth of love). Relief from false knowledge is as great as from confused emotions. Those who honestly inquire with Socrates see their clarified reflection in him, love him as the source of their getting better, and identify themselves through him. Those like Meno or Anytus who remain confused blame him as the source of their confusion. A good analyst shows us ourselves but has no identity himself. As Versenyi says, "We too interpret ourselves into the Socratic problem, and, finding it difficult to separate our person and ideals from those of Socrates, we too come to know ourselves in the Socratic mirror." *Socratic Humanism* (New Haven, CT: Yale University Press, 1963), pp. 183–184.

successors with developing a language for philosophy is a large part of his legacy.

Data on Socrates' life is slight and often inconsistent. In 399 at age 70, he was found guilty of impiety and executed by taking hemlock. He was a manual laborer, likely a stonemason, from a working-class family. How he came to bother people in the *agora* and dine with the upper classes is known as "the problem of Socrates": what is known about the historical man and his ideas and how coherent this is. We have four main pieces of evidence: Xenophon's memoirs, Aristophanes' play, Plato's dialogues, and Diogenes Laertius' biography. No two simply agree with each other. Separating Socrates' beliefs from his progeny, like Plato, is currently a popular research topic.[2]

The search for his person and ideas begins with his influences. It is said Socrates shifted inquiry from nature to human nature, but how did this arise? We know little about his education. As he refused to be a Master over others, so there is no clear Master whom he followed. He likely studied cosmology with Anaxagoras' student Archelaus and language with the Sophist Prodicus. How did nonaristocratic Socrates get to study at all? Many stories of his poverty and ascetic life attest that he was not born into leisure. Other tales that he was a freed slave or subsidized to leave manual labor show the need to explain his life of inquiry.

Socrates' relation to the Sophists is central in his life. Our sources show them both only in Athens, though the Sophists taught in many cities. Athens' secular and cosmopolitan culture fed both their interests. Socrates' usual questions—what is virtue, justice, courage, and so on—like Sophists' rhetoric, were unwelcome in a traditional city like Sparta. Athens' democracy tolerated inquiry, despite a few show trials, just as it tolerated snake oil, superstition, and prejudice. It was the Greek city most open to innovation, leading Santas to say that Socrates was "the only stable thing in Athens in the last half of the fifth century."[3]

---

[2] Thirty years after Taylor's last major study, the 1960s saw many new works on Socrates: Chroust (1957), Guthrie, Gulley, Versenyi, Strauss. In 1971, Gregory Vlastos's *The Philosophy of Socrates*, set an agenda that bore fruit twenty years later in Hugh Benson's *Essays on the Philosophy of Socrates*. Further studies by Brickhouse and Smith, Kraut, McPherran, Navia, Santas, and Vlastos inform this current interest.

[3] Gerasimos Santas, *Socrates: Philosophy in Plato's Early Dialogues* (London: Routledge and Kegan Paul, 1979), p. 3.

As the city's buildings and innovations of its Golden Age (the new Acropolis, Long Walls, port at Piraeus, its growing empire, new means of warfare, rhetorical innovations in the law courts) showed its technical *arete,* it wondered how to use this reason in human affairs. Should reason serve to fulfill desire or vice versa? Socrates and Sophists agree that we are driven by the desire for happiness. The Sophistic being-in-the-moment with its serial need for more satisfaction in the next moment is curiously similar to the Socratic belief-in-the-moment with its need for continual validation. They are both erotic and always on the make. Socrates' restless trips to the *agora* seeking new inquiry partners parallel the repeated displays of the itinerant Sophists. Neither can ever get enough.[4] Both need to continually seduce new partners.

Both Socrates and the Sophists built upon the Eleatics' rhetorical practices and took the individual thinker–listener as the unit of being that could stem the Heraclitean flux long enough to have a conversation. Our beliefs hold us together, and this insight motivated them both. The Sophists tried to manipulate beliefs by using desires, while Socrates tried to strengthen this web by cleaning out the debris and developing some rules for judging which beliefs to save.

We have scattered reports of their activities, often polemical or contradictory, edited or invented by friends or enemies, and collected by energetic but noncritical biographers, such as Diogenes Laertius centuries later. Plato gives the longest portraits of both but is not easily verified. The few surviving Sophists' writings give a limited view of their opinions and use of language and reason. Socrates left no writings at all. The Sophist movement involved dozens of teachers for over half a century, leaving many traces in the speeches of plays, histories, and law courts and in social developments, but Socrates left us only a few: a caricature in a comic play, a friendly student's memoirs, a serious one naming a character for him in his dialogues, and the stories Diogenes Laertius edited. By chance these four sources were the ones to survive,[5] and all require careful consideration.

---

[4] Both appear to enjoy performing. Ryle's *Plato's Progress* imagines king-of-the-hill debates. But for Socrates, performing is a distraction. Beating up a partner prevents hearing what he has to say.

[5] Only Aristophanes' plays remain among Greek comedies. *The Clouds* is one, but other comedies also depicted Socrates as an arch-Sophist. *The Connus* ("Wastrel") by Ameipsias competed against *The Clouds* in Athens, featuring a scoundrel "Socrates." Why in 423 at age 46 is Socrates a popular image of the Sophists? Xenophon's *Symposium* set in 424 emphasizes a moral Socrates. Socrates' military heroism is also in 424 at Amphibolis and at Delium before the truce of 423.

"What must Socrates have been to account for the fact that the Socratics, for all their divergence, could each claim to be authentically Socratic or at least to continue Socrates's work, elaborating the implications of his theories?... Any reconstruction of Socrates's thought and personality not only had to be consistent with Aristotle... [but] also had to make Socrates's opponents' views and accusations at least superficially plausible" (Versenyi 177). The more pieces we can fit together, the better, but we can never know how many more pieces have disappeared and cannot even be considered.[6]

Aristophanes' humor makes it easy not to take him seriously. He has sex jokes about sausages, ejaculation, and buggery; body jokes about flea bites, flatulence and food; and social jokes about aristocratic names, gender identity, and legal talk. In *The Clouds* he has Socrates enter floating in an air-supported basket, communing with the Cloud goddesses. He runs the Thinkery school, where nature study measures a flea's jump in flea feet or sees which end of a gnat makes the buzzing sound.[7] They dabble in astronomy and geometry but major in the new persuasive but amoral rhetoric. His new student is Strepsiades, a farmer caught in the erosion of traditional values. He married for status to an aristocratic wife who desired his money, but he did not become an aristocrat, and his wife and son soon spent the money. Their son scorns rural virtues for aristocratic desires like raising and gambling on horses, causing large debts. He wants Socrates' new logic to talk his way out of his debts. He is a simple man, impatient with Socrates' teaching and naïvely concrete in his own ideas for evading debts: capturing the moon to stop the monthly (moonly) debts coming due, melting the wax tablet of a debt notice to erase the debt itself, or simply killing himself so he could not be prosecuted.

---

[6] Guthrie describes the fads in Socrates scholarship. "The earlier tendency to pick out one source as authentic, and belittle the rest, became somewhat discredited when everyone of the four had found his chosen champion and been held up in turn as the only true mirror... Plato was the first to enjoy this privilege, then Xenophon, then Aristotle; one or two backed Aristophanes, then round came the wheel to Plato again in Burnet and Taylor." *Socrates* (New York: Cambridge University Press, 1971), p. 9.

[7] Most assume this is comic exaggeration, but R. Brumbaugh suggests that if Archelaus followed Anaxagoras into exile, then Socrates may have become "the school's recognized leader, his role in Aristophanes' *Clouds*." The Cloud deities also fit Archelaus' idea of air as the basic stuff (*The Philosophers of Greece* [Albany: State University of New York Press, 1981], p. 126.). He makes sense of why three fourths of our main sources say Socrates' studied nature early. Aristotle's comments about Socrates are philosophy, not history. See H. Cherness on Aristotle on Plato, *The Riddle of the Early Academy* (Berkeley: University of California Press, 1945).

Impervious to lessons about language and argument, he is expelled. His debtors ignore his arguments from nature ("Since the water in the ocean does not increase, neither should the interest on a debt"), only leaving when physically beaten. He persuades his son to enroll in his place, but the new logic brings unexpected results. His son uses it to beat him, arguing if his father properly beat him as a child when he needed it, now the reverse is true, when he thinks his father needs it. As his son goes off to beat his mother, he decides the new logic's danger outweighs the relief it may bring to his debts. So he burns the Thinkery, and the resulting smoke stops any more discourse.

Greek comedy loved exaggeration, distorting and mocking its victims for a laugh. Socrates here leads paying students in a flamboyant study of nature and rhetoric, prefers new gods (the Clouds, Chaos, and the Tongue) instead of the old, leads a corrupt life (stealing to support himself), and condescends to students. Since the audience had to identify the object of scorn for the parodies and lampoons to work, some of this must be true to life. Some of his "Socrates" is historically familiar: physically short, solid, not handsome, impoverished, talks a lot, and not always easy to understand. The Thinkery could be the popular (pejorative?) nickname for an actual place (a marketplace corner?) where he and his companions passed the day. That there even could have been some "school" is possible (see note 5). Other sources agree he studied and discussed word usage. The basket, new nature gods, and stealing disagree with other sources but provide great humor. Dionysian comedy enjoyed defamation and distortion, like speeches "roasting" an honored guest. The charge of elitism makes sense, as most people tried to avoid talking with him. He was an acquired taste. Aristophanes' comedy gives clues to the Sophist-like younger Socrates and his reputation before he met Plato and Xenophon, but we use what we think we know to dismiss the strange or unwelcome aspects of this caricature.

The second source is Xenophon, a career soldier slightly older than Plato, born in Athens sometime before 430. His *Anabasis* tells of the betrayed Greek mercenary army he safely led out of central Persia back to the Aegean. He continued fighting with his army for the Spartans in Asia Minor up to the battle of Coronea (394) against Athens, for which Athens temporarily exiled him. He spent the next twenty years on a Spartan country estate as a country gentleman writing his memoirs. He died in Athens or Corinth sometime after 355. He held to the "traditional values" of his military career and affinity for Sparta. He found a basic compatibility in Socrates, following him in his youth up to his Persian trip in 401. He used him as a character in many of his later writings. Their friendship was not based on philosophy, beyond Socrates promoting moral values. As the new rhetoricians, politicians, and playwrights spread moral and religious relativism, Xenophon valued Socrates' ascetic life and discussing virtue seriously. Like any lover, he may have overlooked their differences since he was engaged in their united front against relativism. Somehow Socrates' moral and religious views were able to attract both Xenophon and Plato. He also admired Socrates as a proper citizen–soldier, who cared for his body and mind. Socrates inspired Xenophon to seek the good life, but he did not go on to examine this life and give an account (*logos*) of it. And Socrates seems to have accepted this. He had perhaps many Xenophons among his followers. In his *Memorabilia*, Xenophon shows he is aware of current philosophical debates, but like his "Socrates," he prefers concrete talk about human affairs over speculation about the cosmos.

> He did not even discuss . . . "the Nature of the Universe" and avoided speculation on the so-called "Cosmos" of the Professors . . . he would argue that to trouble one's mind with such problems is sheer folly . . . he marveled at their blindness in not seeing that man cannot solve these riddles. . . . His own conversation was ever of human things. . . . what is godly, ungodly; what is beautiful, ugly; what is just, unjust; what is prudence, madness; what is courage, cowardice; what is a state, a governor; these and others like them, of which the knowledge made a "gentleman," in his estimation, while ignorance should involve the reproach of "slavishness." (Memorabilia, I, i, 12–17)

The "gentleman" (*kalon k'agathon* = noble and good) was the aristocratic ideal of Xenophon's birth but not of the mason's son. Socrates' new "gentleman" has beauty not from good breeding but from good action, based on personal responsibility for one's own decisions. Doing good makes one look good. Xenophon's ethics often seem little more than the aristocrat and soldier's good manners and social utility.

He intends to praise and defend Socrates by showing what he actually said and did. In his *Symposium*, Socrates twists arguments but not to his advantage. He challenges a young beauty to a beauty contest and typically asks what it is that makes beautiful things beautiful. The response is "If they are all well formed for the purposes for which we respectively employ them, or are well adapted by nature for that for which we want them, they will assuredly be beautiful" (*Symp.* IV). He proves by this that his bulging eyes, nose, and lips are more functional and thus more beautiful. He asks for a secret ballot, with a kiss from the winner to the judges. He does not get a vote, knowing nobody would prefer his functional—but ugly—kisser. He chose to win the argument but lose the vote. Plato's Socrates has similar limited success that leaves arguments open. Is this a Socratic or philosophic trait? Xenophon does not seem to notice such issues. Socrates' aporetic (impasse) search that ends in continued searching (all proposed definitions fail) in Plato is not in Xenophon's report. His Socrates has many of the same pieces as Plato's but is more simply arranged and in a gentler light.

He and Plato take opposite approaches to writing. He is literal and straightforward, not given to metaphors, symbols, irony, or images. He writes his thoughts as they occur, without strategies such as Thucydidean debates or Platonic framing.[8] He includes whatever defends Socrates against his detractors. His *Apology* and *Memorabilia* offer quotations proving Socrates' innocence but often omit who told him. He says Hermogenes reported that Socrates told him before his trial that he had already chosen to accept a death sentence, but when Xenophon, who was absent in Ionia, quotes Socrates' trial speech, he gives no sources.

Xenophon was a prolific writer on many topics. He continued Thucydides' history of Greece, described a country gentleman's life and military adventures, and retold many events in Socrates' life. In his accounts of country living, "Socrates" is more a literary creation (an imaginary friend in Sparta?), while his *Symposium, Memorabilia,* and *Apology* are seen as his version of the historical Socrates. He was soldiering in Asia Minor during Socrates' trial and gives a shortened version of it. "It is not my intention to give a full account of the entire trial, as my purpose is to show that Socrates was firmly committed never to act impiously toward the gods and never to behave unjustly toward human beings" (*Apology* 23). He tries to correct the popular belief that Socrates' words and conduct lost his case. He claims Socrates chose to lose, accepting Athens' offer of execution instead of suffering the inconveniences and injuries of old age (note his pragmatism). His *Symposium* is an elaborate dinner party at the

---

[8] A story within a story within a story makes truth more complicated, as in Plato's *Symposium* or Odysseus reciting his travels in the *Odyssey*.

Sophist-friendly house of Callias where Plato's *Protagoras* also occurs. Xenophon says he was there but does not appear in the story and was under age 10 at the time. There are similarities to Plato's *Symposium* (Socrates gives the same response to the proposal that each guest speak on the given topic), but it is hard to tell who wrote first. Xenophon is the silent observer–reporter, as Aristodemus is for Plato. They must have known each other as followers of Socrates and each other's writings, but neither ever mentions the other. His *Memorabilia* reviews the indictment against Socrates at his trial, using evidence from his life to show the charges were mistaken. Again, who his sources were or what he actually witnessed is not clear.

Louis Navia, in his helpful collection of Socratic testimony, sums up Xenophon's Socrates as follows: "A deep sense of religiosity and piety, an unfailing tendency towards joviality and cheerfulness, a commitment to being useful and helpful towards anybody who crossed his path, a desire to function within the laws and customs of his polity, a keen sense of intellectual curiosity, and an unfaltering attachment to honesty. These qualities by themselves do not necessarily give us the required ingredients for...a 'great philosopher,' although they would certainly go far towards the making of a great human being."[9]

Six hundred years later, Diogenes Laertius wrote eighty-two biographies in *Lives of Famous Philosophers*. Socrates is with the Ionians in Book II influenced by Anaxagoras and Archelaus and influencing Plato, Xenophon, Antisthenes, Aristippus, Aeschines, Phaedo, Euclides, Stilpo, Crito, Simon, Simmias, Cebes, Glaucon, and Mendemus. Trying to be interesting and inclusive, he includes wisdom and gossip, usually naming his sources. He is less partisan than Xenophon and no more philosophical. He does include different versions of stories: Socrates was a slave or free, taught rhetoric or no, made lots of money or took no fees, had one or two wives—maybe at the same time—and did keep Euthyphro from suing his father or not. He enjoyed Socratic one-liners. "To one who said, 'You are condemned by the Athenians to die,' he answered, 'So are they, by nature.' When his wife said, 'You suffer unjustly,' he retorted, 'Why, would you rather have me suffer justly?'" (ii, 35). He says the comedians ridiculed but also praised his simple lifestyle. His stories resemble those in

---

[9] Luis Navia, *Socratic Testimonies* (Lanham, MD: University Press of America, 1987), p. 123.

Plato and Xenophon, with Socrates not very different from in Plato. One nicely describes his unhappy interlocutors. "Frequently, owing to his vehemence in argument, men set upon him with their fists or tore his hair out; and that for the most part he was despised and laughed at, yet bore all this ill-usage patiently" (ii, 20). He also depicts a young and overconfident Plato. "In the course of the trial Plato mounted the platform and began: 'Though I am the youngest, men of Athens, of all who ever rose to address you'—whereupon the judges shouted, 'Get down! Get down!'" In sum, Diogenes offers details but no new directions, mostly agreeing with Plato.

Plato created our most extensive and complex writings using a character called "Socrates." The last fifty years spawned a renewed interest in separating Socratic from Platonic philosophy, encouraged by a positivism in Plato studies.[10] Computers renewed hopes of finding the order of composition for his dialogues and thus the development of his ideas, with an early Socratic Plato apart from (presumed) non-Socratic ideas such as recollection, Forms, political theory, an immortal soul, and so on. A literal approach avoided literary issues, simply equating Plato with "Socrates." And Aristotle was the authority on Greek philosophy.

Around 1860, stylometrics began measuring the frequencies of style elements that changed during Plato's career. This seemed more empirical and less arbitrary than prior attempts to measure themes. It found that many features of word choice and arrangement were shared by a group of dialogues but differed from other groups. Evidence such as the mention of a dated event was then used to date the group, as well as, assuming the *Laws* was the last made, a baseline to arrange dialogues by their stylistic distance from this. This produced the familiar order of composition in early, middle, and late periods. If this order were certain and the thematic content changed in concert with it, then the development of Plato's thought would be self-evident. But the results were more suggestive than conclusive. Tracking different textual features has given different results. "By comparison with the differences that distinguish the final group, those which separate the dialogues of Plato's middle period from all preceding it are not as sharp, connected as they are with the earlier,

---

[10] Those seeking the pre-Platonic Socrates often prefer the pre-Platonic Plato before he turns literary and metaphysical.

gradual development of his style."[11] His "gradual development" as a skilled and careful writer could also include recurrences of earlier styles. Style alone cannot solve thematic development.

Plato's Theory of Forms is often used to track his philosophical growth beyond Socrates. We each create Forms as psychological tools needed in order to think. We authorize their validity. Definition questions move people to recognize and examine this role in giving meaning to language and life. Most recent critics see this theory as an epistemological failure and deny Socrates any role in it. Plato supposedly breaks from Socrates in the *Meno* when the immortal soul, recollection, and Forms appear, and he gives more positive answers to "What is X?" questions.[12] The middle dialogues continue this until Forms are critiqued in the later ones. Such development in clear stages is hotly debated. Cherniss finds these ideas in almost every dialogue. "From among the earliest of the dialogues on through the last... the doctrine of ideas [Forms] is the cornerstone of this thought... a few of the earliest dialogues [may] antedate the birth of the doctrine in Plato's mind; but that is neither demonstrable nor even likely, for... no one has succeeded in saying convincingly [of a dialogue]: 'Here is its first appearance'" (Cherniss, *Riddle,* p. 4). The Forms may even be implicit in Socrates and just made explicit by Plato. His Forms are often imagined to exist in a religious/metaphysical realm, but this is a metaphor for our mind storing what we think we know. Socrates tries to take these Forms out of this dark to examine them, showing that meanings must expand beyond the sophistic Moment to include one's selves over time and to participate through speech in the shared Forms of others as well. Thus, the philosophic life, his entire waking life, is one of dialogue, of testing our ideas and ourselves as he says in Plato's *Apology.*

Whether "Socrates" ever or always was Plato's mouthpiece has no simple proof or resolution. While Xenophon declares his intentions to defend Socrates, Plato gives us no direction. He only appears

---

[11] L. Brandwood summarizes this in "Stylometry and Chronology," in *The Cambridge Companion to Plato,* R. Kraut, ed. (New York: Cambridge University Press, 1992), p. 114. During Plato's active fifty years, possibly "certain doctrines underwent considerable changes... but there is little help in [ordering the dialogues] from external sources or the dialogues themselves" (p. 90).

[12] Recollection in the *Meno* is a source of courage, not knowledge. The geometry problem's answer is an irrational number with its repeating decimals. Socrates' virtue words are similarly indefinable and useful.

in the *Apology* and only speaks in Diogenes Laertius' quote earlier discussed. He is as silent in his writing as Socrates is by not writing. Plato's *Letters* (maybe forged) discuss his approach to writing. His *Second Letter* says of "Socrates," "I myself have never yet written anything on these subjects, and no treatise by Plato exists or will exist, but those which now bear his name belong to a Socrates become fair and young" (314 C), that is, unlike himself or another.[13] Plato may have been clever and faithful enough that he kept both of them from becoming an expert, disguising Socrates just enough to save his from kidnappers. To guess that Plato is Socrates' mouthpiece before he discovered the Forms and then reversed roles could be fruitful but will always be speculation. The issue of literal vs. literary reading will be discussed in the next chapter.

Aristotle's testimony has guided recent efforts to extract the Socratic from the Platonic. Terry Penner offers a good summary.

> Aristotle tells us that Socrates (i) asked only, and did not reply; for he confessed that he knew nothing... (ii) concerned himself with ethical matters only, being not at all concerned with nature as a whole; (iii) was the first to argue "inductively"; (iv) was the first to search (systematically) for the universal, and for definitions—i.e., to ask What-is-it? Questions... but (v) did not "separate" these universals, as Plato did: for Plato supposed... no knowledge of the perceptibles, but only of some other things, the Ideas (or Forms).[14]

Born seventeen years after Socrates died and coming to Athens eighteen years later, Aristotle is an odd authority on him, as neither firsthand nor neutral. He could ask Socrates' followers, but they were competing to claim his legacy and were hardly objective witnesses. Nor is Aristotle objective in showing his methods superior to his predecessors.[15] Like us, he sees his competitors from the superiority of his own view and may not see or discuss inconvenient or irrelevant data.

Several critics list the Socratic versus non-Socrates traits in Plato. Penner finds twelve. Versenyi finds "Socrates" growing more faint

---

[13] Cf. "This is why every serious man dealing with really serious subjects carefully avoids writing, lest thereby he may possibly cast them as a prey to the envy and stupidity of the public" (*Seventh Letter* 344 C).

[14] T. Penner, "Socrates and the Early Dialogues," in Kraut, op. cit., pp. 122–123.

[15] See Cherniss's *Aristotle's Criticism of Plato and the Academy* (Baltimore, MD: Johns Hopkins University Press, 1944).

from early to late, "Artistic unity, dramatic character, presentation of Socrates as a person and an embodiment of his philosophy rather than a mere spokesman for theories, dialectic interchange and real opposition between interlocutors, undogmatic search for definitions and maieutic, aporetic, negative, ironic, elenctic character" (Versenyi, p. 178). He sees a continuum without a specific separation. Gregory Vlastos' last book finds ten marks distinguishing the historical Socrates (early S) from the Platonic (P) (paraphrase mine):[16]

1. The early S does moral and only moral philosophy.

2. The early S has no metaphysical theory of separately existing Forms or a separable soul learning by recollecting prenatal knowledge.

3. The early S claims no knowledge and seeks it elenctically. P seeks and finds demonstrative knowledge.

4. The early S believes incontinence (*akrasia*) is impossible. P posits a three-part soul that explains how *akrasia* occurs.

5. The early S has no interest or expertise in sciences. P has mastered mathematical sciences.

6. The early S's conception of philosophy is populist. P is elitist.

7. The early S is critical of Athens but prefers it (without explanation). P does political theory, from monarchy (best) to tyranny (worst).

8. Both early S and P Should this read "Both S and P"? As written it does not make sense syntactically. Please provide correction. include homoerotic ties in their ideas of eros, but P has "metaphysical . . . love for the transcendent Form of beauty."

9. The early S believes piety is service to a supernatural and ethical deity. "His personal religion is practical, realized in action." P's religion "centers in communion with divine, but impersonal, Forms. It is mystical, realized in contemplation."

10. The early S is elenctic, adversarial, refuting the theses of dissenting interlocutors. Later he posits and opposes his own theses. P is didactic, reveals truth to tractable partners from *Meno* to *Phaedrus*, criticizes his metaphysics in *Parmemides.*, and has new maieutic in *Theaetetus*.

---

[16] Gregory Vlastos, *Socrates, Ironist and Moral Philosopher* (Ithaca, NY: Cornell University Press, 1991).

With Aristotle as one's witness, reading Plato's literary texts literally, and assuming Forms define reality, this list makes sense. However, it is like the pre-Copernican view of the planets in a geocentric universe. Common sense says what we see in the sky, as in the literal text, must be where the answers are. More of this in the next chapter, but clearly your idea of Socrates has a lot to do with your idea of Plato.

I close with one last list, Brumbaugh's Socratic ideas that continue through Plato rather than marking a point of divergence. Later writers agree in attributing to Socrates the statements: "Virtue is knowledge"; "The virtues are one"; "A just man harms no one"; "It is better to suffer than to commit injustice"; and "We shall be better men if we inquire than if we do not; that is a belief for which I will fight in word and deed." All of these positive views have their origins in a new constructive insight into the self and human value (p. 129). And to these I should add the following from the *Apology:*

"The greatest good for man is to discuss virtue every day and those other things about which you hear me conversing and testing myself and others, for the unexamined life is not worth living for man."

"Wealth does not bring about excellence, but excellence brings about wealth and all other public and private blessings for men."

"A man who really fights for justice must lead a private, not a public, life if he is to survive for even a short time."

"A good man cannot be harmed either in life or in death."

"I do not think I know what I do not know."

5

Plato

By Socrates' death the range of topics in philosophy was quite similar to today: metaphysics on the invisible elements and rules of nature, epistemology on the justification of knowledge, ethics and politics on the nature of the good life, logic on the nature of argument and truth. Plato and Aristotle will deal with them all. Each needs to overcome the relativistic skepticism of "man is the measure" for his ideas to gain force for anyone else. Both seek mutual agreement to change the "measuring man" from an isolated individual to a communal being.

The early religious thinkers assigned wisdom to the gods and piety to man. Then the Presocratics developed speculation and inquiry as a way to explore this realm of divine wisdom, often retaining a sense of hubris and skepticism. The Sophists avoided the hubris by moving the source of truth inside each individual. Socrates reversed this "winner is wise" Sophistic approach by claiming wisdom in ignorance and the search for knowledge. He returned wisdom to its religious-like status as larger than any one person, marked by his use of religious imagery and myth. Plato accepted Socrates' truth as the mutual agreement in an indefinitely extended conversation, expanding this further in the dialogue between a writer and his indefinite number of readers. The topics, moves, and problems in his written dialogues encourage the reader to engage in inquiry and continue these issues with the writer. This could only succeed if, like Socrates, he de-authorized himself to avoid the inquiry turning into simply absorbing a dogmatic lesson.

Plato refused the Sophistic onanistic satisfaction of the Moment and reengaged in the Presocratic debates on the power and limits of reason, illusion, and skepticism. Instead of taking sides among the Pythagoreans, Parmenideans, or Heracliteans or opting out like the Sophists, he sought a viewpoint that recognized their several truths as elements within inquiry. After the divisions among the Presocratics on the basic stuff and how to find it, he was a synthetic thinker, seeking the common ground. In this, Aristotle was his apt pupil and coworker.

Plato is often described as a systematic thinker, but his is a system of accommodation, not exclusion. As Socrates' "therapeutic ignorance" could absorb all ideas into it, so is Plato's ever-shifting dialogue able to reflect many points of view for his readers. As we identify ourselves in these views and their criticism, we experience the need for self-knowledge and shared inquiry. Socrates took the idea of philosophy as inquiry from the Presocratics and began the discussion of its nature and maintenance. Plato continued this, trying to systematize the questioning of what you think you know that you know. Philosophy's usual crimes are inertia due to action-crippling thought or uncritical self-righteous action due to assumed logical certainty. Finding a middle way is the focus for the responses of Socrates, Plato, and Aristotle.

Plato moved Socrates' trick of hiding in plain sight to writing. Socrates talked in the marketplace with anyone interested, developing a middle way of speaking that allowed people of very different outlooks and opinions to find some connection to his words. He was a One yet also a Many.[1] Plato writes almost thirty dialogues, continuing Socrates' use of the same words to say different things to different people. Several terms have been used to describe their methods: *elenctic*, revealing the flaws in other people's ideas and lives; *aporetic*, bringing people to the point of knowing that they do not know and opening them to wonder and inquiry; or *dialectic*, arranging the world using the best ideas available and then testing these against all comers. All of these are strategies in the dialogues, each an element in the pursuit of inquiry.

Plato expressed the manyness of human experience, creating dozens of personalities with plausible speeches for famous ones like Aristophanes, Protagoras, and Alcibiades, while also showing unity in the desire and criticism of knowledge. We seek unity in the mutual agreement of definitions and ideas needed to successfully converse and conduct one's life and to guide the Flow of identity-building change. This exposes the assumed power of the Sophistic Moment (for example, Meno's idea of

---

[1] The capitals here suggest the Greeks' technical use of these terms.

different virtues for different people) and tames the Flow of identity-robbing change. He stays anonymous, being everywhere in the dialogues, as Shakespeare in his plays, but in no one place, phrase, or idea more than another. As an encounter with Socrates was a challenge to one's self-esteem, self-knowledge, and identity, so when reading Plato, our search for his ideas becomes the search for our own.

PLATO'S BIOGRAPHY

We have more facts about Plato's life, as he came from a wealthy and famous Athenian political family, yet we still know very little. His father Ariston, who died early in Plato's life, traced his lineage back though Codrus, the last king of Athens, and ultimately to the god Poseidon. His mother Perictione's lineage included Solon, who, in the early 500s created most of the laws and institutions for the Athenian democratic state. This illustrious political past had an ambiguous present during Plato's twenties. Perictione's cousin Critias and brother Charmides were infamous in the Thirty Tyrants (404–403), the oligarchic (rule by "the few," usually the rich) government imposed by Sparta in Athens after the Peloponnesian War. Plato had two brothers, Adeimantus and Glaucon, the main speakers in the *Republic;* a sister Potone, the mother of Speusippus, Plato's successor at the Academy; and Antiphon, a half brother who trained horses, one of Plato's common images. He never married. He apparently lived for eighty years (427–347), the standard length ancient biographers used for a well-lived life, with significant life events at twenty-year intervals. That Plato met Socrates at age 20; established his school, the Academy, and first traveled to Sicily at age 40; wrote his masterpiece, the *Republic,* at age 60; and died at 80 does seem very convenient but not incredible.

Although we have many stories of Plato's early life and adulthood, A. E. Taylor summarizes, "The actual history of Plato's life up to his sixtieth year is almost a blank."[2] Ancient biographers tell us that he traveled to Egypt and Italy, studied mathematics and religion, and followed the teachings of Parmenides or Heraclitus or Pythagoras. All this is interesting but not certain, and much of it depends on information given in the dialogues, taking as evidence that any mention of these people, places, or studies shows he had some direct contact with them.

---

[2] A. E. Taylor, *Plato* (New York: Meridian, 1956), p. 8.

He rejected the public life he was groomed for, either an army career like his brothers or politics like his uncle. His social class was expected to serve in the army, usually the cavalry, and he may have at the end of the Peloponnesian War. His *Seventh Letter* says the Thirty Tyrants invited him to join them, but he rejected their aims and methods. The restored democracy restored his interest in politics, but this soon soured when its leaders pursued the trial and execution of Socrates. As Socrates says in the *Apology*, "A man who really fights for justice must lead a private, not a public, life if he is to survive for even a short time" (32a). In the *Republic* he again warns that "no one who minds the business of the cities does anything healthy" (*Rep.* 496c) and describes the philosopher's place as at the margins of affairs. "Taking this (political injustice) into the calculation, he keeps quiet and minds his own business—as a man in a storm, when dust and rain are blown about by the wind, stands aside under a little wall" (*Rep.*, 496d).

Socrates also addresses here why so few people pursue philosophy. If one excels in both mind and body, like Charmides, Meno, and Alcibiades, it is almost impossible to avoid the allure of the socially valued and valuable paths to success, and none of these escaped. The attraction of social and political favor and power must be broken before philosophy's less immediate pleasure can be experienced. Socrates finds this is rare: only by exile, growing up apart from the ambitions of politics, becoming physically disabled, realizing that all human arts have limits (that expertise in one does not extend to others) or in Socrates' seemingly unusual case, his *daimon* or inner voice warning him from a public career. Socrates' political execution showed the limits of political art and turned Plato to pursue whatever art Socrates did.

Through the young men Socrates meets in the dialogues, we see what it was like to grow up in Athens during the Peloponnesian War. Our search for glimpses of Plato among them is complicated by their different historical natures and that he, unlike most of them, actually turned around (converted) and followed philosophy. Alcibiades in the *Symposium* may be closest to an autobiography. His intensely personal speech describes the effect of Socrates' presence and interactions with him. Socrates makes him examine the basis of his brash self-confidence and apparent power. He is left in confusion, desiring to dominate other people yet realizing he also needs their criticism to reveal his mistakes. That we see Plato here is only a guess. We do see his peers exposed to philosophy but rejecting it, while he, for whatever reason, embraced it.

The dialogues describe the pre-execution world when Socrates, who appears in all but one, was still active. This is when Plato was attracted but not committed to philosophy, and every dialogue questions the nature and value of the philosophic life. The one experience of his youth that he repeatedly depicts is this confrontation with philosophy, the "snake's bite" as Alcibiades put it. The other details of his life—and by implication, ours—are merely chance gifts from the gods.

The two events that scholars use to help us view Plato after age 60 were his *Letters* describing his trips to Syracuse and that Aristotle joined the Academy and became a source of direct information. We have seen how Aristotle discusses the views of others more to clarify his own ideas than theirs. Using the *Letters,* if genuine, as historical documents is also complex. They describe three visits by Plato to Syracuse. On the first at age 40, he met Dion, a young relative of the ruler Dionysius I. He befriended Plato, preferring his ideas on intellectual satisfaction and physical self-control over the luxurious palace lifestyle. When Dionysius II became ruler, Dion asked Plato to come educate him as he had Dion twenty years before. Plato accepted, hoping that a more rational and self-controlled ruler would create a more rational and stable government. Dionysius eagerly pursued his studies as a pastime, but corrupted by thirty years of indulgent living, they had no influence on his rule. His politics of personal gain and intrigue continued, exiling Dion, taking his lands, and forcing his wife to remarry. Tired of being used by Dionysius, Plato returned to Athens. His last visit seven years later tried to reconcile Dionysius and Dion, as well as philosophy and politics. His relations with Dionysius eroded until he was kept under house arrest and grudgingly allowed to go home. Plato and Dion remained friends. He later successfully revolted, only to be assassinated in turn.

It is tempting to link the events of Plato's life to the themes and developments in his writing. Most scholars want his life, as their own, to have a plot, a thread of meaning that provides guidance and security. But reconstructions of Plato's life depend upon which anecdotes are selected and then filled in with probabilities subject to such circular reasoning as this defense of the *Second Letter:* "A strong argument for the genuineness of the letter is the fact that it throws a great deal of light on a particular stage in the relation of Plato and Dionysius that is not illuminated by the other letters."[3] That is, the author thinks it is historical because its content is so useful. However, just because something makes sense does not mean it really happened. This motto should be our constant companion with all Greek biography, including Plato's.

---

[3] L. A. Post, *Thirteen Epistles of Plato* (1925), p. 25. In J. E. Raven, *Plato's Thought in the Making* (Cambridge, England: Cambridge University Press, 1965), p. 22.

Arguing from historical to philosophical biography is like the attempt to derive ought from is. Almost all scholars agree that Plato went to Syracuse. Most agree that the events in the *Seventh Letter* happened. That the development and significance of the *Republic, Laws,* or other works is explained by these journeys is controversial. The idea of the philosopher–kings appears in both the *Republic* and the *Seventh Letter.* "Unless the philosophers rule as kings or those now called kings and chiefs genuinely and adequately philosophize, and political power and philosophy coincide in the same place . . . there is no rest from ills for the cities, nor I think for human kind" (*Rep.* 473e). "The classes of humans will have no cessation from evils until either the class of those who are right and true philosophers attains political supremacy, or else the class of those who hold power in the state becomes, by some dispensation of the gods, really philosophic" (*Letters,* 326b). The letter, however, does not clarify what Plato was trying to do in Syracuse or in the *Republic:* implement his idea for an ideal city, create a philosophic ruler to bring eternal peace and justice, or just try to bring more law and order to a sick city whose fall would further erode the Greek presence in Italy. Or maybe it was an act of friendship, more about Dion than Dionysius. Plato's actions in Sicily could reflect his belief in the practical politics of his day or in the reality of his ideal state, just as his intention in the *Republic* is similarly ambiguous. Neither the visit nor the book can explain the other, though many have tried. His biography provides clues but no program for how we are to read his work.[4]

Literary Background

Parmenides and Empedocles wrote in traditional poetry. Heraclitus used short epigrams. The many books *On Nature* used a simple prose style, as did the later Stoics. Plato was the first to use dialogue, building on Socrates' vision of philosophy as requiring a dramatic exchange between people. Parmenides needed the poetic inspiration of the gods to see beyond the human illusions of plurality in this

---

[4] "The chronology of composition has been a perennial subject of scholarly debate . . . with efforts to establish the outline of Plato's philosophical 'development,' or the lack of any. We have solid scholarly arguments and a consensus about some aspects of the chronology of Plato writings, but this is much too slight a basis on which conscientiously to fix even an approximate ordering of all of the dialogues." John Cooper, *Plato Complete Works,* (Indianapolis, IN: Hackett Publishing, 1997), p. xi.

world. Heraclitus said as little as possible as his words were disappearing as they were being spoken. Plato, like Socrates, understood that drama was the heart of the life of reason—not the stability of the One or the flow of the nameless but the tension that is played out between them.

Plato wrote twenty-six dialogues, with several more likely by him and a dozen or so forgeries in his style.[5] He likely wrote some letters, mostly about his trips to Syracuse, and a few Epigrams. He also gave public lectures, most famously "On the Good," which reportedly few understood. But his legacy is the dialogues. The high quality of his writing is as praised as the meaning is debated. "Men grow weary of the very perfection of Plato, the polished surface of the unfailing literary art, the mastery of the inevitable dialectic, the sense of intellectual adequacy or superiority, the perfect reasonableness, the entire absence of pseudo science and a technical and system-building terminology for the mind to play with, the ironical evasion of unprofitable discussion of ultimates in symbolism and myth."[6] After reviewing his cultural context, we will examine the broad aspects of his philosophy and then how the elements of his art (structure, conversations, myths, and irony) develop these.

Plato's dialogue style grows out of the rich cultural environment of the Athenian Golden Age with its various literary forms, such as epic poetry, dramatic tragedy and comedy, sophistic arguments, history, and memoirs that he blended into his writing. Examining these will help us better see the contribution of each and the unity of the whole.

Most critics believe that Plato wrote tragedies before turning to philosophy, just as Aristotle wrote dialogues before adopting his final lecture-notes style. We do have some fragments of Aristotle's dialogues, while we have no record of Plato's plays. Some say the *Phaedo* is his most tragic dialogue and the *Symposium* most like a comedy. The *Symposium* ends asking if one author could write in both forms, that is, convey both dimensions of human nature. Plato does this in

---

[5] Thrasyllus (first century AD) listed thirty-five dialogues. Nine are now contested, so modern lists vary: Friedlander, thirty-one; Cooper, twenty-six with another three likely; Taylor, twenty-seven.

[6] Paul Shorey, *Platonism Ancient and Modern* (Berkeley: University of California Press, 1938), p. 23.

the speeches of the comedian Aristophanes and tragedian Agathon, showing his abilities as a playwright and perhaps some as an auto-biographer.[7] Whether he ever wrote plays, he lived in the culture of the great Athenian tragic and comic festivals. All of Athens could attend these civic and religious events; over thirty thousand attended Agathon's play before his *Symposium* party. Plato's audience heard drama often, both in the theater and epic poem recitals. They were used to multilayer stories that both entertained and addressed moral, political, and religious issues.

Tragedies and comedies began including more rhetorical exchanges, as in the "new logic" learned by Strepsiades' son in *The Clouds* and Medea and Jason arguing over who better served the other in Euripides' *Medea*. The debates in the histories of Herodotus and Thucydides, like Plato, use historical figures saying historically likely things. Including likely fiction in history was different from Homer's ancient culture stories, which many thought had little historical basis. The tragedies reworked much of this epic material. The comedies used caricatures of living people, with just enough accuracy to assure recognition. This bawdy humor mixed slapstick with sophistication, flatulence and name-calling with discussions of waging peace or the soul's immortality. Any source of humor was fair—ridiculing people's names, relatives, physical qualities, occupations, reputation, sexuality, and so on—the more ludicrous, the better. Reading Aristophanes' comedies is an essential preparation for reading Plato, just as Plato was informed by the raucous style of these comedies before he wrote his own works.

All of these are elements in Plato's style. He writes historical fiction about real people and events. He often alludes to Homer, as Socrates describes the Sophists' house in the *Protagoras* using the language of Odysseus visiting Hades (*Ody*. 315b–d). When Socrates picks up Aristodemus on his way to the *Symposium* party, he describes them as heroic fighters going to Agamemnon's house (174b–c). When Simmias and Cebes attack Socrates' argument in the *Phaedo*, he compares himself and Phaedo to Heracles enlisting Iolaus to help him fight two battles at once (89c). Some allusions are less explicit, as the story in the *Phaedo* of Theseus saving fourteen youths from sacrifice to the Minotaur in the labyrinth. Here the fourteen youths

---

[7] The *Symposium* speeches could be autobiographical, telling Plato's intellectual journey up to the critical moment when he, like Alcibiades, had to decide whether criticism or desire was more important.

visiting Socrates' prison also need saving from the half-rational bogey-man of death. Plato moves heroism from the clash of spears to that of words and ideas.

Humor is a weapon in these battles. As in Comedy, Plato plays on his characters' names. Eryximachus (Gk. "fighter of hiccups and belches") is among the combatants in the *Symposium,* so he is set in battle against Aristophanes' hiccups. Meno ("to remain") will not stay to be initiated into philosophy's Mysteries. Meletus ("care") is careless about the youths he says in the *Apology* he is trying to save from Socrates. Cephalus ("head") holds traditional morals as head of his family in the *Republic.* Theaetetus ("spectator") defends that knowledge is perception in his dialogue. Thrasymachus is a "wild fighter" in the *Republic,* and Polus is an undisciplined "colt" in the *Gorgias.* Good editions translate the Greek names to explain the many puns and even turns of the plot.

There are also humorous incidents. While discussing moderation, Socrates is aroused by young Charmides' open robe exposing his bare body. This amazing body promises an equally amazing mind, worthy of a philosopher's lust. In the *Symposium,* Eryximachus drones on while Aristophanes employs his hiccup cures. The comedian holds his breath through shades of purple, gargles at full volume, and then builds up to the great sneeze, while the doctor explains how his science enables him to control human bodies. In *Euthydemus,* two wrestlers turn into rhetoric teachers, as this is just an easier way of fighting in the ring.

Socrates is another source for the dialogue form. Several historical sources discuss his engaging others in philosophical conversations. According to the opening of Plato's *Symposium,* some were so famous that people would request to hear particular ones. That Xenophon and Plato wrote both an *Apology* and *Symposium* shows that Socrates' dialogue style at these events was well known. Xenophon recalls other Socratic discussions in his *Memorabilia,* and other writers such as Aischines were known to have written more accounts. These written Socratic dialogues were not so much a philosophical genre as a means by his followers to record his words and deeds and keep his memory.

Plato's dialogues developed in a context of dramatized conversations from the tragedies and comedies to the Socratic dialogues and imagined historical debates. Some modern philosophers, such as Hume and Berkeley, have written philosophy in dialogues but lack the drama that grew out of the richer Athenian culture or of Plato himself. We next examine the dynamic ideas that are matched to this dynamic form.

The Search for Wisdom

Recent philosophy avoids grand systematic explanations of experience and the world, while Plato seems to do just this with his Ideal City in the *Republic,* Ideal Forms in the *Phaedrus,* immortal soul in the *Phaedo,* and so on. Many scholars and textbooks assume Plato built the sort of system it is philosophy's duty to expose and reject and use him as a foil. Exposing the errors of his City, Forms, and Soul has become a common exercise, but this Plato may be only a convenient straw man.

Many arguments in the dialogues are easy to knock down, often with suspicious ease. In our litigious, competitive, eristic culture, so similar to ancient Athens, this is usually the end of the matter. But for Plato this is exactly the beginning. A failed argument generates wonder about a better one. Philosophy concerns both the criticism and construction of arguments and ideas. As Alcibiades shows in the *Symposium,* what we find absurd in this work may be just those ideas where our ego protects us from seeing problems in our own lives. "When reading the works of an important thinker, look first for the apparent absurdities in the text and ask yourself how a sensible person could have written them. When you find an answer, . . . when these passages make sense, then you may find that the more central passages, ones you previously thought you understood, have changed their meaning."[8]

Finding absurdities in a recognized philosopher warns us to be sure that our own perspective is flexible enough to incorporate whatever insight may be lurking within these ridiculous-sounding statements. Our desire to be right must be tempered by the dangers of being wrong. The cost of unexamined knowledge from Anytus or Meno to the tyrant in the *Republic* is a constant theme. If Plato has a system, it might be more one of helping us ask questions than of giving answers.[9]

The absurdities of his language and images bothered his audience as much as us. His Socrates says philosophy is the practice of dying, the soul is immortal and reincarnated, philosophers should be kings,

---

[8] T. S. Kuhn, *The Essential Tension* (Chicago: Chicago University Press, 1977), p. xii.

[9] "The attentive reader who looks below the surface will find that Plato usually limits his dogmatic affirmation to one or two elementary principles of logic or morals. He concludes nearly all his subtlest speculations, his myths, and his symbolisms with some such formula as this; 'The rest I would not positively affirm; of this only I am sure.' And that of which he is sure proves to be only some indispensable presupposition of elementary logic or ethics." Paul Shorey, *Platonism Ancient and Modern* (Berkeley: University of California Press, 1938), p.12.

knowing the good is to do it, and the most important work is examining oneself. These are all provocative, and we will see how Plato uses these to expand and clarify the notion of philosophy, as he faced the same issues in the life of inquiry that we confront today. What we find unphilosophical in him may be where we too need to be provoked in our own conception of the relation of our thinking to our world.

The Practice of Dying and Being Dead

Many issues can awaken our wonder and start us on the search for wisdom. Plato uses many characters and topics to offer different means of access into the philosophic life. Among these multiple dimensions to our lives and thoughts, no single revelation provides the ultimate access. Descartes in his *Meditations* removes himself from life as much as possible in order to find such a thread, while Plato's action always occurs in the middle of things. There are removals to the edges of life's confusions: the shelter of homes, the isolation of a prison, the open space outside the city's walls, the gymnasium, but there is always contact with other people and their activities. Thus, as we try to follow the themes of death and life, other threads will weave themselves around our search. Plato does not have a single organizing principle like the One or the Flux. Some say the Good plays this role, but we will see.

In the *Phaedo,* Socrates says philosophy is "the practice of dying and being dead" (64a) and then gives several proofs for the immortality of the soul. Something dies; something lives. This death that can be practiced requires a soul (mind) that can be reincarnated as experienced by Meno's idea of virtue. Meno decides not to practice dying with Socrates and goes to Persia where he really dies. The death Socrates practices is that of our senses and the commonsense world that informs our daily lives. Our assumed reality needs a regular exam and cleaning. Practicing dying, like Cartesian doubt, removes the assumed meanings of our perceptions and pushes us to find more satisfactory reconstructions. Challenging "the given" follows Heraclitus, while the immortal soul and world follows Parmenides, reflected in Plato's many variations of his mythic journey beyond the limits of discursive reason. Plato seeks enough separation from our habit world to awaken inquiry but not so much to encourage fantasy. Practicing death provides this.

Plato's imagery for the life of reason centers on the immortal nature of our *psuche,* usually translated "soul" but better as "mind." This word evolved three meanings, and all are relevant for Plato. Originally it meant the force causing life in a thing. The Latin synonym *anima* provides this in English. Its presence *animates* a thing, enabling it to move itself, as *animals* do. In Homer a dying soldier's soul always had to escape the body because life could not coexist with death.[10] The second meaning as "spirit," our common meaning of soul, developed to describe how the life force lived on in the afterworld of Hades. The speechless, sullen "shades" in Homer evolve into beings that are rewarded, punished, and reincarnated. The life force takes on a life. The third meaning describes what is most lively within us, the mind that moves even when the body is asleep. Socrates plays between these meanings, often using the religious terms and imagery of the life of the soul to help us understand the less well-known life of the mind.

An ascetic practices the death of the body to better appreciate the life of the disembodied spirit. The philosopher practices the death of his ideas to better appreciate the life of the mind. This sounds paradoxical at first. How can any death encourage life unless we are getting mystical here? Why is any special practice needed to appreciate the most lively element within us? Since we prefer certainty to searching, we spend most of our lives trying to think as little as possible. What makes Socrates so odd is that he thinks so much, just as his partners are noteworthy for avoiding, whenever possible, any heavy thinking. As for the mysticism, we will soon see what a trip to Hades looks like.

Since some thinking goes on all the time, the distinction here is one of quality. Most of our thinking is just calculating. We need to decide what to do next and think we know our options and how to evaluate them. We have a formula for how to proceed, punch in the appropriate data, and come up with an answer giving us a clear direction to follow. Much of this calculating does not even reach the level of consciousness, as most of our daily activity is a semihabitual routine.

Philosophic thinking, however, occurs when we have a real problem and are not sure what exactly is wrong or which formula to apply. Socrates' repeated efforts to define the main Greek *aretai*—justice, piety,

---

[10] This is one of Socrates' arguments for the immortality of the soul in the *Phaedo*. It is a good *ad hominem* argument for anyone who speaks Greek. To us it sounds like a simplistic play on words, but it reveals an aspect of the *psuche's* nature, that it cannot coexist with death.

courage, moderation and wisdom—are examples of such thinking. The usual rendering of *arete* as "virtue" can be misleading, with "excellence" or "success" serving us better. Aristotle suggests Socrates'[11] interest in "virtue" reflects a limited moral concern, whereas the issue for both is the nature of human *excellence* in all its aspects and ambiguities. Meno asking how to obtain *arete* is like a college student asking how to be successful in life and is similarly difficult to answer. What major or career or spouse or number of children should I select? Although all "should" questions, these do not seem very ethical in our current usage. They are quality-of-life issues: how to avoid getting in a mess or, the Greek version, how to make myself happy. The Greeks repeatedly heard the problems Oedipus, Agamemnon, Achilles, Priam, and others had in creating whole, meaningful, and satisfying lives.[12]

Such problems unfold over an entire dialogue. A closer look at the *Meno* will show how Plato works with such problems and his use of imagery. Meno is a young man with natural abilities of body and mind. He is used to succeeding like any well-endowed person. His excellence is challenged more as he moves from his rural home to the big city of Athens and then beyond to the world of Persia. In his conversation with Socrates, he is pausing to make sure he is on the right track. But like us, he does not want to dig too deeply. He wants assurance he is right but does not really want to see how he could be wrong. He will agree to calculate, hence the geometry problem, but is reluctant to think.

Meno sees three possible ways to attain excellence and thinks he can fulfill each: an inherited trait or a know-how to be taught or the result of training. As his friends are aristocrats, he feels he shares their superior human traits. Gorgias taught him rhetoric, the highest science, so he sounds like an expert in any field. And he has trained his body and mind to perform. He has all the bases covered, but Socrates eliminates them all. Excellent parents can have mediocre children, so it is not inherited. Rich parents who train their children in every practice also often have mediocre children. Teaching remains, but they can find no teachers of excellence. Such a teacher knows both what excellence is and how to transfer it. Both Socrates and Gorgias admit they cannot.

---

[11] Aristotle, *Metaphysics*, 987a1.

[12] Martha Nussbaum examines this fragility of happiness in Plato and Aristotle in *The Fragility of Goodness: Luck and Ethics in Greek Tragedy and Philosophy* (Cambridge, England: Cambridge University Press, 1986).

With Meno having exhausted the three options, Socrates suggests a fourth: The gods are responsible when human excellence occurs. Meno readily agrees. He does not care if the gods' distribution is a democratic potential in all or limited to their favorites. He assumes he is a favored child of fate, seen in his rising reputation and being voted a general in his early twenties. He will soon invade Persia as a leader in an army hired to overthrow the Great King. But fate is fickle; it is dangerous to be yesterday's favorite. His army is betrayed and captured in Persia. His fellow generals are killed in a trap, but he is saved to serve as a lesson for any future rebels. Meno is slowly tortured over the course of a year and finally dies. His name evokes a strong image of human promise and failure. His torture in life compared to those in Hades.

Meno repeatedly wants answers from Socrates rather than to think on his own. This is Meno's notion of education. You buy a piece of knowledge, and it is handed to you. But Socrates demands active participation, with the student finding the answers for herself. It is similar to the scientific method where the learner's direct experience convinces her that it is true. The structure of the experiment demonstrates to us the truth of the results. Of course, such "truth" is limited by our ability to observe and what we think we observed, but this is also the strength of the scientific method; it is self-consciously fallible and corrigible. Any experiment is only as true as the next time it is performed. The Socratic student, like the experimenter, does not accept any external authorities but proves to herself with the authority of her perception and reason. As these internal authorities are also fallible and corrigible, the knowledge-seeker regularly examines and tests her ideas and beliefs. As we need others to test our experiments, so we need them to test our ideas.[13] The inquiry for both is democratic and open ended.

Socrates' reason to get Meno to examine his ideas is the same as any scientist's to train his student, to improve inquiry in general and ultimately test the ideas of the teacher. Any good scientist wants his experiment, if faulty, to be proven faulty. There is no good in hanging on to falsehoods in science or philosophy. Socrates joins in these dialogues to articulate and criticize his own ideas and those of whoever will talk with him. He is trying to think and needs others to overcome the efforts we all make to short-circuit this process:

[13] *Apology*, 29e, 38a, 39d, and *Protagoras*, 333c.

defensiveness, prejudice, haste, and lack of confidence. Much of his talks deal with these obstacles, and so religion and death enter his talk with Meno.

In the first half, Socrates tries to get him to define *arete*. Meno does not care what it is so long as he has it, but he finally states that it is having the power to get the goods in life. When Socrates pushes him how he knows which goods are really good, Meno teeters on the brink of having to think but saves himself by creating a distraction, calling Socrates a mind-numbing torpedo fish and blocking more inquiry with the "learning paradox." How can one inquire into what he does not know, for either he already knows it and has no need to inquire or he does not know it and could never recognize it even if it were found (80 d–e). This creates a crisis both in Meno's therapy, restoring his soul to health so he can think, and for Socrates' hope of gaining a colleague.

Socrates responds with a story about what others say about this, removing himself like any good therapist. He shifts to a topic of interest to his partner, the wisdom of the Mystery cults. "They say that the human soul is immortal; at times it comes to an end, which they call dying, at times it is reborn, but it is never destroyed, and one must therefore live one's life as piously as possible" (81b). Socrates uses religious imagery to make the mystery and danger of thinking, like death, less scary. Religion creates a safe zone where our ideas can be reworked, similar to play therapy with children.

Plato uses several reincarnation stories in his work, and they are inconsistent.[14] This questions how systematic these ideas really are. One explanation is that these stories are pedagogical and not autobiographical. They are tailored to the student's individual need at this moment. They do not offer final explanation but development of method. Meno's confidence needs a boost, so he can return to participate in the inquiry. The story says a goddess takes the souls of human failures, punishes and purifies them, then forces them to live another life, resembling Socrates' treatment of Meno. Then from this pitiful group arise some who will gain great mental and physical power and reputation. This reversal of fortune starts with the purification available in Hades, giving a new beginning in life. But where is Hades?

Reincarnation here provides Socrates' "recollection," access to the knowledge from all of one's previous lives. "As the whole of

[14] R. W. Sharples, *Plato: Meno* (Chicago: Bolchazy-Carducci Publishers, 1985), pp. 145–149.

nature is akin, and the soul has learned everything, nothing prevents a man, after recalling one thing only—a process men call learning—from discovering everything else for himself, if he is brave and does not tire of the search, for searching and learning are, as a whole, recollection. Thus we must not believe that debater's argument (learning paradox), for it will make us idle, and fainthearted men like to hear it, whereas my argument makes them energetic and keen on the search" (81d–e).

Philosophy tries to explain instead of explain away experiences. The myth of recollection works by explaining away, by eliminating the possibility of evidence and proof. How do we identify recollecting so as not to be confused by an opinion from our present life? The story gives hope that among our ideas are some true ones, but it cannot identify them. It restores confidence for the search, saying not how knowledge is acquired so much as why we might have any. As Socrates concludes, "I trust that this is true, and I want to inquire along with you into the nature of virtue" (81e). Recollection is not a proof but a crutch. Socrates believes in this for support to enable inquiry to continue. The understanding of the life of ideas begins through death and recollection.

Earlier Socrates tells Meno to remain in Athens and be initiated into the Eleusinian Mysteries (76e).[15] Without Orphic reincarnation cycles or Dionysian orgies, it offered a simple practice, *a ritual encounter with death* and assurance that the soul prospers in an afterworld. The initiates then realize they must care for their soul, as it will continue living after the body dies. After the death-type experience and revelation, with no further ritual or practice, life was forever changed.

Philosophy offers a similar initiation into death. The religious Mysteries seek the continued life of the soul after the death of the body. Socrates' philosophic Mysteries seek the continued life of the mind after the death of a basic idea or opinion that supported one's life. (Meno had given so many good speeches about *arete*.) The Socratic Mystery myths give confidence that our minds, if properly prepared, continue to exist in the reincarnation of a succession of ideas.

The *Phaedo's* death scene illustrates this. Socrates devotes his last day to discussing stories about what the next world is like (61e). The

---

[15] For more on the Eleusinian Mysteries , see G. Mylonas, *Eleusis and the Eleusinian Mysteries* (Princeton, NJ: Princeton University Press, 1961).

stories he offers, except for the closing geographical myth, are all arguments about ideas. The world of the afterlife in Hades (Gk. "invisible") is a useful image for discussing our invisible mental soul life. Socrates here offers several interesting but not compelling arguments for one of these invisible inhabitants, the idea of the soul's immortality. He uses Pythagorean arguments known to his Pythagorean partners, helping them see the problems with this style of thinking, just as he did with Meno's ideas of power. Socrates' arguments often have an *ad hominem* element. His audience puts emotion before reason, as fearful to upset Socrates or his ideas before he dies as they are to upset their own. He seeks to stop them from simply agreeing with everything he says and encourage them to attack his statements.[16] When Simmias and Cebes hesitate with their criticisms, Socrates jokes about their concern for his death. (This is his laughingest dialogue.) Death here is a welcomed test, and he invites their counterarguments.[17]

Upon hearing their reasons against immortality, the audience is devastated. "When we heard what they said we were all depressed... We had been quite convinced by the previous argument, and they seemed to confuse us again, and to drive us to doubt not only what had already been said but also what was going to be said, lest we be worthless critics or the subject itself admitted of no certainty" (88c). The death of an idea makes us as depressed as the loss of a loved one. The frame characters even intrude to lament the death of Socrates' arguments. Socrates proposes a formal mourning if they do not return to life. The soul is weak and vulnerable when depressed. "I am in danger at this moment of not having a philosophical attitude about this" (91a).

Greek inquiry sought explanation that could account for itself, as opposed to the supernatural.[18] When a reliable basic idea falls to

---

[16] Socrates' speaking partners often respond in a series of short innocuous assents. Some critics like Cornford feel these contribute nothing and edit them out, but these repeated assents reflect the mindset that Socrates has to break through, which is often shared by the reader as well. We often "yeah-yeah" as we read, cruising in habit mode until we are shaken out of our slumbers.

[17] Death is welcomed but not suicide. We are too involved with our ideas to properly judge their worth, particularly when stressed. Thus, we should not kill our own ideas but test them in conversation with friends.

[18] For the power of speech, compare the biblical Book of John 1:1, "In the beginning was the *Logos* and the *Logos* was with God and the *Logos* was God." R. S. Version (New York: Nelson , 1933).

criticism and dies, we may lose faith in the possibility of *logos* itself, that any account is true or can be given. The *Phaedo* asks why if an idea proves false after we developed, tested, and believed in it, would the same method succeed any better next time? If we are offered reincarnation, why bother? This loss of faith has two aspects, misology and eristic, passive and active. Socrates calls misology (Gk. "hatred of *logos*") the greatest of human evils, the belief that no argument can ever be sound or offer any reliable guidance. Eristic (Gk. "strife") is the attitude of "the uneducated" toward *logos* (91a). For them argument is a competition to display one's power (cf. Meno) and not to evaluate the ideas discussed. They believe the use of rhetoric can reverse opinions on any topic and so do not expect discourse to provide any access to truth.

Practicing dying and being dead prepares us for these dangers of the rational life. We need more confidence about how our ideas work: bringing ideas to criticism, accepting the death of ideas found deficient and the resulting hole in our understanding, passing through the dark night of the soul when no replacement ideas appear, and finally finding a new candidate. This strengthens the soul, giving it a better chance of surviving. It resembles the cycle of falling in and out of love: elation, suspicion, confusion, denial, depression, reorganization, and a new elation. Philosophy prepares us to be depressed. When our world has crashed, when our career, lover, parenting, friends, and so on have failed us or we failed them, then we need to be prepared or face being crushed.

Modern psychological hygiene suggests diversifying our self-image so it has more than one support, toughening it by facing many positive and negative experiences in a supportive environment, and clarifying it by having meaningful discourse with a variety of people. Socrates' practice of soul hygiene is similar. His soul is not dependent upon any doctrinal beliefs. This does not prevent him from having strong beliefs, as he shows in the *Meno*. "I do not insist that my argument in right in all other respects, but I would contend at all costs both in word and deed . . . that we will be better men, braver and less idle, if we believe that one must search for the things one does not know, rather than if we believe that it is not possible to find out what we do not know and that we must not look for it" (86b–c).

He is committed to inquiry, including who he is, but not to its results, which always remain fallible. In the *Phaedrus* he says his primary search is the Delphic oracle's admonition to "Know Thyself." He does not know if his nature is simple or complex; he is not rooted in any one image of it. He tries new experiences, such as the Bendis religious festival, walking outside the city walls, or being gussied up with bath and sandals at a celebrity's dinner. He turns each of these into a self-conscious experience through discourse, trading ideas and criticisms with an endless variety of partners. Socrates' soul hygiene resembles both scientific method and psychotherapy. Perhaps all three are just good thinking, limiting the distortions of place and prejudice by multiplying the conditions in which an idea holds and engaging the most people to clarify what really is being observed and what it means.

Part of the practice of death is Socrates' Hades stories, and we will close with one of the more outrageous ones, the winged, disembodied souls flying in the heavens with the gods in the *Phaedrus*. It offers another weak "proof" of the soul's immortality, in which some see Plato's new religious beliefs. "The immortality of the soul is established by an argument which Plato regarded as incontrovertible," and "from whatever source he may have derived his justification for believing in personal immortality, there can be no doubt that he did believe in it."[19] Yet even these admit how poor the argument is. "Stripped of the terminology of the Ideal theory, this amounts to saying that the notion of life is bound up with the notion of soul, and what it really yields is not (as Socrates maintains) the conclusion that the soul is immortal but the tautological proposition that so long as soul exists it is alive."[20] This view believes that what "Socrates" tries to prove, Plato believes. But with such pitiful proofs, an excuse is needed for Plato's deficient thinking. Hackforth here rationalizes that this effort is at least more empirical (better) than his metaphysical proofs in the *Phaedo* and thus prepares for Aristotle's later Prime Mover argument for god's existence.[21]

---

[19] Hackforth, *Phaedrus* (Cambridge, England: Cambridge University Press, 1972), p. 64; and R. K. Gaye, *The Platonic Conception of Immortality*, p. 39, as quoted in Hackforth.

[20] Hackforth, op. cit., p. 68.

[21] Our culture has caricatured the idealist Plato vs. the empirical Aristotle, unfairly to both. They had different interests but similar visions of philosophy. "That every man is born either a Platonist or an Aristotelian is broadly true, yet not for the reasons usually alleged. It is not true that Plato is a dreamer and Aristotle a student of fact and reality. It is not true that Aristotle is a reasoner and Plato a mystic and enthusiast. It is true that Plato is a reasoner, an artist, a poet, a mathematician, and a symbolist, while Aristotle is a logician, a biologist, a classifier, and an encyclopedist." Shorey, op. cit., 8. For Aristotle on Plato, see D. Hyland, *Finitude and Transcendence in the Platonic Dialogues* (Albany: State University of New York Press, 1995), pp. 169–170.

In this dialogue, this proof makes good sense. That the soul is immortal because it is ever-moving gets the attention and agreement of the exercise-conscious but lazy Phaedrus. He wants to be self-moving but finds himself always moved by others: the speech of Lysias, the order to exercise by Eryximachus, the seduction letters he attracts, Socrates' suggestion to talk rather than walk. His self-movement principle is weak; he needs to strengthen his soul. As Socrates distanced himself from his "proof" by saying, "*If* it has been established that what moves itself is identical with soul" (246a), so he does not claim his description of soul-life must be true. Only a divine description would suffice, so he settles for an image, a self-conscious mix of truth and fiction.

His image of the soul is that of a charioteer and two winged spirit horses, one noble and one base. The horses pull the charioteer around the heavens, traveling with a group of like souls led by one of the twelve Olympian gods, minus the hearth goddess Hestia who, as a homebody, stays home. When hungry, the gods fly beyond the top of the heavens to be nourished by the metaphysical principles that exist there. Metaphysics means beyond nature and examines such questions as why is there something rather than nothing, which cannot be answered from within nature. The usual divine fare of nectar and ambrosia is fed to the horses, while the gods are nourished by the true principles of existence. Strange gods! Philosophy not only brings us to the invisible world of the divine but also provides the nourishment there.

The nondivine souls with one unruly horse struggle to see "the things that are," the unchanging realities beyond the heavens. The few godlike see most, some see only some, and most are too distracted to see any. When reincarnated, the godlike are protected from harm by their true vision. The rest are reincarnated according to how much they saw. Those seeing the most become lovers of wisdom, beauty, or music, while those seeing the least become tyrants. At death all will be judged, punished or rewarded, then reincarnated again. In the myth one can rise up the scale of nine occupations at thousand-year intervals; for us this occurs within. These levels could represent stages from child to elderly, each thinking it knows best only to be awakened by the next.

Reincarnation promotes not fear of god but hope in ourselves. We cling to a shaky idea of life or belief because we fear change is either impossible or impotent. We fear losing what we have; however pitiful, it is better than nothing. We hide in fantasies, dissemble, make plausible excuses, and become rhetoricians. In the *Phaedo's* tailor's cloaks story, it shows how our ideas wear out, no longer fit, stop being effective, and need to be remade or replaced (87b–88b). The *Phaedrus,* as in the *Republic's* Myth of Er, explains we, not the gods, choose our next incarnation. Being uncertain what success is or how to get it, how do we pick a life? By working in a community of critical inquiry, philosophy finds meaning in both death and life. Having seen how the philosopher overcomes death, we can now examine how she pursues life.

The Life of Ideas

Having seen how ideas die, we are now able to examine how they live. Just as religious death talk helps illustrate the life of the mind, so Plato's metaphors from our physical life reveal the life of ideas. Ideas in the dialogues have the qualities and activities of living organisms. Plato's "Socrates" is, at least in part, the idea of philosophy brought to life, and his activities show aspects of the life of ideas as well. Just like an athlete's body, ideas need food and exercise and are always ready to be tested and even overthrown. The ideas in the *Symposium* behave like the bodies of the guests and the wine usually do; they intoxicate, nourish, seduce, impregnate, put on special clothes, and so on. The flute-playing prostitutes are replaced by the rival speeches, competing to seduce the minds of the audience. The *Republic's* promised torch relay race on horses becomes the inquiry relay team of Plato's brothers. Ideas are not passive objects, like documents in a safety deposit box. They have needs such as coherence and offer benefits such as guidance and security.

Being alive, they interact with each other. There is continual adjusting among new arrivals, old standbys, and the world of discourse and experience. Ideas provide nourishment, like the feasts of words in the *Republic, Gorgias,* and *Symposium.* Like athletes, they require testing to reveal their worth, as in the trial in the *Apology,* the horse race in the *Republic,* and the matching of wits in the *Protagoras.* They enter our lives with powerful emotions, as when we gaze in wonder at absolute beauty in the *Symposium* or we throb and sweat on seeing this beauty incarnated in the *Phaedrus.* They wrestle in the *Euthydemus,* intoxicate the *Symposium* guests, and have intercourse when speech impregnates another's mind, as in the *Theaetetus'* midwife image and Agathon's seduction of Socrates' idea in the *Symposium* (175c).[22]

---

[22] Cf. the *Bible* story of the impregnation of Mary by the Word of God.

Ideas direct our lives for well or ill, as with Meno's ideas of power and the goods it gets, Thrasymachus' or Callicles' idea of advantage, and Socrates' idea of the good in its several images in the *Republic*. The need to monitor and maintain this directing function leads to Socrates' claim to be a doctor of the soul, attending the health of its ideas. Socrates' allegiance to Apollo, the god of medicine, emphasizes this special role. Apollo enters Socrates' life at several critical moments. His oracle at Delphi sends him on his life's mission to solve the riddle, "No one is wiser than Socrates." Diotima, who taught Socrates that love is therapeutic, has Apollonian knowledge of the divine and disease, delaying the plague in Athens.[23] And finally, Apollo's festival extends Socrates' life for a month after his conviction.

Socrates' Apollonian medical mission reflects the significant role of ideas in our lives and that their health and nurture matters. "Submit yourself bravely to reason as you would to a physician," Socrates tells Polus in the *Gorgias* (475d). When the *Republic's* idea of the city becomes sick and fevered with Glaucon's demands for luxury, this illness is treated by purging the excess (399e). Phaedrus in his dialogue realizes he has to take care of his aging body but is still careless about taking any idea into his mind. In the *Republic*, ideas are drugs, especially a clever lie that escapes detection (382a–d). Ideas are magical protective charms in *Phaedo*, like the Pythagorean proofs of the soul's immortality (77e–78a). In *Protagoras*, Hippocrates cares what he eats but not about the value of ideas he lets into his mind. He thinks he can be nourished on sophistry and not become a Sophist (313a–314c).

This soul doctor ministers to the health of other's ideas and exemplifies being healthy himself. Plato's presentation of the life of the mind centers on Socrates' activities in the dialogues. The life of Socrates' character reflects the life of the mind. To see this better, we should review the relation of the historical and the dramatic Socrates.

As discussed earlier, the historical Socrates, who wrote nothing, presents an even more mysterious figure than Plato, who writes in such an indirect and confusing manner. The three people who directly knew him variously describe a charlatan, a Unitarian minister, and a philosopher. In deciding what is historical in Plato's characterization,

---

[23] The Peloponnesian War brought Athens' worst plague in 430. Diotima could have postponed the plagues of disease, war, or rhetoric. Her philosophical concern with civic and psychic health reflects Socrates. She keeps pushing him to challenge her teachings (206e, 207c, 208c), as he does to his own audiences, and Plato does to us.

the early dialogues are considered mainly a report of the ideas and methods of his teacher. As Plato's ideas mature and differ from those of Socrates, then the character separates from the historical model, becoming Plato's mouthpiece or a representative of his evolving notion of philosophy. However, Socrates' character can be both historical in inspiration and Platonic in function without being either inconsistent or divided chronologically. Plato's consistent idea of this character could continue through swings in dramatic intensity and complexity, the apparent move away from aporetic (puzzling) endings to dialectical conclusions, and even the relative silence or absence of Socrates himself.

I support the consistent character option. "Socrates," at least in part, represents the idea of philosophy itself come to life and working in the world. He is something other than simply human, more divine like the Homeric heroes. He presents the essential role of our rational ability but also how difficult it is to stay in this role, and even whether it is always desirable. Most of us would not want a slaughtering or deceiving Homeric hero living next door, and we would be exhausted having to face Socrates every day. Socrates is all philosophy all of the time. He demands that we keep realizing our philosophic nature, yet his nature is so monomaniacal that our lives barely seem to touch. He has been called cold and aloof from daily human affairs and emotions and for his tunnel vision that finds value only in life's most critical issues.[24]

Plato chooses this Socrates to represent philosophy, not himself. He is the undistracted love of wisdom. Whether it is the tasty treat of Agathon's or Cephalus' feast, the sexual treat of Charmides' or Alcibiades' naked body or the domestic treat of returning home after war (*Charm.* 153a) or the *Symposium's* all-night party, Socrates seems impervious to them all in his godlike pursuit of philosophy. In trying to give our lives order and meaning, we recreate our world,[25] as when Descartes' *Meditations* mimics the Bible's six days of creation to find a rational order for life or as the *Symposium* speeches reflect the seven competing world orders of their creators. As we can create, we also live with the effects of our creating and must critique the work of

---

[24] G. Vlastos, *Socrates, Ironist and Moral Philosopher* (Ithaca, NY: Cornell University Press, 1991); and M. Nussbaum, "Irony of the Historical Socrates or Philosophy Itself?" *The New Republic*, Sept. 16 & 23, 1991, pp. 34–40.

[25] The Greek gods only ordered the stuff of the world and did not create it. A god creating the universe out of nothing would have been absurd.

our ideas. Socrates can dwell in this create–critique nexus beyond ordinary human endurance. In army camp he once stood in thought for an entire day and night, an action he repeats while waiting for the dinner and small talk to end at Agathon's party (*Symp.* 220c–d and 174d–175c).

Philosophy as Plato presents it through Socrates is an activity of necessarily endless striving (*eros*) for humans. Our mental creations are never complete and never stay put, which is why Socrates' work is never done. A reader who thinks she is making progress toward wisdom is confronted with the parade of failed characters and ideas that, as in any scientific experiment, show there are many ways to be wrong, and whatever happens to work at this moment may turn out to be wrong as well. Scientific "truth" is only as good as the next experiment; the guiding ideas in our lives are only as good as the next account and defense we can give of them.[26] Socrates is always ready to start over, to take nothing for granted, to test his ideas and himself every day.

This endless searching could be seen as tragic in its futility, as when Oedipus's reasoning leads to his horrifying collision with its limits, yet there is also nobility in his refusal to subject his inquiring mind to the gods' will. Reason gives us inquiry on life's important questions but deprives us of certainty and closure. As David Roochnik put it, there is a tragedy of *logos* "because it cannot achieve a moral techne (art, skill, technique), a stable body of reliable knowledge able to tell us, in fixed terms readily teachable to others, how we ought to live."[27] Plato knows the repeated thwarting of this desire for stability and happiness will overcome normal humans. Socrates is the more-than-human ideal of reason. He can face tragedy continuously and not be destroyed. We can participate in his strength and also measure our limitations.

Most of us first meet Socrates in the *Apology*, where for both historical and dramatic reasons he defends his way of life. The historical Socrates was tried by his fellow citizens, found guilty, and sentenced to death. Plato here has a unique opportunity to give a

---

[26] True belief is as good as knowledge in directing our lives except that it is unstable. What we find believable is always subject to change and may even abandon us, like the statues of Daedelus in the *Meno* (97d–98a).

[27] David Roochnik, *Of Art and Wisdom* (University Park: Pennsylvania State Press, 1996), xii; and *The Tragedy of Reason* (New York: Routledge, 1990). Both show Plato's philosophy as critiquing our basic ideas.

defense of the philosophic life. How much Plato could deviate from Socrates' actual words is much debated. Those who date this dialogue close to the event feel it must be close to Socrates' own words, while those who think its composition was later admit more creativity on Plato's part. Like most disputes over Plato's life, our current knowledge cannot resolve this.

This is a portrait of a person doing this odd thing called philosophy, with the oddness not removed or glossed over. Socrates is not made pretty here. He is possessed by a *daimon* or inner voice telling him what not to do. He spends his days accosting his fellow citizens about their ideas, claiming this invasion of privacy is a divine mission. He spends little time with his impoverished family but mentions it when convenient. His singular commitment to seeking wisdom suggests that he is better than other people, whom he berates for attending to material goods more than to the health of their souls. On meeting Socrates, we might join the jury's mutterings against this man.

Socrates' crustiness soon becomes a reflection of our own. Philosophy enters when Socrates distinguishes the unconscious crust of opinions or prejudices the jury has formed and the fully conscious judgment their legal role demands. Images of Socrates and philosophy lived in their minds for many years. They knew Aristophanes' charlatan named Socrates and debated the value of those itinerant Sophists, who offer youths short cuts to political success, stir up their hopes, then leave after taking their money (*Meno* 91b–92d). Sophists, philosophers, and fancy talkers were all the same thing in popular opinion. But on this day the people are on jury duty, where they could use some help finding the truth, and philosophy has the stage to make its case.

Popular opinion and common sense will have to fail before the jury is willing to engage any more critical faculties. As discussed previously, we prefer to calculate rather than think, to use rather than test or develop our habitual ideas. At his trial Socrates discusses the need to test our ideas and ourselves, giving a clear example of this process. To be on trial is a philosopher's dream. His entire city demands an account of his ideas and critiques them. The jury has nothing to do but examine ideas and those who hold them and to consider what exactly is the good of their city. The law courts gave the opportunity, and Socrates took advantage of it, using it to do philosophy with his fellow citizens.

Socrates first addresses the prejudices that subvert the jury's ability to inquire. We are always in the midst of our ideas. We cannot judge well unless we take into account our prior ideas concerning both what and how we judge. The objective juror is a fantasy. Thus, the traditional charges against Socrates (atheist, rhetorician, corrupter) reflect typical limits we, and the jury, put upon our own inquiry: certain ideas are off limits; rhetoric is how other people talk; problems are caused by bad people, not bad explanations. Total inquiry is too time consuming, so we exempt those basic ideas that are too risky, painful, or complex to change. We claim to know who tells lies or not, and besides, punishing a scapegoat is easier than fixing a system.

Apollo's oracle that no person is wiser than he sets Socrates on his lifelong course of self-examination. Most people believe knowledge of the world is fairly direct and that no one is particularly better at this. As Meletus says here (24e) and Anytus repeats in the *Meno,* all Athenian citizens are equally able to instruct proper behavior in the youth (92e). Socrates turns this commonplace into an inquiry into what it is we claim that we all know. Excepting the skills of craftsmen, this knowledge turns out to be mostly opinion. The claim "we all know certain things" becomes "we all think that we know," and "no one is wiser" refers not to superior knowledge but equal ignorance.[28] Shared ignorance, like shared knowledge, diminishes our interest in inquiry until we see that inquiry can also result in well-founded opinions that, when true, guide our lives equally well (*Meno* 97a–99c). Common sense prefers stable knowledge. Only after this fails do we reluctantly turn to philosophy and the work of creating reliable opinion and the constant criticism to maintain it.

The oracle's ambiguous message that "no one is wiser" sets up the Socratic revolution in our ideas. The oracle tested people by their interpretations. When the oracle told King Croesus a great kingdom would fall if he invaded his neighbor, of course it was his own. We join Socrates in wondering if being wiser means he is the wisest of all. This is his meaning that he alone knows he does not know, but this is hardly an exclusive advantage. He pushes the comparative "wiser" to the superlative "wisest" in order to reveal the positive and shareable

---

[28] How quickly the comparative becomes the superlative. Six lines later Socrates asks, "What then does [Apollo] mean by saying that I am the wisest?" He makes explicit for us our reading of the ambiguous comparative "wiser." Yet if "no one is wiser," then all can be equally wise.

"wise" with a better understanding. The world of ideas is a great democracy. "No one is wiser" does not segregate the wisest but unites us all in the same ignorance, wisdom, and inquiry. Knowing that we do not know, we need mutual inquiry to find what we can know, or at least agree to.

That philosophy is necessarily democratic is essential to Plato's thought. Although democracy mostly values freedom for the pursuit of individual desires, this is also where criticism is most unrestrained and potentially honest. It is no accident the *Republic* takes place in the Piraeus, a democratic stronghold. When the ideal government and its degenerate forms are described in *Rep.* Book 8, democracy is the only regime where thinking is allowed. The others each have a defined good and no place for inquiry. Even the ideal aristocracy of the philosophers becomes so refined that calculation replaces inquiry. There are systems for education, career selection, and eugenics. A human mistake in calculating this last area, the nuptial number controlling reproduction, causes the system to destruct. Our irresistible and tragic hope (cf. Roochnik) that reason can find a stable foundation for our lives is again dashed. Plato made such a well-founded edifice to give us practice surviving such a wreck, knowing this "ideal" construction would fall apart. "A city so composed is hard to be moved. But, as for everything that has come into being there is decay, not even a composition such as this will remain for all time; it will be dissolved" (546a).

If the best does not reproduce itself,[29] it disappears in the city, taking with it the true measure of all things. It is replaced in both city and soul by the traditional measure of worth—honor. A timocracy of the honorable arises. As tradition falls apart, a more concrete idea of good emerges, the goods. Oligarchy reigns, the rule of the few with the goods. Next the goodless many think their desires also count and take power for the people, the *demos*. They define power by freedom from restrictions, including those on thinking. The people compete, as we do today, to have the greatest desires and means to satisfy them. If one succeeds beyond all others and enlists them to help him achieve even more satisfaction, his desires become the social rule. He becomes a tyrant. As he rules over others, so his desires rule him. Socrates imagines the futility of satisfying all one's desires as continually pouring water into a leaky jar (*Gorg.* 493b) or as a "pelican's life," eating and defecating at the same time

---

[29] This also describes language and culture between generations.

(494b). Four of these political and soul states are controlled by external values: the experts' best, the culture's honor, the goods of the few, or the desires of the most powerful. Only in a democracy is the idea of value up for grabs. Only here can inquiry occur.

Realizing Plato's philosophic need for democracy contrasts sharply with his infamy as an antidemocratic ideologue. After World War II he was blamed with Nietzsche for helping Hitler develop his totalitarian ideas,[30] and current textbooks say philosophers can only be kings if they are not democrats.[31] This opinion reflects the approach that takes any of Socrates' statements as an end product, as dogmatic assertions of Plato's truth. Assuming Plato is authoritarian encourages these interpreters to find hierarchical systems in his thinking, which makes him seem more authoritarian and then more hierarchical, and so on.

Realizing the dialogues' democratic elements helps break this self-reinforcing cycle of interpretation and supports the view that Socrates' statements are part of a process and cannot be understood in isolation. This process is similar in each dialogue yet expressed differently according to the varying context and participants. Philosophy tries to bring our ideas to criticism, and this takes a period of orientation and practice to overcome our reluctance, as shown by Socrates' partners. Socrates' own purpose is to examine further his own life and ideas. Many images of Plato, such as Ryle's where he arranges king-of-the-hill argument contests, make him appear more competitive than cooperative.[32] Yet what Socrates keeps asking of his partners is to join him in seeing through each other's conscious and unconscious defenses and tricks. Criticism by the best person would be best and even sufficient, but Plato has taken us here before. We do not know

---

[30] The most famous example of this accusation is Karl Popper's *The Open Society and Its Enemies* (Princeton, NJ: Princeton University Press, 1966).

[31] That Plato is not politically correct is a common theme. "Plato's fundamental vision is hierarchical and aristocratic, rather than egalitarian and democratic. His epistemology and metaphysics reflect and encourage this kind of highly discriminating orientation. . . . If you believe in the fundamental equality of all people, you may be suspicious of Plato's belief in the superiority of those who have supposedly escaped the Cave and seen the Good. If you are skeptical about the possibility of any human being discovering the 'truth,' you will probably have difficulty with the idea that only these exceptional, enlightened individuals are more fit to govern than the rest of us." Douglas Soccio, *Archetypes of Wisdom*, 3rd (Belmont, CA: Wadsworth, 1998), pp. 138–139. That Plato awakens critical abilities does not fit into this vision.

[32] G. Ryle, *Plato's Progress* (Cambridge, England: Cambridge University Press, 1966).

who is best. There is not a human "best" that can adequately account for itself. So any proposed aristocracy (rule of the best), even that of philosophers, can only justify itself if it includes everyone. Philosophy requires criticism based on pluralism and democracy more than dogma.[33]

Socrates democratically talks to everyone he encounters, but not everyone talks to him. Most are too busy making money or running their lives to talk with him or trouble about anyone else. Most people most of the time and all of us some of the time choose not to think. It is rarely in our interest to disrupt what we are doing. Socrates talks to everyone to help them identify their golden, self-ruling nature, as in the Myth of the Metals. In the *Republic* Socrates suggests their developing city could use a story, a noble and useful lie (382c–e), about the presence of different metals identifying each person's basic nature. The rulers contain gold, the auxiliaries have silver, and the farmers and craftsmen have iron and bronze (415a–d). This story seems to justify a natural aristocracy, with some people born rulers and others to be ruled, but the story soon self-destructs. Each person has to be carefully examined to determine which metal is present, which is not easy. Golden parents do not always produce the golden children they should. Identifying the metal is as difficult as identifying the basic nature in the first place.

This analysis of social classes further breaks down in its parallel with the soul. The metals distinguish both types of people and parts of the soul. Thus, each soul contains all of the metals (cf. Anaxagoras). We all have a golden, reasoning nature that is usually obscured by our iron, acquisitive part. Gold is thus democratically present in everyone. What looks like support for hierarchy and privilege becomes another argument for inquiry, the need to determine the traits of a good ruler and to examine each person for their presence. The readers hunting for the just man throughout this long book know this task is not as easy as determining the presence of gold. This evaporating explanation shows a pattern in the dialogues where accounts that initially appear dogmatic when examined internally destruct. This initial inflexibility gives way to a more responsive discourse that can examine beneath this surface.

---

[33] Three decades ago the American Philosophical Association debated whether it could afford domination even by a majority, much less an aristocracy, without losing the critical edge that the widest participation provides. Following Plato they finally decided for more inclusion.

The lives of ideas create much of the drama in the dialogues, centering upon Socrates as an illustration of how to live this "life of reason."[34] This section has examined reason coming to life through him and will end with more examples of the life of ideas from the *Republic*.

Ideas come to life not to replace the things of this world but to help us work with them. The idea of injustice comes to life in the unjust man who hides himself using the Ring of Gyges, just as the unjust rhetorician hides behind his just-sounding words. They are flushed out of hiding in the chapter on the tyrant, which reveals the effects of following the idea of injustice. Thrasymachus, like Callicles in the *Gorgias*, thinks he can change one aspect of his beliefs and behavior without affecting any other. He believes an advantage over others must be an advantage to himself, seeing only the goods he will get and not the potential losses. The tyrant's portrait in Book 9 vividly depicts this life and losses. He is isolated by his own power. Words mean what he decides, and people only say what they think he wants to hear. Language increasingly disconnects from experience. He creates a culture of systematized deception, just as that of philosophy is one of truth telling.

The need for mutual criticism demands mutual truth telling. There is no guarantee that truth will be told other than good will arising from mutual need. When Meno asks Socrates what answers he gives, he responds, "A true one, surely, and if my questioner was one of those clever and eristic debaters, I would say to him: 'I have given my answer; if it is wrong, it is your job to refute it.' Then, if they are friends as you and I are, and want to discuss with each other, they must answer in a manner more gentle and proper.... the answers must not only be true, but in terms admittedly known to the listener" (75 c–d).

Philosophy tries to communicate clearly so that one can receive in return a worthwhile judgment on the ideas presented. While Callicles claims rhetorical flourishes will leave Socrates dizzy and helpless, Socrates counters that it is truly spoken judgments that will dazzle and cripple Callicles (*Gorgias* 526e–527a). When confronted by a divine being revealing the truth about his soul, he will not know how to respond because he can only be deceptive or clever. He is unaware of the effects his ideas have in his life. Socrates' afterlife myths serve to move us beyond the moment and illustrate these consequences.

---

[34] Cf. John Herman Randall's helpful introduction *Plato: Dramatist of the Life of Reason* (New York: Columbia University Press, 1970).

The promised feast in Cephalus' house is only in the ideas they are consuming, a meal eaten too quickly to digest in Book 1, so Plato spreads out the banquet over nine more books (354b). The proposed torch relay race on horseback similarly only occurs as Plato's brothers pass back and forth the light of inquiry in their hunt for justice. The idea of the city is born and nurtured, becomes fevered and purged, grows up to find waves of criticism, realizes in midlife that criticism is beneficial and needs to be incorporated, and so makes the apolitical philosophers the rulers. As most citizens care more for money than their souls, so philosophers are too busy caring for their souls to be concerned with politics. They rule only from their interests in social stability, a large educated class, and open communication. They rule to avoid being ruled by a worse person, just as we test our ideas so that we are not ruled by a worse one when a better one is possible.

Truth, Sophistry, and Rhetoric

Many Athenians saw little difference between philosophers and Sophists. Both were sharp talkers and logic choppers, using persuasive arguments in their self-interest and suspected of lying. Philosophers claim the criticism of their ideas requires mutual truth telling, while rhetoricians say only the plausible is persuasive. Socrates is ambiguous, always talking about cooperation yet frequently using rhetorical tricks.

Socrates has four dialogues with major Sophists and several with minor ones, usually asking them to explain their *techne* (skill). The *Phaedrus* and *Symposium* feature rhetorical displays and commentary. In the *Apology* he is accused of being a Sophist making the weaker argument seem the stronger. Aristophanes uses Socrates as his model Sophist in *The Clouds*. When he arrives at the Sophists' house in the *Protagoras,* the doorkeeper takes him for a Sophist. In the *Phaedrus,* separating philosophy and rhetoric is an explicit theme, while the *Symposium's* competitive love speeches examine persuasion more implicitly. The *Sophist* pursues a funny and confusing topology of human activities, at last defining the deceiving Sophist from the truth-seeking philosopher and statesman. We now need to examine further why philosophers must be committed to seeking the truth, just as they are to criticism in the death and to democracy in the life of ideas.

While Sophists like the *Phaedo*'s Evenus have no interest in the practice of death, they share other interests with philosophy (61b–c). They flourish in a democracy with public discussion of new ideas. They attract the youth of the city, particularly those with political aspirations. They raise questions about the foundations of traditional values and spread cultural relativism. Their practice requires a facility with language and logic. Although their presentations may be clear, they leave a degree of confusion in their wake. They both breed skepticism.

Socrates uses rhetorical devices, manipulating similarities and differences in language to force acceptance of his logic even when others doubt his conclusions apply to real life. Hippias' complaint is typical: "Oh, Socrates! You're always weaving arguments of this kind. You pick out whatever is the most difficult part of the argument, and fasten on to it in minute detail, and don't dispute about the whole subject under discussion" (*Hippias Minor* 369c).

We can see how similar they are in practice. In the *Symposium,* Agathon uses his Sophistic training to create ambiguity and twist his argument. First he proves that Love is self-controlled. "Everyone admits that self-control is mastery over pleasures and desires, and that no pleasure is stronger than Love. If then all pleasures are weaker than Love, Love must be the master and they his subjects. So Love, being master over pleasures and desires, will be in a preeminent degree self-controlled" (196c). We accept the ambiguous phrase "no pleasure is stronger than Love" as "Love is the strongest of all pleasures," but then Agathon gets his conclusion by reversing it to mean "Love [not being a pleasure] is stronger than [all] pleasures." Since this is a possible meaning, we are convinced by the form, if uneasy on the content.

He then proves Love's courage. Love captured Ares, god of war and lover of Aphrodite according to Homer. "Now the capturer is superior to the captive, and the capturer of the bravest of all other beings will necessarily be the bravest of all beings whatsoever" (196d). Here "the capturer is superior to the captive" is ambiguous. The capturer defeats the captive in one area: wits, tricks, strength, patience, or sexuality. But superiority in one area does not apply to every area, yet this is what Agathon does. The superior capturer must be braver, as well as superior in any other quality. Again the meaning Agathon wants is in his phrase, so we accept it. Even if uneasy, we cannot dwell on such doubts while trying to keep up with the flow of his speech.

After the *Meno's* geometry lesson, the issue is how knowledge relates to what is teachable. Socrates offers a hypothesis to help their inquiry, "Or is it not plain to anyone that men cannot be taught anything but knowledge?" Socrates can cajole and bully like a Sophist. Calling something "plain" or "obvious" should put us on alert, as

Agathon's "everyone admits" seen previously. Such phrases use our intelligence against itself, for we ought to see what everyone else does.[35] Here "anything but" supplies the ambiguity. Socrates makes a syllogism with the premise "Virtue is knowledge" and the conclusion "Virtue is teachable." His major premise, then, should be "All knowledge is teachable," but he says "All teachables are knowledge." If "all V is K" and "all T is K," then no conclusion follows. He even calls attention to his logic, but Meno is oblivious (88c). When it finally sinks in, a confused Meno wonders "whether we have investigated this correctly" (96d).

Hippias' concern and Meno's wondering show a key difference in philosophy's use of rhetoric. Socrates' arguments are questioned by his audience. He not only welcomes this but specifically sets it up, while Agathon seeks an emotional response over an intellectual one; the audience should be consumed by the beauty of his words and left entranced, not inquiring. Socrates questioning Agathon after his speech stresses this change in purpose. Socrates uses rhetoric as a tool of self-examination, *leading to* questioning instead of avoiding it.

Sophists prefer longer speeches before large audiences with little opportunity for reflection or questions. This is Thrasymachus's strategy in his first long speech in the *Republic*. Having spoken, "he had it in mind to go away, just like a bathman, after having poured a great shower of speech into our ears all at once" (344d). Plato's Sophists say they need long speeches to fully express their ideas and are always ready to give one, while they reluctantly participate in Socratic question and answer. The Sophist wants as little attention on him as possible, just as he makes his audience feel homogeneous and not individually responsible. His arguments try to be transparent in the light of common sense and avoid attention to themselves. He needs to know and use the dispositions and prejudices of his audience. Indeed, the best argument is one that does not appear to even be arguing; just providing information or facts. Rhetoric's first goal is to hide that it is even rhetoric.

Socrates, however, prefers one-on-one short statements, gaining his partner's assent to each step of the argument. His speech intensifies the focus on himself and his partners. "My object is to test the validity of the

---

[35] We easily adapt this extralogical support for our arguments. The Hackett edition's *Apology* Introduction uses "obvious," "surely," and "certainly" in the space of three sentences to support its historical accuracy. Such words can reflect that our arguments exceed our evidence.

argument, and yet the result may be that I who ask and you who answer will both be tested" (*Protagoras* 333c). He disturbs his audience by calling their prejudices into question. In *Meno*, Anytus says he knows all about Sophists but never met one, just like Meno thought he knew all about virtue and the slave boy how to do geometry. Anytus opposes the Sophists undermining traditional values, but these values were already eroded by war, politics, and greed. The Sophists are the symptom, not the problem. In a similar way rhetoric is the symptom. It reveals the places where we lack *logos*, claiming knowledge without proper evidence. Like a litmus test for ignorance, its presence shows the absence of knowledge. Rhetoric by nature is self-concealing but, if guided by philosophy, reveals both itself and the soul it represents.

This helps explain why Socrates' rhetorical use is sharpest in talking with the famous Sophists: Gorgias, Protagoras, and Hippias, plus Thrasymachus, Euthydemus, and his brother. He is accused of defending views contrary to public opinion, common sense, and logic only to display his skill.[36] In *Gorgias,* he argues it is better to suffer wrong than do it. In *Hippias Minor,* he says those who commit injustice voluntarily are better than those who do so involuntarily (376b). In *Protagoras,* he twists the poet Simonides' words to support his claim that no one does evil voluntarily. In *Republic,* he says the advantage of the stronger is to care for the weaker. The Sophist would argue such unpopular positions tongue in cheek to display his skills. Socrates uses his unpopular positions to confront his audience with their moral responsibility and question the adequacy of common sense. He opposes popular opinion not to promote his skills but to expose their flaws. He ironically uses a sophistic strategy to undermine the sophistic dogma that all opinions are true.

Socrates argues these unpopular views rhetorically to put his audience on guard. When we know we are hearing rhetoric, we go into thinking mode. In Plato's image, we become hunters of logic and illogic. As we watch someone failing against Socrates' skill, we see the possibility of our own failing. This can lead us to confront some of our own risky issues. We are brought to consider critiquing the key ideas in our life because we see examples of the costs if we do not. We do not want our beliefs supported by tricks, not of Socrates or the Sophists.

---

[36] Gorgias was known for a speech praising Helen as being innocent of any wrongdoing and not responsible for starting the Trojan War.

Rhetoric's exposure causes inquiry both into itself and the ideas that it is hiding and protecting. Thus, Socrates uses rhetoric in his primary task of examining his life. In *Phaedrus*, Socrates explains that a true rhetoric (very like philosophy) requires knowledge of all types of people and speech and how to properly match them. "When he is not only qualified to say what type of man is influenced by what type of speech, but is able also to single out a particular individual and make clear to himself that there he has actually before him a specific example of a type of character which he has heard described, and that this is what he must say and this is how he must say it if he wants to influence his hearer in a particular way—when, I say, he has grasped all this... he can be said to have perfectly mastered his art" (271e–272a).

Knowing all this, if possible, would give great power, and the use of this power is the last aspect of rhetoric to examine. What determines if this power is used beneficially, for either the one who has it or the greater society? What society would permit its citizens to have such destructive abilities without controlling their use? Traditional forms of governing rely on some sort of involuntary control: Aristocrats need to prove their innate goodness, timocrats need to deserve public praise and avoid blame, and oligarchs need to show their wealth serves social good and stability. All these means are indirect and open to failure, as Socrates shows in *Rep.* Book 8. Only democracy has an intrinsic reason for limiting one's power; it leads to more freedom, as social stability permits the fewest restrictions on one's pursuits. Citizens uniting into a faction, however, can upset this stability. Their united power gives them an advantage and better satisfies their desires. If this faction gains power, then the same logic applies to itself; its own parts compete until the strongest emerges. Thus, the tyrant comes into being, with no conscious need and little ability to control his desires or care for anyone.

This problem of making congruent the benefit to the individual and society is a constant tension in Athens and the dialogues. The Ring of Gyges in *Rep.* Book 2 turns a person invisible, so he can embark on a life of crime without fear of punishment. Rhetoric also gives its users a cover, the appearance of being just, so they can do as they please without being discovered. To help resolve this, it is time to discuss "The Cave," Plato's most famous, and most quoted out of context, image. First let's see the story and then examine the context. In *Rep.* Book 7, Socrates "makes an image of our nature in its education and want of education" (514a), describing people living as prisoners in a cave who can only look forward. Behind them a fire provides light and in front is a wall upon which all the items we see in our world appear. Other people move these objects behind the prisoners and make noises appropriate to them. Passing in front of the fire, their objects make shadows on the wall in front of the prisoners, who experience these shadows and echoing sounds as their real world.

It then asks what would happen if a prisoner were freed. When he turned around and went up to the cave opening, moving his previously restrained body would be painful and the sun's light blinding on his dark-adjusted eyes. In this dazed state he could see neither outside nor the things passing on the wall and would yearn for the familiarity of the shadows. If forced out of the cave and into the sun, he would gradually get accustomed to the greater light, clearly seeing the things that made the shadows, as well as the sources of light, the stars and sun.

Socrates gives this story his usual disclaimer that "a god, perhaps, knows if it happens to be true," then explains that "in the knowable the last thing to be seen . . . is the idea of the good; but once seen, it must be concluded that this is the cause of all that is right and fair in everything . . . and that the man who is going to act prudently in private or in public must see it" (517b–c). The appearance of the idea of the good is the climax of the search for justice and answers the question why anyone would be just or tell the truth. This idea appears in the better light outside the illusions in the cave; it is the explanation that makes sense of all the rest.

While seeing the good in the sun's light sounds remote to our daily lives, having an idea of the good is a fact of our psychology. We organize our lives using a hierarchy of ideas to make decisions. The most basic idea directing our welfare is our idea of our good. The most basic idea of the universe's welfare (how things should be) is our idea of universal good. All our actions follow this idea of our own good. Thus, Socrates claims we cannot choose to do evil (*Prot.* 345e) but only have a deficient idea of our own good. With so many other ideas resting upon it, the good is buried deep inside our thinking and difficult to examine or change. It is the most critical idea for the "practice of dying and being dead" but also the most difficult to approach.

If to know the good is to do it, how to first educate the philosopher–rulers to find it? How can this good be described and taught? Socrates gives us a series of images said to be the good's offspring: the Sun, the Divided Line, and the Cave (506e). Respectively they illustrate that we have an idea of the good; it is hidden under the layers of images, beliefs, and calculations of the Line; and examining this idea requires leaving our usual life experiences in the Cave.

The Cave experience recurs in many dialogues, with a few starts toward conversion but no completions. Meno begins to turn when he wonders in his dialogue (96d and 97c), or even better, Alcibiades in the *Symposium* when he gets the "snake bite" from Socrates (217e–218a). His idea of good is physical and mental power, starting with his own superior body and mind. But when he offers himself to Socrates and is turned down, his life-organizing idea is shredded, pushing him to the brink of examining what is really good in life, but he falls back.

Even a Sophist wants the truth when his own ideas are at stake, and Socrates flushes them out from hiding by attacking their ideas of the good. Protagoras in his dialogue claims to easily teach the virtues, but Socrates argues that each virtue also requires wisdom and is thus more difficult to learn. Courage is the last virtue they discuss, primary for rhetorical success and for Protagoras. When defending his own ideas, Protagoras becomes less rhetorical, even rejecting public opinion as his truth and examining his own idea (353a). At the end of the dialogue this idea has failed. He is at the door of the Cave, blinded by the light he could use to find a new idea. He too experienced Socrates' "snake bite" but is also unable to leave the Cave. He becomes a truth-seeker when his own truth is at stake, if only for a moment.

The Cave story ends with the person now used to the sun's light returning to the cave. The dark would blind and confuse him much as the light had before. When asked what he had seen above, there would be no comparable Cave experience he could use to explain his own. People would say he came back worse than before and want nothing to do with his out-of-cave adventure. But these are the adventurers who fill the ranks of philosophers, seeking to find the light or *logos* that illuminates the most. Ruling the city, our language, and ourselves is a necessary pastime on the way to implementing the next breakout.

Settings and Structures

The Flux, the One, and the Moment each present separate truths that Plato considered deficient but contributory toward a practice of inquiry. He expressed his dynamic vision of harmonizing these in a literary presentation, but whether he could have used a literal equivalent is an ongoing debate. Does philosophy require drama or not tolerate it? To see, we will examine the philosophic roles of some of his dramatic devices. With each element integral to the dramatic and philosophic whole, this is best seen by examining an entire dialogue in detail, a task beyond the present book. A good guide to start is Koyre's *Discovering Plato,* discussing the *Meno, Protagoras, Republic,* and *Theaetetus.*[37]

Philosophy may seek tranquility but begins in our frustrations and enthusiasms. Plato's dramatic approach serves to track the drama in us, both our emotional and logical responses. The characters are full of emotions. They get angry when defeated by Socrates. They get embarrassed and blush: Thrasymachus(*Rep.* 350d), Hippocrates (*Prot.* 312a), and Euthydemus' brother (297a). They are in love (Lysis), afraid for their reputations (Crito) or of death (Cephalus), and worried about their children (Lysimachus and Melisias in the *Laches*). As Socrates works with his partners' responses, so Plato works with ours. The release of emotions can expose the ideas they have been defending. Emotion, like rhetoric, is useful in finding the defenses that shield our ideas.

It has long been debated how the dialogues inform or interpret each other. Thrasyllus made one standard edition four hundred years after Plato, ordering the dialogues in nine tetralogies, perhaps after the tragic theater's trilogy plus a satyr dance. Some use links in the dialogues; others have little thematic unity. Plato's relation to this order is uncertain. The three linked groups are Socrates' trial and death (*Euthyphro–Apology–Crito–Phaedo*), the *Republic–Timaeus–Critias* series told by four friends (the fourth by Hermocrates is not known), and the *Theaetetus–Sophist–Statesman* series also lacking a promised fourth, the *Philosopher.* Later Neoplatonists made new pedagogical tetralogies, using the order for initiation into universal knowledge, from *Alcibiades* to *Timaeus.* Many scholars agree the drama affects the arguments in a dialogue but disagree if one drama joins all dialogues, as in this proposed ascent to certainty.

---

[37] A. Koyre, *Discovering Plato* (New York: Columbia University Press, 1945).
P. Friedlander's *Plato,*3 vols. (Princeton, NJ: Princeton University Press, 1969) discusses all of the dialogues. C. Griswold's *Self-Knowledge in Plato's Phaedrus* (New Haven, CT: Yale University Press, 1986) is a good close reading of a single dialogue.

Plato uses a variety of settings and speakers to stage his dialogues. Two thirds occur in a well-defined setting. Three fourths occur in a group of over two people. Two thirds use direct narration by an anonymous and invisible narrator. But none of these majorities coincide. Each dialogue asks why these elements are used in this situation. Socrates is alone with his partner in eight dialogues, but how does this intimacy affect the content? In the *Phaedrus*, he and Socrates are alone in an isolated romantic spot where legend said a god ravished a young girl (229). Phaedrus is attractive and provocative, but Socrates turns this steamy scene from seduction of bodies to that of speeches, such as the one Phaedrus is memorizing. The occasion uses the image of sexual intercourse (Phaedrus is reading a trashy speech) to examine our mental impregnating of others with ideas that can reproduce and grow.[38] As this matures, we consider this brainchild as our own and suffer the parental inability to assess their children. Socrates says he is a midwife in the *Theaetetus*, helping the idea-pregnant bring their idea to the light of day to see if it is whole and healthy or just hot air (149a–151d).[39]

Ideas are sexual in the dialogues. Socrates' young friend in the *Protagoras* fears becoming like the Sophist whose ideas (children) he hopes to carry away inside him. In the *Symposium*, Diotima challenges male homosexual superiority, arguing the need for procreation against the sterility of homosexual physical or mental activity. Our mental lives need contact with different ideas for criticism and cross-fertilization. Socrates has a knack for attacking the center of his opponent's ego, here their homosexual maleness and later his refusal of sex with Alcibiades, destroying his idea that his super-stud self is the Good.

The setting in many stories reflects the ideas under discussion and reveals the effects of holding them. Religious beliefs have political effects in the *Euthyphro*, *Apology*, and *Phaedo*. What you love shapes what you are, as the seven *Symposium* speakers illustrate. The *Republic* occurs in Athens' seaport the Piraeus, where new religions and ideas flourish outside the city and its traditions, a place of moral and civic

---

[38] Being awakened by a clock radio shows how easily a tune can be inserted into one's brain and how hard to remove. The same goes for ideas that are heard or read. Prophylactics for the ears might be needed.

[39] Victorian Jowett sees this internal hot air as a "wind egg," combining fertility and emptiness. Use of several translations avoids becoming hostage to one person's idea of Plato or of the proper language for philosophy.
Plato, *Theaetetus*, trans. Jowett (Indianapolis: Bobbs-Merrill, 1949).

instability where Socrates is waylaid and revolutionary ideas discussed. Phaedrus in his dialogue also opens himself to change outside the city's walls, pursuing a new speech and exercise program. Ideas give Euthydemus and his brother a new arena for wrestling. Cephalus travels to Athens to hear about Parmenides, who believed travel was impossible.

Several dialogues occur just after a sophistic display. Socrates sees the exhibitions in *Euthydemus, Laches,* and *Hippias Minor* and arrives just after those of Gorgias, Protagoras, Cratylus, and Ion. There are other competitive arenas like the gymnasia and wrestling schools. Socrates usually refuses to make a display speech but then turns around and does so, as in his long comment on Simonides' poem in the *Protagoras,* trading etymologies with Cratylus, quoting long passages from Homer with Ion the rhapsode, and capping the rhetoric of Lysias's speech with his own in the *Phaedrus.* He blends enough with his partners to use their terms and arguments, then turns these against them.

Five dialogues use a framing technique, setting one story within another to better examine it. In the frame, two people discuss the main action after it occurred, one anxious to hear all the details. Only in the *Phaedo* is the subject of interest Socrates. In *Parmenides,* Cephalus wants Plato's brother to recite the meeting of Parmenides and young Socrates. A friend in the *Symposium* wants a racy story to occupy a tedious walk. The *Theaetetus* is a memoir of its dying namesake. The *Protagoras's* companion wants the latest news of the Sophist. The dialogues rarely present philosophical encounters. People are usually looking for a good story or talk that Socrates then turns into philosophy.

We each read within our own frames of reference. Plato's frames pull our framing into consciousness, for example, the *Symposium's* first scene. Apollodorus (Ap), a fanatic Socrates groupie, tells a story from another groupie, Aristodemus (Ar), to a business friend as they walk to town.[40] Ap begins with a story to establish his authority, while Plato uses this opening to question his own authority. Ap tries to convince us to believe him, while Plato raises issues to make us doubt him. He stirs the issue of truth instead of settling it, putting us on guard for what follows. Ap claims our trust by saying he did not attend but got his story from Ar, who did. He also verified the facts

---

[40] Aristodemus *tries* to be Socrates by looking and acting like him. He goes barefoot and arrives at Agathon's as his surrogate. Apollodorus imitates by saying his words. His business is to "know what Socrates says and does every day" (172c).

with his hero Socrates. But we are told that Phoenix's inferior version is also circulating. As questions arise about the truth, Plato warns us his frame will not be very critical, between a businessman desiring only entertainment and Ap too smitten with Socrates to criticize. Ap promises to retell all he was told but later admits, "Ar did not recollect precisely everything that each speaker said, and I do not recollect everything that Ar told me, but I will tell you the most important points in each of the speeches that seemed to me worth remembering" (178a). (So much for recollection.)

Ap's preface and story is framed by his already retelling it two days ago, just like the party itself is framed by Agathon's victory and first drunken party two days ago. The recital by Ap is framed for us by the faulty memories of Ap and Ar and the noncritical listening of the companion. This elaborate setting helps us consider our own contexts and memories. Communication of events and ideas is always filtered through interest, memory, and purpose. Our ideas have histories that affect what we think they mean. The frames emphasize our distance from the story's events, with Socrates' editing only adding confusion. The story demands to be examined, providing good practice.

Conversations and Dialectic

The primary conversation in every Platonic dialogue is between Plato and the reader or better between the reader and her idea of what is being presented in the dialogue. We cannot ever converse directly with another person but only with what we think the other person is saying, doing, intending, and so on. All conversations are ultimately with ourselves, the Sophists' truth of being-in-the-Moment. But this self is not impervious to outside influence or incapable of change. This self can become beyond the limitations of the Moment. A conversation can make us see information previously ignored and show us contradictions in our thinking, fantasies in our desires, illusions in our interpretations of people and events. We can respond to any of these, but we usually do not.

Plato's characters are historical people, and their natures impact their talk. These people have habits, prejudices, intentions, reputations, desires, emotions, attachments, and so on. They do and say accordingly and not merely for the sake of Plato's plot or philosophy. For example, characters often respond to Socrates with a series of short affirmative answers, like teenagers. This is not using their assent to gain ours as well, but rather shows us how the character thinks. It is tempting to believe these long stretches of minimal response can safely be elided from the text, like Cornford in his *Republic*.[41] These semimindless responses show the tempo of the experience, both the character's way in the story and the reader's way in his dialogue with Plato. We nod in our "you must be right since you're so smart" mode until we are struck by the sublime or ridiculous, as also arouses the dialogue's nodding head. Then we blurt out an emphatic "No!" or "Yes!" and the real engagement begins. Socrates sets this up, lulling us to accept his authority and then zapping us with something we cannot swallow, for example, the coed naked wrestling class in the *Republic*. This reflects our reluctance to disturb an authority, as Simmias and Cebes try not to upset the condemned Socrates or to face the upset of having to think for themselves.

The people conversing with Socrates are rarely philosophers, except-ing Parmenides and the Eleatic Stranger. There are some famous Sophists, such as Gorgias, Hippias, and Protagoras, and some less famous, such as Thrasymachus and Callicles, and some ridiculous, such as Euthydemus and his brother. There are soldiers such as Meno, Alcibiades, Laches, Polem-archus, Nicias, and Plato's brothers, Glaucon and Adeimantus. There are young men full of promise, such as Charmides, Lysis, Theaetetus, Philebus, Menexenus, and those not so promising, such as Phaedrus. Euthyphro is a self-proclaimed religious seer; Ion, a rhapsode performing the Homeric poems; and Lysias, a speechwriter for everything from law courts to love courting. There is Timaeus, bringing his ideas about nature from Italy. There are old men with the wisdom of their experience, such as Crito and Critias and the Cretan, Spartan, and Athenian in the *Laws*.

There are many types of people in Plato but few philosophers or displays of philosophical talk between evenly matched sides. Rather, the dialogues usually start from a question about a common problem: how to succeed, raise children, know a friendship will last, face death, recognize justice or love or a Sophist or statesman; in general, how to live better rather than worse and appear smart and not foolish. Socrates' response is to turn his partner from a piecemeal view to a more holistic inquiry of the basic ideas and terms involved and their links with our other ideas. This process is dialectic, meaning to converse or argue and more specifically, to examine the connections between ideas. In the *Phaedrus*, Socrates describes the two aspects of this reasoning.

---

[41] F. M. Cornford, *The Republic of Plato* (New York: Penguin, 1945), Preface.

The first method is to take a synoptic view of many scattered particulars and collect them under a single generic term, so as to form a definition... and make clear the exact nature of the subject one proposes to expound.... That definition may have been good or bad, but at least it enabled the argument to proceed with clearness and consistency.... (The other method is) the ability to divide a genus into species again, observing the natural articulation, not mangling any of the parts, like an unskillful butcher... I am a great lover of these methods of division and collection as instruments that enable me to speak and to think (and call those who can do this) dialecticians. (265d–266c)

The dialogues start with the partner's question (any starting place) and lead into this more comprehensive inquiry. The vehicle for the first method is usually defining a broad value term (a virtue), a human relation (friendship), or an emotion (desire for pleasure or fear of death). Socrates uses the specific problem to raise questions about the related basic ideas, but the partner only wants a quick Band-Aid and to get on with life. He wants to succeed, not know what success really is.

For the second method of dialectic, we must revisit the order and typology of the dialogues. Linking this order to his theory of ideas has been a major issue of the last century and affects how his use of dialectic is discussed. Circularity is always a danger in arguments that base interpretations on the order of composition. Though the sequence is said to determine the content, often the content is used to justify the sequence. Stylometrics, as we have seen, analyze the frequency of elements in a person's writing style and group Plato's writings according to his unconscious use of such elements. In theory this reveals a chronology of the writer's habits, changing slowly over fairly stable extended periods. It finds three broad kinds of dialogues sharing similar habits of style, with debate over which dialogues belong in which of the three stylistic periods. In the first, Socrates seeks definitions of a word like "justice," and the talk ends without one being found. Some see here the historical Socrates in the current debate about when "Socrates" speaks for himself, when for Plato, and when for philosophy.[42] The middle period has more dramatic

---

[42] Gregory Vlastos organized and inspired much of this recent inquiry. He lived a long and productive life, publishing for over forty years. A good example is "Socrates," *Proceedings of the British Academy* 74:87–109. A summary of recent work is his final book, *Socrates, Ironist and Moral Philosopher* (1Ithaca, NY: Cornell University Press, 1991).

complexity, a less abrasive Socrates moving beyond definition to dialectic and more willing, able, and satisfied partners. The last period seems more stark with less drama; Socrates on the sidelines or not even present in the *Laws,* the partners almost too willing or "tractable," and the analysis or dialectic more central and intense. Stylometrics can sort the dialogues by similar styles but cannot limit a style to only a certain creative period or get consensus on the necessary membership or meaning of these groups (see Note 4).

Dividing the dialogues into time periods could as well be into types of conversation, which might help avoid turning claims of chronology into philosophical development. The Greek word *sunousia* (being with), like our "intercourse," means both conversation and sexual encounter. We have seen Plato use sex as a metaphor for philosophy. In the *Symposium,* this word describes Agathon's drinking party as an "orgy," but the only sexual activity is between ideas. "Socrates'" actions could then divide into three types of intercourse: (1) on the make, as he tries to connect with reluctant inquiry partners, (2) in relationship, as he works through difficult issues with attentive partners, and (3) with other lovers, where he takes a seat to let others speak, or in sum, (1) seeking a partner, (2) having a partner, and (3) changing partners. This sounds unusual but better shows the continuity of philosophical vision by seeing the need for mutual criticism in a community of discourse. Other thematic links could also describe the philosophic unity of the dialogues, or neutral names, as types One, Two, and Three for the current Early, Middle, and Late. The following lists are alphabetical and help one follow discussions using such groupings.[43] The lists vary among commentators.

---

[43] L. Brandwood, "Stylometrics and Chronology," in *The Cambridge Companion to Plato,* R. Kraut, ed. (Cambridge, Endland: Cambridge University Press, 1992), pp. 90–120. Kraut's introduction divides the dialogues as follows:

Early	Late Early	Early Mid.	Late Middle	Late
Apology	Euthydemus	Meno	Symposium	Timaeus
Charmides	Hip. Major	Phaedo	Republic	Critias
Crito	Lysis		Parmenides	Sophist
Euthyphro	Menexenus		Theaetetus	Statesman
Gorgias	Republic I		Phaedrus	Philebus
Hip. Minor				Laws
Ion, Laches, & Protagoras				

Type One	Type Two	Type Three
Alcibiades Major	Phaedo	Critias
Apology	Phaedrus	Parmenides
Charmides	Republic	Philebus
Clitophon	Symposium	Sophist
Cratylus		Statesman
Crito & Euthydemus		Theaetetus
Euthyphro & Gorgias		Timaeus
Hippias Major & Minor		Laws—generally
Ion & Laches & Lysis		assumed to be
Menexenus & Meno & Protagoras		written last

Now we can finish our discussion of dialectic. In the *Phaedrus* quote previously discussed, Socrates spoke of two methods of reasoning. The first tries to discover the "one in the many" by asking for a definition. What is virtue (*Meno*), moderation (*Charmides*), friendship (*Lysis*), or piety (*Euthyphro*)? The second method tries to determine the relations and distinctions between the items defined. This method is discussed in Type Two works like the *Phaedrus* and is demonstrated in the Type Three. In the *Republic*, several types of cities are constructed and five types of government examined, but there is no effort to explain "city" or "government" by *diaeresis,* the complete classification of their defining and distinguishing features. This occurs in the third type, like the search for the *Sophist's* Sophist, where several defining features are tested (angler, merchant, warrior) to see which is most productive in classifying him.

Inquiry into definition is continuous through the dialogues. Too much gives the One; too little, the Flux. Socrates journeys to Hades in the *Protagoras* seeking such definitions and his soul doctoring ministers to their health. Definition is the rhetoricians' playground, switching meanings between relative and absolute, individual and group, by culture or nature. It is also the basis of philosophic exchange and criticism. The illusions in the Cave show how difficult definition can be. Philosophy cannot enter the *Republic* until criticism is present, until after the young men raise the problems in "the three waves" in Book 5 (457c, 457d, 472a). Then the effort to clarify leads to the higher education in the images of the good: the Sun showing the life-defining power of our idea of the good; the Line showing the mass of opinion, images, and formulae we have to distinguish from knowledge; and the Cave showing that these opinions and images pervade our definitions and require our conscious removal from these habitual ideas in order to examine more fully our foundational ideas such as that of the good.

This concern with definition and dialectic leads us to this section's last topic, Plato's Theory of Forms. Much of recent Plato research concerns his development of this theory. The dialogues discuss Forms as the true definitions of things, like shapes in geometry. Perfect shapes (lines, angles, circles) could never be drawn and thus never be physically seen. But we can understand such a concept and even see it "with the mind's eye." "Form" (cf. Note 1) shares this union of knowing and seeing, conceiving (definition) and perceiving (a thing's shape). The Greek word *eidos* unites these two branches of meanings, as we alternately speak of Plato's "Forms" or "Ideas." Greeks consciously played with this dual meaning, as in the tragedy "Oedipus Rex," which turns on the hero's inability to know the truth of what he sees. The blind wise man Teiresias can "see" Oedipus' situation as both husband and son to the same woman. Sophocles floods us with variations of *eidos* keeping the seeing and knowing issue always before us.[44]

The Greeks linked these phenomena because Forms have this psychological reality.[45] We picture things to ourselves, from daydreams to definitions about the good. Most of these images seem clear, as my idea of my dog. Some are quite vague, especially those with conflict, such as the ideal child or parent. Like Sophocles, Plato repeats this linking of knowing and seeing, as in the *Meno*'s geometry problem, where the answer is a line that can be known only as seen, as its length is an irrational number. The same is true with virtue, as Socrates and Meno agree they have seen virtuous people yet are unable to describe exactly what makes them so. Socrates using images as a prelude to knowledge also builds on this psychology. We need to see a thing before identifying it.

The Form thus presents an ideal answer in the necessarily ideal world of our minds. Ideal here means the definitions and relations that we construct in our minds, not as opposed to real things but as an attempt to inform them. A Form represents our current best (ideal) idea of a definition. For abstractions or stipulations like circles and

---

[44] Roochnik (op. cit.) uses this story to show the tragedy of reason's need to know but inability to do so, especially on life and moral issues.

[45] Psychology is an issue in all the middle dialogues. *Republic* begins seeking justice in the soul. *Phaedrus* examines rhetoric to see how the soul works. *Symposium* examines love, and *Phaedo* the fear of death.

triangles, the Forms we construct usually suffice, as they do all the things such shapes are supposed to. But for worldly things like trees or chariots and qualities like courage or love, we cannot simply stipulate our Form (though linguistic tyrants like Thrasymachus try). We believe in our Forms because they serve us well, but sometimes in our daily conversations or interactions, they fail. However, since we see the world through our ideas, how can we alone critique their adequacy?[46] To say Plato chose the ideal over the real is common but misleading. He examines the *psuche's* natural process of making and criticizing ideals, trying to inform our notion of reality with the best ideas possible. The Theory of Forms is not an escape from but a description of our mental processes. When a partner reaches an *aporia* (impasse) in trying to define a concept, then his old Form has crashed and he needs a new one. Finding one is often an "Aha!" process, involving an insight as we suddenly grasp the new Idea or Form that fits. But the perfect fit today might not be so tomorrow, as seen in the *Symposium's* search for our perfect "other half." The new idea replaces the old if it more adequately explains our experience. The immediacy of "seeing" a Form supplies the momentary certainty of our knowing but also increases our ability to see more in the future. Human sight or insight is never a final determinant of knowledge but can certainly serve the cause.

Stories and Myths

There is a tension between *muthos* (story, myth) and *logos* (reason, argument) in Plato's dialogues, with shifting similarities and differences. Socrates often chooses to present an argument by telling a story. Story space gives a more neutral environment for examining ideas than argument space. In *Gorgias,* Socrates describes the afterlife in Hades, "Then listen, as they say, to a very fine *logos,* which you may consider a *muthos,* but I regard as a *logos;* for I want you to take everything I shall say as truth" (523a). Phaedo says Socrates spent his last day "engaged in philosophical discussion" as usual (59a). Yet

---

[46] "He will mind the city...we have gone through that has its place in speeches (*logoi*), since I don't suppose it exists anywhere on earth. But in heaven, perhaps, a pattern is laid up for one who wants to *see* and found a city within himself on the basis of what he *sees*. It makes no difference whether it is or will be somewhere" (*Rep.* 592a–b). Religious readers may feel ideals need to exist in a special realm, and such fantasies are easy but not necessary to entertain, and Plato did not. We construct new ideals to live better than we did with the old. Ideals are not a substitute for life but hypotheses (threads) to be tested in life.

philosophy here becomes "most appropriate for one who is about to depart yonder to mythologize and examine tales about what we believe that journey to be like" (61d–e). He then gives several arguments for the soul's immortality before ending with another grand story about Hades. In the *Republic* when they are cleaning up the city's education, they begin with the stories about the gods because these are the basis for our values later in life. In *Symposium*, Socrates gives his *logos* on love by telling the story of his love lessons from the divine Diotima. He claims to know love-matters (177e) yet explains this knowledge with the story instead of a rational account. Plato stresses its fictional nature by including pieces of the prior speeches and making Aristophanes comment on it (212c). Phaedrus in his dialogue asks if Socrates believes the myth about their place. He replies that demythologizing stories would distract from his Delphic oracle job to know himself. He accepts common beliefs about traditional myths to save time for examining himself,[47] which entails remythologizing himself, seeing if he is "more complex and furious than Typhon or a gentler and simpler creature" (230a).

Philosophers like their arguments neat, eliminating the ambiguities of language by reducing it to the symbols and forms of logic. Socrates does the opposite, dressing up his arguments as stories. Some of his *logos* stories use simple direct language, as in *Phaedo's* arguments or *Meno's* geometry problem, but why use *muthos* at all? Arguments ensure that we know what we think we know by fastening down our opinions so they do not wander like Daedelus' statues in the *Meno*. Stories do not provide logical proofs with premises and conclusions but act more like hypotheses, positions from which to begin inquiry and to hold while waiting for something better to appear. There is no simple proof that unjust people will be unhappy or happy in life. The *Republic's* Ring of Gyges story shows the argument for happiness; the descriptions of the tyrant and of Er's visit to Hades show the argument for unhappiness. The Er story, like all his reincarnation stories, shows this use of hypotheses. Regardless of our past, assume we can choose a new life now and try it, as the souls in Hades choose a new life on earth or Socrates chooses a life of inquiry in the *Meno*. "I would contend . . . that we will be better men, braver and less idle, if we believe that one must search for the things one does not know,

---

[47] Compare this with Descartes' accepting the culture he was raised in while awaiting a better one in Part Three of his *Discourse on Method*.

rather than if we believe that it is not possible to find out what we do not know and that we must not look for it" (*Meno*, 86b). Arguments can be developed for such a hypothesis, as for the Sophist hypothesis that philosophy is not a proper adult activity, but none of them yet seem to be conclusive.[48]

Myths, then, are not supernatural doctrines beyond questioning but give us images to promote discussion and evaluation. Plato's myths do not express mystic certainty but his desire for certainty when simple argument can be found. Myths do not prove but can give us new perspectives to aid in inquiry. One of the best stories is by Aristophanes in the *Symposium*. I will end this section by showing how his images help focus the discussion and advance our ideas. Aristophanes is the middle speaker at Agathon's party. The first three base their ideas on, respectively, the poets' traditional values, the Sophists' cultural relativism and utilitarian values, and the physician's objective natural science. Each self-destructs: Phaedrus wants to emend divinely inspired poetry, Pausanias promises to deliver excellence but retains the lover's right to lie, Eryximachus shows love balances all things yet he can exempt overeating. Each begins with love as a great outside force (the god Eros) but ends by locating this force in his own ego, respectively, as the power of attraction, seduction, or maintainance of proper balance.

Aristophanes' love is an erotic need beyond our control that fate helps fulfill by creating a perfectly matched other half just for me. He understands the desire for completeness, which the first three egos saw only as immediate gratification, and our inability to achieve this. He describes our origin as double people, with two bodies attached at the stomach, two faces on one head, two sets of outfacing genitals for external fertilization "like grasshoppers," four arms and legs, and so on. These people tried to gain the gods' power and were punished by being split in half, thus creating us. If we do not behave, we will be split again, rendering our mouths, sex organs, and other things inoperable. After the split, Apollo sewed up our stomachs, creating the navel; our heads turned around (remember the Cave); and our genitals moved to the front so we experience some of the old wholeness when we copulate.

But how do we find our other half? You have *sunousia* and experience the fit. If it is the best possible (you judge), then this is your

---

[48] Callicles wants to beat some sense (force as argument) into an adult who is still philosophizing (*Gorgias* 485c–d). Thrasymachus claims Socrates' clinging to philosophy is infantile (*Rep*. 343a, 345b).

one and only. But after seeing more of the world, some good-looking fits might make you question your earlier judgment. You try a few and find one that is everything you ever imagined, but then your imagination moves on. New ones keep appearing, and your body keeps changing. We need to spend our lives[49] going belly-to-belly with every other human being to finally judge which fit is best. If you forget match number 302,783, you need to start over. What are the key criteria to keep track of? What is the *diaeresis* of "fit?" Aristophanes' story destructs on the physical level (so many bodies, so little time) and points us to the philosophical level. He is the first speaker to define love, "the desire and pursuit of the whole" (193a). We cannot gain completion on the level of bodies and their changes. Our only hope is on the level of soul or mind.[50] This is how Socrates spends his life, seeking someone to help him find completion, to share his views, his ideas, his criticisms—even his Forms.[51]

Socratic Irony

Our last element is Socrates' irony. This problem is what students experience when a teacher uses "Socratic method." If the teacher knows the answer, why doesn't she just say it instead of playing "Twenty Questions," and if she does not, how will the class ever find something that she cannot?[52] It seems like a charade with the teacher using a veil of false ignorance to encourage the class to make some predetermined discovery.[53] It is the same with Socratic irony. In his claim that he knows nothing, it seems that he is hiding something. There is more to what he is saying, giving us a double meaning. Socrates uses irony to express what he sees in an idea, but his

---

[49] His version of self-examination is to see what partner matches us.

[50] Continuous sex with an endless series of partners is a type of completion, always being in the process of being completed, like the idea of god as continually creating. But our bodies cannot take it. Mental intercourse has more promise of constant activity, as in Socrates' routine.

[51] The *Encyclopedia of Philosophy* entry on Plato dismisses the *Symposium* as lacking clear arguments and containing nothing philosophic.

[52] This is Meno's "learning paradox." Recollection does not solve it but gives faith to do so. It is not self-verifying and can be mistaken.

[53] The Socratic method now means teaching by asking questions but without the original commitment to ignorance. Teachers already know the answers to their questions, losing the potential for shared discovery.

audience does not, linking his fuller meaning with their lesser meaning in the same expression. Socrates borrows the ambiguities that nourished the Sophists, but for education rather than manipulation. His claim that virtue is a gift from the gods in the *Meno* expresses this difference. To the uncooperative, Socrates sounds sarcastic and nasty, while for the willing, the multiple meanings help them work through the complexity of the problem.

Friedlander analyzes Socrates' use of irony as, "The concept (of irony) may waver between dissimulation, hated or despised, playful hide and seek (a common idiom of the intellectually brilliant and critically suspicious society of democratic Athens), and dangerous concealment, feared or admired. Indeed, friends as well as enemies could talk about Socrates' irony with very different meanings."[54]

In this third concealing type, the listener is made to feel uneasy, that more is happening unlike anything that is already known. This is when irony, like the good Socratic method, can help lead into a new realm of possibilities. The ironist does not know the answer; she knows what does not work and where inquiry might be continued. As Friedlander explains, "Socratic irony, at its center, expresses the tension between ignorance—that is, the impossibility to put into words "what justice is"—and the direct experience of the unknown, the existence of the just man, whom justice raises to the level of the divine." [55]

We can see that there is something we call just or a Sophist or the diagonal of the square, yet these cannot be so simply described. The ironist may be more advanced in the inquiry, knowing more of what does not work and that her listeners also need to experience how these do not work in order to understand the inquiry. For common sense that lives in the literal and univocal, irony is a capricious multiplication of puzzles and is only for the pleasure of those who like such puzzles.

Clitophon in his short dialogue criticizes Socratic irony and method, just as *Parmenides* critiques the Forms. He claims Socrates keeps getting people ready to do philosophy and to care for their souls by defining key terms like justice, which will make them just. But they never get the definition or the action. He claims Socrates is all talk, and talk for its own sake, "You say that men are unjust because they want to be, not because they are ignorant or uneducated. But

---

[54] P. Friedlander, *Plato*, Vol. 1, (New York: Harper & Row, 1964), p. 138.

[55] Ibid., p. 155.

then you have the effrontery to say, on the other hand, that injustice is shameful and hateful to the gods. Well, then, how could anyone willingly choose such an evil?! 'Perhaps he is defeated by pleasure,' you say. But isn't this defeat involuntary if conquering is voluntary? Thus . . . the argument shows that injustice is involuntary, and that every man privately and every city publicly must devote to this matter greater care than is presently the norm" (407d–e).

Clitophon ironically accepts Socrates' call to inquire but also demands some closure. He asks the pupils, "O you most distinguished gentlemen, what are we actually to make of Socrates' exhorting of us to pursue virtue? Are we to believe this is all there is, and that it is impossible to pursue the matter further and grasp it fully? Will this be our lifelong work, simply to convert to the pursuit of virtue those who have not yet been converted so that they in turn may convert others? Even if we agree this is what a man should do, should we not also ask Socrates, and each other, what the next step is? How should we begin to learn what justice is? What do we say?" (408d–e).

Clitophon wants his inquiries answered and claims Socrates misleads and finally obstructs this. "When I had endured this disappointment, not once or twice but a long time, I finally got tired of begging for an answer. I concluded that while you're better than anyone at turning a man towards the pursuit of virtue, . . . your ability to praise it so well does not make you any more knowledgeable about it. Now that's not my own view, but there are only two possibilities: either you don't know it, or you don't wish to share it with me . . . . You're worth the world to someone who hasn't yet been converted to the pursuit of virtue, to someone who's already been converted you rather get in the way of his attaining happiness by reaching the goal of virtue" (410b–e).

A simple division of the dialogues is between the Socratic that end with such an *aporia* (impasse) as Clitophon complains of and the Platonic that deliver the answers Clitophon wants. Some people even think this dialogue, if genuine, is the transition between these two phases, leading up to the *Republic,* when Clitophon hears justice defined as he desires. I think this division reflects our sharing Clitophon's desire for answers more than a change in Plato. We do find justice in the *Republic* and love in the *Symposium* and the Sophist in his dialogue, but we find these within complex webs of particular conditions, reconstructions of ideas, and attempted proofs that often fail. The greater complexity in these later inquiries hedges their solutions, qualifying answers as incomplete as the *Meno*'s solution that the gods give us virtue.

And yet Clitophon should get some answer. What is the good of all this preparatory behavior? Philosophy is a communal activity, and inquiry, with its intrinsic need for mutual criticism, requires maintenance of the community more than packaged answers that can be carried away for individual use, like the rhetorical tricks or cooking recipes one has paid for. Answers freed from further inquiry put an end to philosophy, thus ending the need for both a democratic social order, where self-interest leads us to share information and arguments, and mutual truth-telling, which is our only hope of limiting rhetoric.

Clitophon here believes there is no truth in a situation or speech other than what someone, preferably himself, can impose upon it. His beliefs give him all the answers he will ever need. He is the measure of all things, so that what he *believes* to be to his advantage really is to his advantage (340b). He cannot be influenced by what Socrates or anyone else says, and so his response in the *Republic* is silence. This is the world of the tyrant, which at first seems filled with great noises, the seductions of the constant stream of desires, and the actions of the constant stream of efforts to fulfill them. But at the center of this activity is Clitophon's same silence. There is no *logos* in the world of pure desire; it has nothing to say. If our life is to be more than the leaky jar in the *Gorgias* and our inquiry is to advance beyond silence, then we need to answer Socrates' invitation to join in the mutually critical philosophic community. Plato describes the difficulties of such citizenship but also its chief reward: that when asked to account for one's life, to give one's *apology,* one will have something to say.

6

Aristotle

Aristotle's presentation of philosophy seems familiar at last. He articulates the topics that philosophy still uses today, in each summarizing all prior Greek thinking and explaining the structure of its proper inquiry. In textbooks he is when philosophy begins to sound normal: inquiries into everyday experiences and opinions instead of the metaphysics of water, air, and fire; a straightforward essay style with no more poems, myths, or dialogues; no fantasies of all things dissolving into the Flow or the One. Contrary to Platonism, he finds order in our daily world instead of imposing forms upon it. He is a main guide to the prior history of Greek philosophy.

On the surface he seems to deviate from these prior thinkers, especially Plato. He promotes his innovations but may overstate differences to stress his ideas. Since opening his own school, it has been debated whether he and Plato are more alike or different. Recent opinion supports difference, following Raphael's "The School of Athens," a portrait gallery of the Greek philosophers with Plato and Aristotle balanced in the center. Plato carries his *Timaeus* and points up to the heavens while Aristotle carries his *Ethics* and gestures ahead into the world of experience. Raphael saw them as equals, yet some think Plato's concerns with the heavens and metaphysics are no longer relevant. He uses stories for arguments, morbidly dwells on the soul and death, questions any action to a standstill, and examines the self to the exclusion of all else. Aristotle is more familiar, like a modern scientist dealing with real things, from mollusks to political constitutions.

Irving Berlin opposes these two approaches to life, the wideranging many-sided fox versus the single-minded, stolid hedgehog. "A great chasm exists between those who relate everything to a single central vision, one system less or more coherent or articulate . . . a single, universal, organizing principle in terms of which alone all that they are and say has significance—and, on the other side, those who pursue many ends, often unrelated and even contradictory, connected, if at all, only in some *de facto* way . . . [They] entertain ideas that are centrifugal rather than centripetal, their thought is scattered or diffused, moving on many levels, seizing upon the essence of a vast variety of experiences and objects for what they are in themselves."[1]

Berlin's distinction is evenhanded but incommensurable, with famous thinkers on both sides, but the wily fox soon caught our fancy, while the stodgy hedgehog was as old-fashioned as his British name. Plato is his prime hedgehog, while Aristotle runs with the foxes.

This raises a problem for our Aristotle. In his *Nicomachean Ethics,* to hit the mean we must adjust our sense of it away from any predisposed attraction toward either extreme. If our current culture inclines us towards things Aristotelian, we must adjust accordingly. He may be too easy and comfortable for us, obscuring the edge of his analysis and criticism. If he is our model of objectivity and analysis, this may only reflect current scientific bias and miss his concerns with the quality of life, ambiguities of language, and development of reason. Tredennick gives this stereotype: "As a thinker, Aristotle is essentially logical and analytical; and these qualities are almost inevitably accompanied by the limitations of literal-mindedness and lack of imagination. Both merits and defects can clearly be seen in his criticisms of earlier systems, whose inconsistencies he can ruthlessly unmask, but whose more abstruse points he frequently misunderstands."[2] Our image of Aristotle may be so "Aristotelian" that we miss his similarities to Plato.

Yet similarities must exist if Aristotle resided amicably with Plato for twenty years in the Academy. Both wrote dramatic dialogues for most of their lives. Why Aristotle at the end switched to writing lecture notes we do not know, any more than why Plato wrote at all after Socrates did not. As Plato possibly tried to complete Socrates, so Aristotle did to Plato. Plato tried to make writing speak; Aristotle tried to present the Forms through the dialectic of things instead of

---

[1] Isaiah Berlin, *The Hedgehog and the Fox* (New York: Simon and Schuster, 1953), pp. 1–2.

[2] H. Tredennick, *Aristotle: Metaphysics* (Cambridge, MA: Harvard University Press, 1933), p. xxx.

thoughts. Socrates feared writing would turn philosophy's dynamism into an authoritarian rule of scripture. Plato feared that direct talk about things would freeze into the One or melt into the Flux, denying any space for a conscious life worth living. We will examine Aristotle's response first in his biography, writings, and relation to his predecessors, then in his individual works and vision of the life of ideas.

BIOGRAPHY AND WRITINGS

We have as much information on Aristotle's life as we do for Plato and, as usual, more stories and assumptions than facts. He was born in 384 in the northern Ionian Greek colony of Stagira, near Macedon.[3] His father Nicomachus (like his son, names skip a generation) was physician to King Amayntas II of Macedon, likely living mostly in Pella, the nearby capital. His mother Phaestis came from Chalcis, Stagira's mother-city, where Aristotle took refuge at the end of his life. His parents died when he was young, and a relative named Proxenus raised him in Stagira. At 17 he went to Athens and became a student of Plato. How and why this happened is unknown, nor are there any stories of similar young men coming to school in Athens. Whether this school was like Socrates in the *agora* or an apprentice relation with the learned teacher, we do not know. They shared interests and spent time together, but how many, how long, how often, and how organized, we do not know. Perhaps Plato moved the *agora* talks to a spot where only those interested would attend and pursue projects of mutual interest.

Aristotle stayed twenty years with Plato, until the latter's death in 347. He became known for his Platonic-style dialogues, closely arguing both sides of an issue, and much admired in antiquity. Only a few fragments remain. We know nothing of what he did in school. Political disputes between Athens and Macedon, in which he played no role, caused his relocations. Just before Plato died, Macedon–Athens relations deteriorated. Philip, the new king of Macedon, whose earlier invasion was stopped north of Athens by illness, returned. The Athenian orator Demosthenes then delivered his first anti-Philip speech and spent his last thirty years rallying Athens against

---

[3] Because of his birth in Stagira, he is known as the Stagirite. Parmenides' hometown similarly gives its name to Eleatic philosophy.

this menace. Demosthenes had the same life span as Aristotle (384–322). No stories relate them, but he would have fought anyone connected to the Macedonian court.[4] He wanted to rebuild the last century's glory days of the Periclean Empire, the citizen–soldier, and an isolated Greek world. His reactionary vision distracted Athenians from admitting that citizens would rather pay mercenaries, Greece no longer was isolated nor was the independent city–state viable. We will see if Aristotle could see any better.

In 347, life for a friend of Macedon in Athens was tenuous, so Aristotle left, returning only in 335 when Alexander crushed the revolts after Philip's death and regained hegemony. He only begins his own teaching at the Lyceum twelve years after Plato's death. During his absence, one can imagine the struggle to define the proper account of Plato's works. His nephew Speusippus had inherited the leadership of the Academy but alienated peers with his mathematical— or even Pythagorean—approach to Plato. Critics debate the effect on Aristotle's motives toward Plato's ideas. Was he the student wanting to show his own ideas superior to his teacher's, or was he like-minded with Plato (twenty years is a long time) and his criticisms directed against the Platonists, who misrepresent his notions? Tredennick, who translated both, suggests a basic rapport: "Aristotle's thought is always struggling against Platonic influences, which nevertheless generally emerge triumphant in his ultimate conclusions. His great contribution to philosophy was on the side of method; but it was Plato, acknowledged or not, who inspired all that was best in the thought of his great disciple."[5]

Retreating from political events in Athens or the Academy or wanting to see more of life, Aristotle left Athens with some Academy friends for Assos in Ionia, ruled by Hermeias, a former Academy student. For three years he studied there and married Pythias, Hermeias' niece. Next he lived a year in Mitylene, probably with Theophrastus, his successor at the Lyceum, pursuing his biological studies on these trips. Then King Philip asked him to tutor his son Alexander, age 14, which he did for eight years until Alexander

---

[4] How to control demagogues like Demosthenes was always an issue. Plato tried community of inquiry; Aristotle, a hybrid demo-oligarchy.

[5] H. Tredennick, *Aristotle: Metaphysics* (Cambridge, MA: Harvard University Press, Loeb, 1933), p. xxx. Tredennick has a Platonic bias, but his point still holds. Aristotle shares much with the inquiring Plato but not the systematized prisoner of the Forms created by his followers.

became king when his father died in 336. The Greek cities tried the traditional revolt when the ruler of a foreign occupying power died but lacked a unified leadership. A year later they lost, and Thebes was razed. He safely returned to Athens and started his school in the Lyceum grove, probably subsidized by Macedon, as Alexander, like his father, supported Athenian culture.

Aristotle ran the Lyceum for the next twelve years. His followers were called Peripatetics apparently because he walked while he talked in a covered walk (*peripatos*) on the property. He wrote lecture notes (*acroasis*) for school use and popular pieces for an outside (*exoteros*) audience. Only the lecture notes survive. He had many famous collections of materials and data, from 150 civic constitutions to chronicling all athletic festival winners. We know little about how the school worked, if students conducted their own research, or how his collections were used. He again left Athens during the next revolts when Alexander died in 323. This time he attracted a politically motivated charge of impiety, like Anaxagoras and Socrates, and took the invitation to leave. He reportedly said that he would not permit Athens to sin twice against philosophy. He fled to his mother's town of Chalcis and died a year later, perhaps of indigestion. The revolting Greek forces again lacked leadership and trust and were again defeated in a year. The Macedonians finally decided to silence Demosthenes. He also fled Athens and committed suicide rather than be killed by his lifelong foe.

Aristotelian studies continued at the Lyceum for several hundred years, with several rebirths before the Emperor Justinian in AD 529 closed all Athenian pagan philosophy schools for good. The founders were more flexible in their ideas, while their progeny wanted them clear and distinct. As Plato's followers mistook the myth for the message, Aristotle's mistook the systematizing for a system. Application of reason turned into its incarnation. Inquiry became encyclopedias.

Aristotle's writings of fifty to two hundred books do have an encyclopedic breadth. As some titles are repeated or ambiguous, the final count is difficult to calculate. Jonathan Barnes samples the one hundred fifty titles in Diogenes Laertius' catalogue: "Justice, the Poets, Wealth, the Soul, Pleasure, the Sciences, Species and Genus, Deductions, Definitions, Lectures on Political Theory, Art of Rhetoric, the Pythagoreans, Animals, Dissections, Plants, Motion, Astronomy, Homeric Problems, Magnets, Olympic Victors, the River Nile." He then comments, "There are works on logic and language; the arts; ethics and politics and law; constitutional history and intellectual

history; psychology and physiology; natural history—zoology, biology, botany; chemistry, astronomy, mechanics, mathematics; the
philosophy of science and the nature of motion, space and time;
metaphysics and the theory of knowledge. Choose a field of research
and Aristotle labored in it; pick an area of human endeavor, and
Aristotle discoursed upon it."[6]

Aristotle ran like Berlin's fox or dog, turning all of his experience
into an inquiry. By constantly formulating the uniting *genera* and the
differentiating *species* of every object and event he encountered, he
controlled the One and the Many by keeping them in dynamic
tension, balancing their relationship instead of resolving it once and
for all. His broad range is not a compendium of unified knowledge
but an agenda for the continued application of reason. His breadth
shows reason is a satisfying and satisfactory way to deal with all the
areas of human experience. Medieval Christian science, however,
gave him a unifying vision, like God for whom all inquiry ends in
closure, not criticism.[7]

As J. H. Randall said, "Aristotle's writings are 'systematic' only in
the common thread of the distinguishing and organizing power of
analysis. [His] individual 'inquiries' are in no sense systematic. They
start with problems, *aporiai;* they grow and radiate from those problems.
But he never answers more than a small part of the problems he initially
states; and he ends by defining further problems. The Aristotelian corpus
can be said to present a totality, not of results, but of problems. It is the
problems that are for him primary, the systematic interest secondary. For
the later Hellenic systems, it is the primary concern."[8]

All his surviving works are the lecture-notes variety. They are
not the polished texts that we usually find in a library. They are at
times sketchy, incomplete, lacking detail and references, or citing
works we no longer have. Some were revised several times but often
piecemeal, leaving some parts that used older terms and images. In
this unfinished form, more interested in problems than results, a
powerful mind is asking us to think along with it. While his treatises
appear so different in conception, style, and approach from Plato's

---

[6] Jonathan Barnes, *Aristotle* (Oxford, England: Oxford University Press, 1982), pp. 2–3.

[7] Aristotle is a culture hero in Dante's *Divine Comedy* but like all non-Christians cannot
attain absolute knowledge. The Greek philosophers are pleasantly talking and walking in
Limbo, lacking only certainty. Philosophy in Hell has problems; philosophy in Heaven
has answers.

[8] J. H. Randall Jr., *Aristotle* (New York: Columbia University Press, 1960), p. 31.

dialogues, they also try to capture the dynamism of Socrates' spirit of inquiry.

About thirty of his surviving works are considered genuine, while another sixteen are spurious. His works are often cited with Latin names, as for most of the past two thousand years commentary on Greek texts was written in Latin. The following list with English and Latin names has all his surviving works in the order and grouping of the standard Bekker edition.[9] Works are measured in books or the number of scrolls used. Thus, the ten books in the *Nicomachean Ethics* are each similar in length, averaging about thirty pages in Ostwald's edition. The ten books in Plato's *Republic* also average thirty pages in Bloom's edition. However, the average number of Bekker pages per book in the multibook works in his edition varies quite a bit from ten to twenty-three, with most at the low end. The number of books, if greater than one, is given in parentheses following the English name. An asterisk (*) signifies the work is considered spurious.

Categories	*Categoriae*
On Interpretation	*De Interpretatione*
Prior Analytics (2)	*Analytica Priora*
Posterior Analytics (2)	*Analytica Posteriora*
Topics	*Topica*
Sophistical Refutations	*De Sophisticis Elenchis*
Physics (8)	*Physica*
On the Heavens (4)	*De Caelo*
On Generation and Corruption(2)	*De Generatione et Corruptione*
Meteorology (4)	*Meteorologica*
On the Universe*	*De Mundo*
On the Soul (3)	*De Anima*
On Sensation and Sensibilia	*De Sensu et Sensibilibus*

[9] The uniform citation system for Aristotle is based on Immanuel Bekker's nineteenth-century Berlin edition. All good translations use Bekker reference numbers to compare. The first number is the page in Bekker, the *a* or *b* is the left or right column, and the last is the line number.

On Memory and Recollection	*De Memoria et Reminiscentia*
On Sleep	*De Somno*
On Dreams	*De Insomnis*
On Divination in Sleep	*De Divinatione per Somnum*
On Length and Brevity of Life	*De Longitudine et Brevitate Vitae*
On Youth, Old Age, Life and Death	*De Vita et Morte*
On Respiration	*De Respiratione*
On Breath★	*De Spiritu*
History of Animals (9)	*Historia Animalium*
Parts of Animals (4)	*De Partibus Animalium*
Movement of Animals	*De Motu Animalium*
Progression of Animals	*De Incessu Animalium*
Generation of Animals (5)	*De Generatione Animalium*
On Colors★	*De Coloribus*
On things Heard★	*De Audibilibus*
Physiognomonics★	*Physiognomonica*
On Plants★	*De Plantis*
On Marvelous Things Heard★	*De Mirabilibus Auscultationibus*
Mechanics★	*Mechanica*
Problems★	*Problemata*
On Indivisible Lines★	*De Lineis Insecabilibus*
The Situations and Names of Winds★	*Ventorum Situs*
On Melissus, Xenophanes, Gorgias★	*De Melisso, Xenophane, Gorgia*
Metaphysics (14)	*Metaphysica*
Nicomachean Ethics (10)	*Ethica Nicomachea*
Great Ethics★ (2)	*Magna Moralia*

Eudemean Ethics

On Virtue and Vices★   *De Virtutibus et Vitiis*

Politics (8)   *Politica*

Economics★ (3)   *Oeconomica*

Rhetoric (3)   *Rhetorica*

Rhetoric for Alexander★

Poetics   *De Poetica*

The usual approach to Aristotle follows Bekker's sequence, examining the subject groups in order. The series looks so systematic it is tempting just to follow it. But Aristotle did not have an overall plan like this of the totality of human knowledge. He criticized the Platonists for such use of preconceived solutions rather than letting the situation speak for itself. He describes and classifies the things in the world, so he can discuss them and find out what they are. He builds an ever more adequate scaffolding, making the world ever more accessible to us, but the scaffolding is always the means to understanding, not the substance to be understood. He is on the make instead of having it made.

Some think our taste in philosophy is a predisposition that is hard to expand.[10] Aristotle, however, thinks we need to develop broad tastes if we are to live a good life. "Living under the sway of emotion, [most] pursue their own proper pleasures... and they avoid the pains opposed to them. They do not have a notion of what is noble and truly pleasant, since they have never tasted it. What argument can indeed transform people like that? To change by argument what has long been ingrained in a character is impossible or, at least, not easy. Perhaps we must be satisfied if we have whatever we think it takes to become good and attain a modicum of excellence" (*Ethics* 1179b13–19).

My goal in what follows is to provide a taste "of what is noble and truly pleasant" in Aristotle. After a brief discussion of each work, showing the patterns in his method and the breadth and variety of his contributions, I will then examine in more detail the *Nicomachean Ethics* to see how he actually goes about the business of inquiry. The results of this reading will be summed up in an Aristotle Survival Kit to help us be less frustrated, confused, or lost when reading his work.

---

[10] J. Barnes in *The Cambridge Companion to Aristotle* (Cambridge, England: Cambridge University Press, 1995), pp. xviii–xix, discusses taste as a factor in choosing to read past great thinkers. Whether its presence forms a natural elite or its absence is remediable is debated.

LOGIC

Bekker begins with the six works on logic known as the Organon, that is, an instrument or tool. Aristotle describes the elements of language used in arguments and then determines how to arrange these into good arguments. He is the first to name and explain the syllogism. Earlier people used these logical forms; Aristotle enabled the discussion of them by developing vocabulary and showing how they worked. He did not invent logic but did invent its systematic study. He tries to be complete in these discussions, tediously repeating similar points. This a good place to begin' seeing how he uses language, argument, inquiry, and science, but for him there are many starting places, which all eventually meet. This one does serve as the base for his project, like Plato's, to distinguish philosophic from rhetorical argument.

The *Categories* studies individual words to determine the ways in which they can be said, such as distinguishing univocal (synonyms) from equivocal (homonyms). "Animal" means the same whether applied to dog or cat, but "hand" is different referring to a living hand or a statue. Also, words may be derivative (paronymous) where one gives a different but related word its name, such as grammar to grammarian. Recent critics, e.g., say that Parmenides was just confused about derivative senses of "is." Aristotle also distinguishes how words connect to each other, whether "present in" or "predicable of" a subject. In the first case, the word is neither part of a whole nor exists apart from the subject—as the green in green grass. In the second, green is also predicable of (grass is green), while beings such as Socrates are neither predicable of nor present in. These beings are substances (things with a stable identity, dog as dog) distinguished from the words describing them, "remaining numerically one and the same, it is capable of admitting contrary qualities" (4a10–11). The same person is old or thin or asleep or their opposites. Substance is the first of his ten types of *katagoria* or predicates. The others are quantity, quality, relation (greater, double), place, time, position, state (condition; for example, armed), action, and affection (what is done to something). In *Metaphysics,* these ways of speaking are also ways of being, "for thinking and being are the same." Other elements described are types of opposites and various uses of the words "prior," "simultaneous," "motion," and "have." It readies us for thinking well, showing the linguistic bases for the rhetoricians' tricks.

On Interpretation concerns the combination of noun and verb into sentences that are either true or false. These propositions will form the premises for syllogisms. He examines how changes in a proposition—universal or particular, affirmative or negative (contradictories or contraries), possible or impossible, contingent or necessary—affect their truth status when used as syllogistic premises.

Prior Analytics examines all the arrangements of pairs of propositions sharing a common term into arguments called syllogisms, the building blocks of reasoning. He examines what happens to truth in an argument as propositions change. Medieval thinkers gave the four types of propositions each an identifying letter to help describe this process.

A	universal affirmative	All dogs are mortal.
E	universal negative	No dogs are mortal.
I	particular affirmative	Some dogs are mortal.
O	particular negative	Some dogs are not mortal.

These then have the following logical relations:

A and O, E and I are contradictories—not both true and not both false.

A and E are contraries—not both true but possibly both false.

I and O are sub-contraries—possibly both true but not both false.

A syllogism has two premises with a shared term ("dogs") as follows:

All dogs are mortal.

All Dalmatians are dogs.

Therefore, all Dalmatians are mortal.

Aristotle saw there were only three ways or figures to arrange the middle terms, first in both premises, last in both, or diagonally arranged as in the dog example. Then for each figure there are sixteen combinations of the four types of propositions in each of the two premises. Of these forty-eight, he finds fourteen valid forms. He was the first to identify and explain this basic structure of demonstrative or deductive logic.

The *Posterior Analytics* next sees how the valid syllogisms can be used in the demonstration of scientific knowledge. Such knowledge begins from *archai* or starting principles, which cannot be demonstrated but impress us as self-evident. There are three types: axioms (the law of excluded middle), definitions (set meanings of terms, tells "what"), and hypotheses (assumptions about existence, tells "that"). We grasp these premises immediately. Repeated memories of the same thing create a single experience useful to both artisan and scientist (100a7). Scientific knowledge is demonstrated when the premises are "true, primary, immediate, better known than and prior to the conclusion, which is further related to them as effect to cause" (71b20–21). He then details which circumstances meet these conditions or not.

The *Topics* examines dialectical reasoning with probable premises. This includes most of our talk and inquiry, as they are not limited to the necessary truths of science. *Topoi* means places or situations where the subject–predicate relation defines how the argument proceeds. There are four: *definition,* when the predicate belongs essentially to all subjects (humans are rational animals); *genus,* when it belongs to other similar subjects as well (dogs are animals); *property,* which belongs always but not to the subject's essence (dogs can roll over); and *accident,* which belongs only sometimes (some dogs are black). For each place where argument occurs, he provides a "supply of arguments" to respond to these problems.

The *Sophistical Refutations* examines Sophistic reasoning using rhetorical premises with fallacies. Aristotle says he is the first to systematically expose the fallacies of such refutations, for the Sophists gave more examples than explanations. His concern is the eristic arguments used by "those who argue as competitors and rivals to the death." They have five ways to defeat their foes: refute them, show he used a fallacy, lead him into paradox, reduce him to solecism (use of ungrammatical expressions), or reduce him to repeating himself, babbling. The fallacies remain the same today, giving a useful view of ancient greek verbal street fighting.

PHYSICS AND CHANGE

The next group is the physical (*phusis* = nature) treatises: the *Physics, Meteorology, On the Heavens,* and *On Generation and Corruption,* offering Aristotle's improvements to the Presocratics' views of the principles and elements of the universe. The *Physics* is the most general of these. It is a theoretical inquiry (no resulting action or product) into things that change and exist separately from our ideas of them. The other theoretical inquiries are mathematics about things (numbers) that neither change nor exist separately and theology about things (gods) that do not change but do exist separately. He views nature as an orderly change, opposed to Parmenides' frozen world or Heraclitus' endless Flux. Prior thinkers questioned the basic stuff of the universe and how it underwent change. He did not experience any special basic stuff, only the substance of things, or better, their substantiality. As in the pre-Homeric universe, the stuff is just there, uncreated and changeable. He explains change by describing its four causes: material, formal, efficient, and final. Material is "that out of which a thing comes to be" (the bronze of a statue). Formal is "the form or archetype, the statement of the essence" (humans are rational animals). Efficient is the source of motion making the change. Final explains why the change occurred, toward what outcome, "for the sake of what." Animals eat to survive and exercise for health. These constitute knowing a substance: what it is made of, how it is formed (defined), what forces act upon it and what changes occur to it. These last two form his idea of potentiality. Things respond in certain ways to certain causes. My dog reacts to my voice but my car does not. My dog learns to sit but the car doesn't.

Parmenides would feel untouched by this. Apparent order does not make the World of Seeming any more real. Aristotle relished the order he saw in experience, yet outside of demonstrative science, he never felt this order to be final or definitive. If our ideas about the World of Seeming are subject to change, this does not make this world any less real. This is his reply to Zeno's problems with motion. We can never experience infinity, as it is only potential, never actual. Zeno's notion of an indivisible moment when the flying arrow is at rest, and that time is made up of such timeless moments so that at any time the arrow is at rest, assumes an actual infinitesimal. Outside of the movie *The Matrix,* we do not experience the arrow standing still except as an abstraction in our mind. Zeno and Parmenides reply that there only is the mind. He replies that inquiry into the world of seeming provides more mental pleasure than the rhetorical victories of Zeno's arguments.

For Aristotle, nature is the principle of motion and change, and most of his *Physics* explains motion. Each meaning of "is" (here the first four categories) has a type of motion, defined as "the fulfillment of what exists potentially, insofar as it exists potentially." The four types are increase and decrease (quantity), alteration (quality), locomotion (place), and generation and corruption (substance). His predecessors explained motion using four aspects (infinity, void, time, and self-moving) that they mistook to be conditions of motion. We just discussed infinity. His idea of space requires both motion and contact and sees bodies as having something like a place field around them (like gravity but no force) as they approach and make contact. He rejects the Atomists' Void as unnecessary and useless, raising more issues than it solves, such as there is no direction in the void but there is on earth (stones move down), things move through many media that are not voids (water), and what sustains motion in a void (no theory of inertia). Time is the number of motion, an index registering its movement but not separately moving itself. There is no absolute time, as each soul does its own counting. His last question is "Was there ever a becoming of motion before which it was not, and is it perishing again so as to leave nothing in motion?" (250b12). Why begin or end? The Big Bang is a good Aristotelian reply—no knowable beginning, no end. Something banged, and something caused the bang to bang. The universe expands; the universe contracts. Repeat. Something itself unmoved (for a causal chain cannot be infinite) caused the first motion. This unmoved mover is indivisible, without parts or magnitude, exerting an infinite force unchanging in its relation to what is moved and occupying the circumference as things there move fastest and must thus be nearest the mover. The Unmoved Mover, an incorporeal being encompassing the universe, moves the heavens by their attraction to its perfection.

On the Heavens examines motion in the sky and beyond, starting from the Unmoved Mover. It feels more Presocratic with less direct experience requiring more logical assumptions than data. "Throughout there is evidence of a very considerable amount of close observation, rendered to a large extent nugatory by a priori theorizing."[11] For example, to explain the limits on change beyond the moon, he needs a new motion-only element, unlike the multichanging earth elements. Reason, not observation, requires this element be disconnected from the others we do observe. Needing some account, he created the most reasonable hypothesis. Heavenly bodies have this simple and unchangeable substance and express these qualities in circular motion, which can go at a uniform speed in the same direction forever. Under the fixed stars, the planets (Gk. "wander") move in apparent zigzags that are really segments of intersecting circles, each sustained by minor unmoved movers. He thought fifty-five subordinate unmoved movers and circles could do the job, with the original one moving the outermost sphere of the stars. The

---

[11] David Ross, *Aristotle* (New York: University Paperbacks, 1953), p. 110.

earth rests at the center of the universe (nowhere to go) and is spherical. His estimate (10,000 miles) was not that far from its actual size of 24,900 The book's second half explains the motions of the four sublunary elements. Each has a natural place: fire up, air and water between, and earth down. As there are many mingling motions on earth, these elements are stirred up instead of settling out in their natural order.

On Generation and Corruption discusses the combinations and mixtures of the earthly elements. He critiques prior views, especially the Atomists and Pluralists, with little good to say of Empedocles. Coming into being and passing away are changes in substance instead of a becoming from nothing and into nothing. As substance changes form it becomes something new and stops being what it was. The sun's annual cycle drives the cyclical changes in all living things, nutrition and reproduction in both plants and animals. Change by acquiring a new quality differs from growth, which only alters in size. Growth occurs in all parts of the being and does not change its nature. Change occurs when an agent actualizes potential in the patient. Whether the agent–patient interact because alike or unlike as argued previously, he typically answers, "both." There must be a relevant likeness to relate at all yet also a difference to make the change; similarity in genus, difference in species. Elements, after entering a compound, are still potentially what they were before and can be separated in speech if not in action. A combination is the new material throughout, not little pieces of this and that as in Atomism or Pluralism. The primary qualities, hot–cold and dry–wet, account for how the four elements enter into change. Hot and dry tend to produce fire, hot and wet to air, cold and wet to water, and cold and dry to earth. Earthly bodies are compounded of all four elements: earth as most common, water giving shape and coherence, air and fire as the contraries needed to make a compound.

His last *phusis* work examines elements combining in the near-earth region of weather and like phenomena and on-earth changes due to hot–cold and dry–wet. *Meteorology* (study of high or hanging things) is our study of weather but Aristotle's look at all the phenomena between the earth and the moon. Beyond the moon, astronomy studies the unchanging heavenly bodies. Change in the atmosphere results from the Heraclitean idea of exhalation or evaporation from the sun's heat on water and earth. Earthy exhalations are hot and dry, light and flammable, rising high in the air. Watery exhalations are cold and wet, heavy and dense, staying closer to the earth. These naturally settle in layers: fire and air in the sky, water and earth on the earth. Exhalations cause different activities in each layer. The fiery has shooting stars, comets, and the Aurora Borealis. The airy but damp has the weather: rain, clouds, hail, and snow. The water on earth has rivers, springs, floods. The earthy has earthquakes, winds, and thunder (dry exhalations). Optical effects in the sky, like rainbows, occur because very small droplets reflect only color and not objects. The hot–dry and cold–moist use exhalations to move and connect with the things they change. Heat with some cold generates new bodies on earth, which putrefy if they become cold inside and hot without. Heat makes existing things ripen or boil. Dry makes things hard, white moist makes them soft. Most of this study concerns simple bodies. Composite natural bodies (organisms) have parts (organs) that similarly change (digestion is a type of boiling) but also interact with the body as a whole. So we move from simple to living compounds.

PSUCHE—THE LIFE FORCE OF THE SOUL

One must here decide whether to follow Bekker and discuss the soul or discuss animals before humans or place the "meta (after) physics" book after the physics. I will follow Bekker, but other orders of reading are also worthy and stimulating. *On the Soul* is the most general study of life. It has caused many controversies, including how our rational faculties operate, Aristotle's distinction of form and matter, and how much, if any, of the soul is immortal. Eight related short works, collected in *Parva Naturalia* or *Short Pieces on Nature,* inquire how soul and body work together in the areas of sensation, memory, sleep and dreams, growth, and corruption in living things and respiration.

He begins with his usual review and rejection of his predecessors' and peers' ideas. The life force in all living things was the soul; to be *empsuche* (in-souled) meant to be alive, and its nature had been examined for centuries. Where and how was it connected to the body? Did it live on after the body died? Many felt the soul caused motion and must somehow move itself. Democritus thought the soul was hot, as it caused motion in others; Pythagoreans and Empedocles that it harmonized the body; Platonists that it was a self-moving number. These theories of the soul fail to specify "the reason for their union (of body and soul) or the bodily conditions required for it . . .

Interaction (of these) always implies a special nature in the two inter-agents" (407b15–16 and 19). For Aristotle the soul only exists together with the body. The soul does not have elements, parts, harmony, motion, or a separate existence. It is "the first grade of actuality of an organized natural body," that is, not the active conduct of life but the ability to do so (as when inactive in sleep) (412b5). Soul is the form of the body's matter. The two can only exist together and are made for each other. Wood cannot become a human nor our soul, a dog.

The soul enlivens in three ways, cumulative like the point, line, plane series in geometry. The nutritive soul is simplest, involved in feeding, growth, and reproduction. It is the soul in plants and simple animals. Most animals in addition have a sensitive soul to sense and respond to the environment and enable desire and movement. The rational soul occurs only in humans. It is debated if he gives souls to the unmoving divine intelligences who cause the celestial motions, as these pure actualities lack matter, and all souls must be in union with bodies—more of this in the *Metaphysics*. He then describes how each faculty of the soul works. The soul in animals is centered in the heart. The brain's convoluted surface of blood vessels is seen as an evapo-ration cooling system. Nutritive soul directs the flow of similar matter into the body, controlling growth and reproduction. Sensation is also an assimilation, a becoming "like." The sense organ becomes like the things sensed, but unlike food, only the form is taken in. Each sense organ has a different media that conveys its aspect of the environ-ment, such as the water in the eye permitting it to take on any form that enters. The sensing soul directs sense activities and has an aware-ness of its own, the common sensibles: size, shape, duration, rest or movement, unity or number. These are derived from several senses, not just one. Imagination also arises from sensation. It activates the bits of perception held in potential by the soul after receiving them. The *Parva Naturalia* tells how if general sensation is lessened as in sleep, these fainter percepts can be seen as in dreams or memories. Imagination is also the source of desire, which is the source of movement. All of these are operations of the sensate soul.

Rational soul is hardest to observe and thus to understand. He argues by analogy that as digestion extracts the nutritive form from another body and adds it to its own, so sensation receives the sensible form of another into itself, and thought receives the intelligible form from another, making it its own. Sense data wanders about the soul, breaking out in imagination, dreams, and memories apart from any stable system of ideas. He controls the intelligible forms with two working principles: passive intellect, which like a sense organ becomes what it perceives; and active intellect that already has in itself all knowledge and a few problems. As the passive can become all things, like a material cause, so the active can make all things, like an efficient cause[12] (430a11–12). Like the Sun in Plato's image of the Good, his active intellect acts like light, enabling colors to be seen. Its activity parallels the focusing of digestive heat to draw out the nutritive forms or the raising of awareness of sensations by the common sense. Nutritive forms serve growth, sensible forms serve desire and satisfaction, and intellectual forms serve the desire to know. The *noetic archai,* the active intellect's insight into first principles and definitions makes knowledge initially appear and then stabilizes it into ever more complete accounts (contemplation). The active intellect appears in only fifteen lines (Book 3, Ch. 5) oddly lacking in detail. It is described as separable, impassive, unmixed, and essentially active. "When this mind is set free from its present conditions it appears as just what it is and nothing more: this alone is immortal and eternal and without it nothing thinks" (430a22–25). Such immortality is not religious, as active mind is impersonal, but it links us more powerfully than merely sharing the same form.

Sense and Sensibilia begins with an overview of the *Parva Naturalis.* From *psuche* in general, he turns to human issues in the "the four pairs": waking–sleep, youth–age, inhalation–exhalation, and life–death. He adds a fifth, health–disease, but does not develop it. This first work reexamines the senses to prepare for the four pairs. His goal of symmetry tries to match the five senses with the four elements: sight–water; smell–fire; hearing–air; touch–earth; and taste, like touch, is also earth (elsewhere taste requires a liquid medium). Sensible objects are also symmetrical with seven types of colors, smells, and flavors, but he refers sound to *On the Soul* and omits tangibles. He asks if sensation is a divisible process and finds sight immediate, sound and smell less so.

On Memory and Recollection treats stored images and ideas. As memory occurs also in nonhumans, it must not be due to reason alone. The common sense distinguishes fresh sense and thought images from older stored ones and thus creates conscious memory. The young and old have difficulty with memory as the soul-body lacks the correct moisture-making thought, and sense images bounce too much on the dry or

---

[12] Things in nature have the four causes, but forms (like the soul) are one of these causes and seem unlikely to in turn have the causes themselves. This is the only place he speaks of a form having matter.

get stuck in the wet and become unavailable (450b). Recollection is an inference or search from one impulse to another in the past, which only humans can do. Remembering is a different process, as the slow-witted remember better but the quick recollect better. Dwarfs and children have poor memories, as their large foreheads weigh on their perception organ, scattering impulses and disrupting linked lines of recollection.

The next three works deal with sleep and dreaming. Sleep is the unconscious and resting part of the daily cycle of the common sense (the heart). It is induced by the reversal of normal distribution of thick and thin blood in the body during digestion. When we eat, the thick rises, is cooled in the brain, and descends to the heart where it slows the common sense until digestion is complete and the thin again rises. Dreams are stimulations of the imagination that are always present but only perceptible when consciousness is asleep. They have a different origin from the reduced sense perceptions that are felt as we sleep. Whether dreams are a special medium for predicting the future, Aristotle cannot decide. If they are, it arises from some people being sensitive to slight changes in phenomena, which they only see when asleep.

The last three parts treat the maintaining of life, what interferes with this and finally ends it. Plants and animals vary in life spans with no visible quality clearly causing this. There are tendencies, for example, land animals and large animals tend to live longer. Internal heat and moisture promote life, and their waning brings death. Males must avoid expelling too much seed or sweat and drying up, but they do tend to be warmer and thus live longer. Trees live longest, as their sap is resistant to drying. Blooded animals die due to over- or underheating. Consuming fuel too quickly is as deadly as too little fuel. Respiration is a cooling mechanism to prevent overheating. It involves water in water animals and air in land animals. Air moves from the lungs to the heart to regulate the vital heat. The blood pulse is due to the arrival of food in the blood to the heart where it is heated and expands before contracting to receive the next food, sending a pulse (heartbeat) through the liquid. Death in old age is relatively painless, as it is just the fire burning out.

ANIMALS

We have five of Aristotle's works on animal structures and activities: the *History, Parts, Movement, Progression,* and *Generation of Animals.* They fill over 350 Bekker pages, over one fourth of his surviving genuine writings. His *History* (Gk. "inquiry") *of Animals* is twice as long as any other work. He loved to observe animal lives in detail to determine what structures did what activities and how and to compare structures and activities among different kinds of animals. His careful observation saw the heart developing first in a fertilized egg. His comparative anatomy saw that cetaceans were mammals at a time when others limited mammals to land. He describes five hundred animals and classifies them by natural function—what tasks they perform and how, so animals classed together act similarly, such as how they bear their young.

The *History* is descriptive and concerns "the nature and the number of the parts of which animals are severally composed," while the *Parts* is more theoretical and examines "the causes that in each case have determined this composition," that is, what *functions* they perform, such as reproduction, copulation, growth, digestion, waking, sleep, locomotion, respiration, and so on. Activity displays the true nature of a thing, and he tried to determine which activities or functions are intrinsic to the existence of each being. He classified the various expressions or adaptations of these general activities common to most animals. The two functions most critical to life are nourishment and reproduction, followed by respiration to maintain the vital heat. Nourishment and respiration both operate through the blood in most animals. They are centered in the heart, whose heat completes digestion and is controlled in turn by respiration. In the heart, the soul also digests, directs sensation through the common sense, and thinks. His main division in animals is between those with or without blood, similar in concept to ours between vertebrate and invertebrate. The bloodless tend to be smaller with similar simple systems, while the blooded are larger with similar, more complex systems. The main system he examines is reproduction. Only two kinds of blooded animals have live births: land and sea mammals. Two of the blooded egg layers have perfect (hard shell) eggs: birds and then reptiles and amphibians together. The imperfect egg layers cross the blooded boundary, as fishes are the last blooded before we enter the bloodless with cephalopods and crustaceans. Insects are next as vermiparous. He mistook the larvae for eggs, not seeing the real ones. Then come mollusks that reproduce in a slime or by budding, and finally zoophytes that spontaneously generate out of slime. These eleven types are also in descending order of heatedness and thus of the respiratory activities to deal with it. A good classification reflects the order of complexity in several systems, and Aristotle's reflects his main three.

The *Movement* and the *Progression of Animals* are both brief with a similar link as the *History* to the *Parts*. The first describes how animals produce movement with muscles, bones as levers, and so on, while the second describes the use of these systems in animals' motor activities. The last biological work is the *Generation of Animals,* one of life's two required functions, including the sexual process in bloodless animals, the roles of males and semen versus females and menstrual discharge, the stages in embryo development, inherited qualities, sex differentiation, and secondary characteristics. Semen, like mother's milk, is a changed form of blood, made foamy by a special *pneuma* (breath, wind, or spirit) like the celestial ether. The female's material contribution is also a blood product, but lacking the heat and *pneuma* to make the blood foamy, it stays closer to blood, as in the menstrual discharge and placenta. This seminal *pneuma* provides the form for the female's matter. All animal males and females differ similarly (except courageous females in bears and leopards), "[T]he female is softer in disposition... is more mischievous, less simple, more impulsive, and more attentive to the nurture of the young; the male, on the other hand is more spirited, more savage, more simple, less cunning."[13] Humans have these qualities "to their perfection" as our "nature is the most rounded off and complete.... Hence woman is more passionate than man, more easily moved to tears, at the same time is more jealous and querulous, apt to scold and strike... also more prone to despondency and less hopeful, more void of shame or self-respect, false of speech and deceptive, and of more retentive memory... also more wakeful, shrinking, difficult to arouse to action, and requires less food" (608b1–14).

METAPHYSICS

"All humans by nature desire to know." So begins Aristotle's *Metaphysics,* his most general study. Scholars have long debated what the project and subject here really are. Each inquiry and science concerns one subject area of experience: psychology—the life force or

---

[13] His two-sided thinking often uses the Greek "men... de," "on the one hand... and on the other," to distinguish two viewpoints or meanings.

principle, ethics—human good, politics—human associations, biology—the faculties of living things, and so on. But this inquiry incorporates all other inquiries, as broad as experience itself, an inquiry that is both most basic and most perfect and finished—the one "it would be most fitting for God to have" (983a6), so it must be the most godlike, the most primary and perfect aspect of experience, one that God partakes in but does not define, that is, existence itself, being as being. We share being itself with God, though God's existence is unlimited. Aristotle gives several names to this subject: wisdom, the study of being as being, first philosophy, theology. Is this a progression from human to divine (the most cumulative or summary), or is each itself a legitimate perspective, with God's view being just one among the others? Issues about its name and content reflect the difficulty of defining this experience and what we can know about it. *Metaphysics* is the most abstract and difficult of his works and deserves its fame as one of philosophy's Bermuda Triangles. Many a student has sunk beneath its pages, never to be seen again. But there is hope. His method here is consistent with his other works, so we can keep our wits as he tries various approaches to his subject and finds that several names, each from its own perspective, fit very well.

Later editors likely organized these materials but not as clearly or coherently as his other works. The second book was inserted after the first edition. Several books fit poorly if at all. Book 11 restates the problems from Book 3 and repeats sections of the *Physics*. It lists things to keep in mind more than develops the argument. Book 12 aptly discusses the pure form of the unmoved mover but ignores the previous demand that form and matter exist only together. Book 5 is a philosophical dictionary of mostly but not all relevant terms. Again, it is convenient but not exactly needed here. Yet, the work does follow his usual method: a general overview of his topic; common and expert opinions, especially his predecessors; problems that arise and how he can answer these. Most of the books clearly respond to the problems. Some people see a clever progressive structure; others see a later editor taping together odd bits.

Descartes' way of negation or doubt and Plato's way of images carrying us between myth and logos sharply contrast with Aristotle's way of affirmation or accumulation. Descartes in his *Meditations* could make everything disappear except existence, of which he was only an imperfect part. The completion or perfection of this existence he calls God, the necessary being of existence itself. When he tries to know about other beings, he does not find much. His encounter with being explains his certainty about clear and distinct ideas but does not order the world for him. This organizing ability of being itself is presented in the winged souls myth in Plato's *Phaedrus,* where the gods are nourished *"huperuranos,"* outside the universe, the same meaning as *"meta-phusica,"* beyond the realm of nature. They are nourished directly by seeing the things that truly are, the being of beings. This feast refreshes their wisdom, enabling them to better run the universe. But our souls get only partial glimpses of this wisdom and end up still wanting more. "All humans by nature desire to know."

Aristotle's inquiry into being follows his usual method: accumulate as many relevant pieces as possible then try to organize them. What the *History* accumulates, for example, is then ordered in the *Parts.* The more abstract the science, the more difficult this will be, and here is the science of all sciences. Everything is relevant but only in kind or type, as individuals do not differ in being. And as substance is the most comprehensive kind or type, the only things to accumulate are the ideas about it, which is what he does. Other heaps he organized by such distinctions as the three types of soul, the two essential and various other functions of living things, the three types of pleasure, and so on. For this science, he offers several organizing schemes: the causes, the categories, and substance as form and matter versus incorporeal substance. As he himself asks, is there really one science here and if so are humans able to know it?[14] If there is one grand science of being, could it freeze the world back into the Parmenidean One, or could one greatest being at least lessen the reality of other beings? Aristotle seems more tentative here, always making sure that this really is a science to be sorted out.

A coherent analysis of the text has been the despair of many scholars. A general overview of the books will help readers see the whole and better connect the parts:

Book 1: How the idea of wisdom has developed in culture and history. His new approach to wisdom as knowing a thing through its four causes, which prior thinkers failed to do.

---

[14] A thing is known by an essential distinction within a type. God, as beyond type, cannot be known but only described by difference from us (pure form and total actuality) and by negations of attributes (eternal, unchanging, incorporeal). The pure mind *(nous)* in us is like God, sees basic truths and moves ideas by beauty. Other mind just calculates, like the planets trying to be circular. We are to *nous* as the stars are to God.

Book 2: Philosophy studies the highest truth and seeks to know through causes.

Book 3: Fourteen problems facing a first philosophy or science of science. These make a rough outline of what follows.

Book 4: The science of being *qua* (as) being is introduced and senses of being (categories) discussed. This science includes primary distinctions (genus-species, whole-part, and so on) and axioms such as the principle of noncontradiction.

Book 5: The dictionary of thirty philosophical terms or groups of terms.

Book 6: Distinguishes theology as a theoretical science from physics and mathematics.

Books 7 & 8: The crux. Examine being as substance, whether essence, universal, genus, or substratum. Substratum wins and is examined as either form, matter, or combination. Form wins. The difficult relation of form and matter remains. "Substance is the cause or form that puts matter into a determinate state. It is that in a thing that is distinct from its material elements."

Book 9: "The terms being and non-being are applied first with reference to the categories, next to the potentiality-actuality of these (or not) and thirdly to true and false."

Book 10: Being as a unity in the different categories.

Book 11: The review of Problems from Book 3, restating parts of Books 4 and 6 and parts of the *Physics*.

Book 12: Three kinds of substance: changing and sensible, unchanging and sensible (heavenly objects), unchanging and nonsensible (gods). Nonsensibles, as pure unmoved form, are exempt from the matter requirement and make the heavenly objects move in circles. Divine activity is "thought thinking itself," maybe doing logic (pure form, no matter) or seeing the pure being (all substance, no accidents) of all things.

Books 13 & 14: Relations of substance and numbers. Pythagorean and Platonic conceptions. Ideas or Forms only exist separately in thought and not as apart from sensible substances. Numbers cannot be first substances.

There are three main paths through this work, as noted. The first analyzes objects using the four causes, including that form and informed matter only exist together and never apart. The second moves to primary substance and then to separate substance as God. The third studies being as being in itself. It is a continuing test of ingenuity to reconcile these different approaches. Aristotle certainly had all three on his mind and seems to feel they all lead to the same end.

ETHICS AND POLITICS: "THE PHILOSOPHY OF HUMAN AFFAIRS"

The *Metaphysics* ends the "*Peri Phusis*" part of Aristotle's writings, and we now begin the "*Peri Anthropos*" part, those works about human activities that are not simply by nature but are mediated by our deliberation: ethical behavior, political organization, persuasive speech, and poetry. As these studies have "so much variety and irregularity," they are not sciences in the strict sense of universal demonstration. "When the subject and the basis of a discussion consist of matters that hold good only as a general rule, but not always [as by nature], the conclusions reached must be of the same general order" (NE 1094b20–21). Even defining what the subject is in these areas will not always be easy.

The *Nicomachean Ethics* is accessible and coherent and displays his methods so well that we will discuss it in greater detail after completing this survey of the concepts and procedures in his works. Readers may elect to read the extended discussion of the *Ethics* following this section first, as Aristotle has it preceding the *Politics,* or wait until the overview ends and then see his ideas in a more careful and detailed exposition. For those who continue here, the necessary connections from the *Ethics* will be explained to provide the context for the *Politics*.

Like the Sophists, our modern curriculum separates the studies of ethics and politics, while Aristotle presents these as one necessarily unified inquiry to attain the best human life. Ethics describes attaining happiness by actualizing our functional excellence in reason, while politics describes the essential role of the state in promoting and maintaining these rational activities and their social value. Humans are by nature political animals (NE 1097a11, Pol. 1253a3), making the state a necessity, "a creation of nature" (1253a26). Politics is the master science because it "determines which sciences ought to exist in states, (that) each group of citizens must learn, and what degree of proficiency each must attain . . . and legislates what people are to do and not to do, its end seems to embrace the ends of the other sciences. Thus it follows that the end of politics is the good for man" (1094a28–1094b8). Politics is not supreme in a hierarchy of knowledge but has day-to-day control of the other sciences and shapes our thinking about life and human potential. The study of nature may be informative but does not even occur without the law's agreement, as current laws on teaching "creation science" show. On the one hand, politics makes decisions with values from ethics, even its own constitution. On the other, ethical values only develop within the limits of education and inquiry as determined by the state, so they are mutually dependent (Aristotle's typical analysis).

Along with education and law, our choice of personal habits also affects the growth of our rational lives. All human activity seeks to attain happiness, which appears when our action leads to pleasure and not pain, and more lasting pleasure makes more lasting happiness. Most behavior results from habits and not conscious decision. These habits describe a person's most likely actions and thus define her character (*ethos*) or the type of person. Aristotle's ethics concerns the development of proper habits in our ordinary or characteristic behavior. Politics and habit (whether character or constitution) are limiting and stabilizing factors, while ethics and inquiry are extending and actualizing factors.

Aristotle found the defining function of the human soul to be reason. Thus, in the *Ethics* the good of human nature is "an activity of the soul [mind] in conformity with virtue or excellence." As this activity becomes more excellent, that is, complete, self-sustaining, and enduring, so do its resulting pleasure and happiness. The *Ethics* is a progressive education in developing ever-more satisfactory and enduring activities or habits of the mind. The key initial habit is to deliberate instead of acting on impulse. By trying to find the Mean, we choose to avoid extremes in behavior that lead to mistakes and regret. The Mean is the "just right" action between extremes of too much or little that lead to unhappiness, as courage is the Mean between cowardice and recklessness. Political organization and laws provide both the education to develop good Mean-selecting habits and the social stability and material sufficiency to allow one to pursue these choices. Politics provides the context for the pursuit of the best life. In a typical Aristotelian move, the political (or practical, physical) supplies the means for the ethical (or theoretical, rational), acting under its direction and for its sake yet with its own value, as ethics cannot exist without politics. Each has a type of priority, and keeping these distinct will avoid confusion. Remember his rhetorical skill; he knew clear distinctions defeat rhetorical fallacies, just as blurry ones help us believe them.

At the end of the *Ethics,* Aristotle returns to politics to complete his "philosophy of human affairs." Any study of ethics only affects those already concerned about how best to behave. Those confident (no problems) or despondent (not worth it) about their behavior are untouched by argument. Words "can cause a character well-born and truly enamored of what is noble to be possessed by virtue, they do not have the capacity to turn the common run of people to goodness and nobility. . . . They do not even have a notion of what is noble and truly pleasant, since they have never tasted it. What argument indeed can transform people like that?" (NE 1179b8–17). Most are habituated by the frequency of chance events, while few consciously develop habits by controlling these conditions (cf. Note 30). Humans' natural function is to reason. Fulfilling this is a naturally pleasing good but does not occur automatically, as in other living forms. Our growth, unlike trees and cows, requires choices. Actualizing our greatest functional potential creates the greatest happiness, which only occurs if we temper our appetitive soul and promote the rational one. Few natural aristocrats are born inclined toward reason over passion, but proper education and maturing can help the rest of us make this inclination our second nature.

Politics and the law accomplish this renaturing in three ways. It limits excessive behavior that upsets individual and social stability by punishing those who cannot control themselves. It determines the educational procedures that promote developing deliberation in the young. And the law's rationality is a model and guide for behavior. Thus, "someone who wants to make others better . . . whether they be many or few, should try to learn something about legislation, if indeed laws can make us good" (NE 1180b23–24). Politics' ethical purpose is to use legislation and constitutions to enable people to actualize themselves.

Now we can move to the *Politics* itself. In the *Ethics* we act either from the impulse of desire or the choice of deliberation, the "higher" part of our nature and source of a greater happiness. The *Politics* has a parallel analysis where rulers (legislators) can either satisfy their own desires or act for the good of the whole state, with the entire state being more stable and happy in this case. Humans can live on the nutritive or sensory level but not be truly human unless also rational. The state must meet material or cultural needs of citizens but is most actualized (reasonable) in meeting their rational needs. Respect for reason leads to respect for the welfare of each reasonable person. We need physical, sensitive, and mental growth to actualize our whole soul.

Plato and Aristotle share an analysis and agenda for persuading the "spirited," those strong in both appetites and reason, to follow reason.

The Sophists favored nature and desire in this debate (*nomos / phusis*) that arises when traditional values are questioned and changed. Conventional values are subject to change, while natural (or supernatural) values, as necessary, are dangerous to ignore. Customary values also support limited (for example, class) interests, while natural values promote the good of all. "Adultery, theft, and murder" seem bad by nature, yet cultures with a different idea of property used theft in training children to be stealthy warriors. If the state and its laws are merely conventional, this encourages "might makes right" in Greek politics where the democrats' numerical superiority struggled against the oligarchs' monetary superiority. Some third thing, preferably natural and necessary, needs to broker a truce between the many's desire for freedom and the few's desire for wealth. For Plato and Aristotle, this is virtue.

Plato's *Republic* and Aristotle's *Politics* both discuss individual and political justice, the making and unmaking of states, the best political state, and belief in the best life as based on reason. Though Aristotle uses more details from his collection of 150 constitutions and criticizes Plato for denying family and property to his rulers and failing to see the constitutional Mean between democracy and oligarchy, the two inquiries agree more than they differ, following mostly the same purpose, agenda, and solution.[15] Both show the state's natural origins from a simple union of families, that the relation of virtue (especially justice) in the state is parallel with that in the individual, that justice is the completion of virtue needed by all the classes in the state, and that politics serves ethics. Both describe an ideal state ruled by good men with a special state-regulated education to help them become so. The good citizen in each is defined by ability to rule and be ruled in turn.[16]

Despite these similarities, each has a different persuasive strategy. Plato's characters (and audience) build a sequence of cities to experience how each serves their interests and which interests are most important.

---

[15] Aristotle initially critiques a naïve popular version of Plato or Socrates, then ends up agreeing with a more sophisticated "in the strict sense" one. For example, he faults Plato for depriving his rulers of private property, yet his own rulers do not need property and reject it as distracting, so agreeing with Plato. What Plato does dramatically, Aristotle does pragmatically. He attacks errant readings of Plato while keeping the core of his insights.

[16] "He who greatly excels in beauty, strength, birth or wealth or on the other hand who is very poor, weak or disgraced, finds it difficult to follow the rational principle" (1295b7–9). The first do not know how to obey or the second to command. Most people think too much or too little of themselves to rule and be ruled. Compare this to Plato's account of why most talented people do not go into philosophy at *Rep.* 421D.

The group jointly offers questions and solutions, while Socrates seems to best grasp the overall discussion, just as philosophy is the engine of inquiry but not its final resolution. The sequential discussion shows the state and its citizens mutually developing and defining each other. The good person and state develop together. The best citizens have the reasoning to understand the full potential of state (or soul) for happiness. Thus, seeking justice in the state helps find it in the individual. His politics and ethics are as interdependent as Aristotle's.[17]

Aristotle abandons his early dramatic dialogues for the more subtle dynamism of inquiry itself.[18] In any experiential study, a new case could require revising the understanding of types and particulars. Such inquiry learns from the failure as well as the success of the explanation. His model for the legislator to follow for laws and citizens (and texts) is the athletic trainer with regimens and bodies (Book 4, Ch.1). The able trainer has four aspects to his knowledge: the absolute best training, the different types for different bodies, the degrees of training for those who do not want the most, and the best common form adapted for most people. The able legislator similarly knows the absolute best form of government, the best given actual circumstances, how various states arise in various circumstances, and the best form for most states. "Best" here differently describes the state in each of these situations. Not all his best states are the same or interchangeable, so a literal reading or quoting is just as misleading as with Plato.

Since human studies begin in the middle of things, the *Ethics* develops with digressions whose contributions only become clear later. There is no simple linear advance as in the natural sciences. The *Politics* similarly gathers different topics to develop its focus. The *Ethics* says inquiries on human affairs need this searching, as they lack a clear and necessary starting point (*arche*), so the *Politics* pursues two strategies, reflecting the two poles of the *nomos/phusis* debate. The

---

[17] It is debated if the ideal state and education (Books 7 & 8) should come at the end or in the middle (after Book 3), as they do in the *Republic*. We need to know the best before using it to make order. Peter Simpson's translation nicely argues this. His view is a refreshing change from those who find faults rather than reasons. *The Politics of Aristotle*, trans. P. Simpson (Chapel Hill: University of North Carolina Press, 1997).

[18] J. B. Bury in 1900 before the Aristotle renaissance finds him dull and lacking fire. "The republic of Aristotle's wish is not quickened like Plato's by striking original ideas; it is a commonplace Greek aristocracy with its claws cut, ... refined by punctilious education, without any expansive vitality, and like Sparta leaving no room for the free development of the individual citizens. If the cities of Hellas [used this], they would hardly have done what they did for European civilization." *History of Greece*, 3rd (London: Macmillan, 1952), p. 836.

first seeks the natural elements and compositions of politics (for example, the rich and poor plus a middle class or the virtuous, or the types of workers or constitutions, or offices in the state—judicial, executive, and legislative, and so on), while the second defines the political structures and procedures that help develop good humans. The first is typical Aristotle, to observe and classify what is seen in nature, while the second is "for a purpose," to see which political order makes the most good humans. Like humans, the state may have a first or a second nature, its own natural activity or what humans assign to it. Since different perspectives yield different political elements, it seems not naturally but only humanly defined, with the current best form only the result of current human interests. But he also wants a state as natural to support his political ideal: that it naturally develops from the social need for the family, village, and *polis;* that a state's constitution acts like a person's character, giving it substance and predictability (1295a39–40); and that states are happy when fulfilled and stable like people. The *Politics* opens with much nature talk: the natural slave,[19] the natural hierarchies in human relations, the natural associations leading to the political state, nature personified as a godlike force, for example, "Nature does nothing in vain" but also "Nature cannot always accomplish (what) she may intend" (1255b3). This nature talk obscures the naturalness of the state. It is natural only through the need of our nature and does not have any nonmetaphorical nature of its own apart from this need.[20]

Plato's state in the *Republic* shares this *nomos/phusis* hybrid approach, searching for justice on two fronts, the personal and the political. By watching the growth of a new state, he sees when justice naturally arises, and as in the *Ethics,* it comes after the other virtues as their uniting principle. Once found in the state, justice can be found in the individual, both in inquiry and practice. The political discussions serve to define and develop justice in the individual. Protagoras might divide civic from personal virtue, but Socrates would not. The *Republic's* most important political structure may be that of the

---

[19] Natural slaves may be his most controversial idea. Slaves, wives, and children lack the rational ability of men and thus are naturally ruled by them. Natural slaves have mental defects, requiring others to rule them. He rejects war-related slavery. As half the people in Greek cities were slaves, he suggests using slave-like menials, many of whom also cannot rule themselves because they are too uneducated or poor to use their reason.

[20] Some of Aristotle's "nature talk" refers to the naturalness of logical relations; X naturally follows from Y. Compare this to Descartes' "light of nature."

interlocutors in Cephalus' house, with their need for and practice of a democratic exchange of ideas.[21]

Plato dissuades the spirited men from seizing political control as oligarchs or tyrants by showing their need for honest criticism. Aristotle shares this concern. He thinks Greek spiritedness arises as the Mean between the physically desirous and strong northern peoples and the rational but lazy people of the East. He finds three types of constitutions and their perversions (monarchy–tyranny, aristocracy–oligarchy, polity–democracy) and with historical evidence shows that the demise of the warrior class has eliminated three of these: monarchies, aristocracies, and tyrannies. Rarely, a demagogue assumes tyrannical power in a democracy but not for long. The real game is between oligarchy and democracy, as it was between Sparta and Athens. He invents a new constitution, the polity, as the Mean between these extremes, incorporating the good while avoiding the evil of each. He uses his rhetorical genius to make the polity appear as a democracy to democrats and an oligarchy to oligarchs. It gives each the core of what they want while educating them to accept the tempering qualities of their adversaries. The property basis of the oligarchs helps to harness the anarchy of the democrats' freedom, while the broad participation in democracy keeps the oligarchs from pursuing too narrow self-interest. Decisions by larger groups are less likely to express extremes. An aristocracy of good men is his ideal, but a polity is the best realistic form with its compromises, taking the best of the worldly and avoiding the worst.

Most people lack the maturity to know their own good and are unable to be ruled by a good king or aristocracy. The polity persuades them that to support the public good (commonwealth) is really to follow their own, however ill-informed, ideas of their own good. Just as democracy in the *Republic* is much less lethal than tyranny, Aristotle's polity unites rich and poor to at least not destroy each other and maybe even see that freedom needs temperance and property needs justice.[22] The political realm at its best is where the ethical can occur. As polity seeks the public Mean, it prepares us for pursuing the personal Mean of ethics. The final description of education in the

---

[21] This is similar to Richard Rorty's idea of conversation in a liberal democracy but with a little more *eros*. Popper's bogeyman of a fascist Plato is an unimaginative postwar relic.

[22] Aristotle seemed to be well aware of the Hobbesian state of nature. "Where absolute freedom is allowed there is nothing to restrain the evil which is inherent in every man" (1319a1).

ideal state then returns to the *Ethics*. His last image, like the contemplating soul in the *Ethics,* is the complete actualization of the city, that is, the citizens, nurtured in virtue, assume their duties as legislators and to rule and be ruled in turn.

RHETORIC

Aristotle claims to be the first to systematically study and practice rhetoric as well as logic. Rhetoric is a branch of dialectic or logic dealing with the probable, contingent, and nearly true instead of the necessary and absolutely true. It is not a science, lacking any subject matter of its own, but is rather the art of persuasion. When the truth is known, the demonstrations and syllogisms of dialectic organize the conversation most effectively. But if not known, rhetoric provides the principles of analysis and practice for persuasion. "Rhetoric is the ability to observe in any given case the available means of persuasion" (1355b26).

The Sophists began teaching rhetoric in the mid-fifth century to people wishing to speak more effectively in the Greek law courts and assemblies. Plato attacked their claims to teach political science, to separate it from ethics, to make something true by persuasion, and to make an art out of a series of successful ploys. Some say Aristotle critiqued Isocrates' idea for a school for political education using these points. Yet if political practice is to help develop virtue in all citizens, it needs rhetoric to persuade as well as laws. As the sciences need the tools of logic, so human affairs need the tools of rhetoric. He explains the methods of rhetoric to better use it and avoid its abuses in any speech about debatable topics, those with plausible or contingent premises and outcomes. He warns that "rhetorician" can be a pejorative term and is careful to separate sophistry from rhetoric and dialectic. "What makes a sophist is not his faculty but his moral purpose, while 'rhetorician' may describe either the speaker's knowledge of the art or his moral purpose . . . and 'dialectician' describes only the person's faculty" (1355b17–22). It is not what a person does but why he does it.

To clearly separate rhetoric from dialectic, Aristotle develops a parallel vocabulary to deal with persuasion about probabilities rather than demonstration about necessities. The rhetorical syllogism is a less rigorous version that he calls the *enthymeme*. Induction becomes use of examples. Probability and signs replace necessary premises. These elements describe a way of arguing that is less formal and adjustable for an audience not trained in dialectic. "The duty of rhetoric is to deal with such matters as we deliberate upon without art or systems to guide us, in the hearing of persons who cannot take in at a glance a complicated argument or follow a long chain of reasoning" (1357a3–4).

Aristotle defines three primary areas of human deliberation and rhetorical persuasion: the justice of what occurred in the past (legal accusation), the expediency of what will occur in the future (exhortation in political disputes), and the honor of what is happening at present (the praise or blame in a ceremonial speech). Book 1 shows how persuasion works in each. The time distinctions make this division look more definitive than it is, for example, justice, as the supreme virtue in ethics and politics, is really the subject of all three. Praise depends on beliefs about the past and affects future courses of action. Modern exhortation is practiced more in advertising than politics, but the differences blur.

He gathers descriptions of rhetoric in action to develop the most useful account of how it works. "Our various definitions must be regarded as adequate, even if not exact, provided they are clear" (1369b31). He is describing "how it is done" instead of prescribing, as in the Sophists' how-to books. Thus, he describes first situations in which rhetoric takes place, then the elements or dimensions determining if the persuasion succeeds. He finds three such elements: the believability of the speaker and of the words spoken and the audience's readiness to believe. This structures most of the inquiry, with the first and second discussed in Book 2 and the third divided into the forms of argument ending Book 2, with style and arrangement in Book 3.

Aristotle agrees with Plato's *Phaedrus,* where the best rhetorician must not only know more than his audience but as much as possible in order to answer all questions and not mislead himself. Both see rhetoric as a needed tool for thinking about and discussing the uncertain and contingent situations of most human affairs, occupying far more of our thinking and speaking than dialectic. The sophistic and eristic use of rhetoric is a perversion that should not define the whole. The study of rhetoric uses the other human studies, applying their best understandings to life situations in order to live better by clarifying the probable. The rhetorician must know the form and content of any study and the most common opinions about it as well, for these often obstruct the persuasion of an audience.[23] One must

---

[23] Note how this parallels his own method.

understand not only a topic but also the common misunderstandings of it and how to address these. For each topic he gives general directions for arguing ("sources for the means of persuasion"), simple associations that are easily grasped (if not always correct), such as what hurts our enemy helps us or if it is expensive or everyone wants it, it must be good. His extended examples of what people consider to be good and relatively good and pleasures give an impressive view of our human condition (I, 6–7 and 11). His discussion of "nontechnical" persuasion (laws, authoritative opinions, contracts, testimony under torture, and sworn oaths) reads like a law-school textbook. Some topic summaries differ from his more complete studies, such as listing nine virtues instead of the twelve moral and five intellectual ones in his *Ethics*. The *Rhetoric* usually reflects common usage, what people will most easily hear. Efficacy, "a sufficient account for our present purpose," is the standard here (1366b23).

Earlier rhetoric handbooks aimed at law court speeches, especially how to inflate or debase character and manipulate the emotions of the jury. Aristotle includes these, detailing how ten emotions affect us and our audience, support an argument or not, and are aroused and quieted. Human discourse exists in a context of emotions; we always respond with varying degrees of emotion and reason. The concern is not whether to introduce emotion but to be aware of its presence and what to do about it. Similarly, basic character traits (young–old, wealthy, well-born, and so on) are an element in any attempt to persuade, for both the audience's opinion of us and their preferences in their other opinions.

He then details the parts of rhetorical arguments: enthymemes, examples, maxims, twenty-eight types of argument for enthymemes (similar to the *Topics*), and nine types of fallacies (fewer than the *Sophistical Refutations*). A logical enthymeme is a syllogism with a premise or conclusion implied but not stated. This can be true of rhetorical enthymemes but not necessarily. They involve plausible reasoning, as their connection with maxims or proverbs shows. Audiences enjoy an abbreviated version of an argument they know and readily identify with the folk wisdom of maxims, suspending their critical judgment.

After what needs to be known and said in a rhetorical presentation, Aristotle last considers style and arrangement. He believes simple prose can communicate without Gorgias-type poetic effects, which can be artful and "charm" but are overrated. "The way a thing is said does affect its intelligibility, but is not so important as people think. . . .

Nobody uses fine language when teaching geometry" (1413b10–12). He approves of wit, visualization, and metaphor to help involve an audience. Metaphor engages by making an association not seen before, as learning is naturally pleasing. For arranging the sections of a presentation, he also keeps it simple: Introduction, Statement of the Case (narration), Argument (includes interrogation and counterargument), and Epilogue. He agrees with Gorgias's strategy on humor: "Kill your opponent's earnestness with jesting and his jesting with earnestness." He also advises using jests that befit one's character. "Irony better befits a gentleman than buffoonery; the ironical man jokes to amuse himself, the buffoon to amuse other people" (1419b3–9).

POETICS

For Aristotle, human beings by nature desire to know, seek happiness, and are social and political. The *Poetics* adds that we are also natural imitators, which is the basis of poetry and the fine arts in general. "Imitation is natural to man from childhood. He is the most imitative creature in the world and learns at first by imitation. Learning something is the greatest of pleasures.... The reason of the delight in seeing the picture [or any art] is that one is at the same time learning—gathering the meaning of things.... People created poetry out of their [imitative] improvisations" (1448b5–23). Nature then guided this process it began. "Only after a long series of changes the movement of Tragedy stopped on its attaining to its natural form." Aeschylus brings in a second actor and dialogue, Sophocles a third actor and scenery. It evolved from dancing to dialogue and trochaic to iambic as "Nature herself found the appropriate meter, for it is the most speakable of all." He uses Nature to impose order on his four "irregular" inquiries on human affairs, but this Nature is an extension of our nature. This nature is a conclusion from data, not a theological insight; systems grow out of observations, not vice versa. Our theatre with more actors, prose dialogue, and often no music or dance he could easily accept—and see its naturalness.

The *Poetics* examines tragic and epic poetry, with a final section on comedy being lost.[24] Tragedy represents one complete action, if possible within a single day, on a serious topic with characters that

---

[24] Umberto Eco imagines this text's fate in his *The Name of the Rose.*

speak for themselves and are better than most of the audience. Comedy uses characters that are worse and involves them in the ridiculous, "a mistake or deformity not productive of pain or harm," that is, something laughable. Epic uses narrative (storytelling) about serious subjects, including several connected actions over an extended period of time.

He brings systematic terms and distinctions to these activities to enable discussion and criticism. He saw the imitation of life in theatrical plays as a natural outgrowth of childhood play. Modern nonrepresentational art questions this universal quality of imitation. But his evidence makes a strong case, notably his vivid depictions of music's emotional qualities. Greek belief in the emotional effect of different musical modes was as sophisticated and far-reaching as ours. Music represented human emotional life as much as sculpture our physical one.

The most debated part of his account of tragedy is his notion of catharsis. Tragedy must have "incidents arousing pity and fear, wherewith to accomplish its catharsis of such emotions" (1449b28). There is a special pleasure in this, "the tragic pleasure is that of pity and fear [through] incidents that strike us as horrible or piteous" (1453b12–16). Catharsis can refer to religious purification or medical purgation, with scholars supporting each. A missing part of the text may have clarified this, but the simpler explanation is purgation, like the pity in romance novels or the fear in horror movies. We get pleasure from vicarious emotions that in real life would upset or debilitate us. Feeling pity and fear in serious but not in trivial situations reflects our good character, but this apparently is not the issue here. Ross parallels Aristotle's description of the emotional effects of music from the *Politics*.[25]

> Any experience [emotion] that occurs violently in some souls is found in all, but with different degrees of intensity—e.g., pity and fear, and also religious excitement; for some are very liable to this form of emotion, and under the influence of sacred music . . . [are] thrown into a state as if they had received medicinal treatment and taken a purge; the same experience then must come also to . . . other emotional people . . . all must undergo a purgation and a pleasant feeling of relief; and similarly also the purgative melodies afford harmless delight to people. (*Pol.* 1342a5–16—Loeb)

---

[25] David Ross, *Aristotle* (New York: University Paperbacks, 1949), p. 283.

We often overintellectualize Greek culture. Like us, they want to be entertained, and catharsis explains one part of this process.

Every audience is interested in being educated. "To be learning something is the greatest of pleasures not only to the philosopher but also to the rest of mankind, however small their capacity for it." Most tragedies involve one of the dozen or so epic noble families in which horrors occurred, often parents killing children or vice versa, as well as incest and revenge. These stories were known from childhood, so the entertainment and education were in the telling. This heightens the experience, comparing the current to prior versions, for example, the power of metaphor to reveal a new meaning. "The greatest thing by far is to be master of metaphor. It is the one thing that cannot be learnt from others; and it is also a sign of genius, as a good metaphor implies an intuitive perception of similarity in dissimilars" (1459a5–7).

He again advises less is more in his description of effective tragedy. The plot carries the weight of the play, with characters appropriate but not distracting. Diction should be "clear but not common" and can include unfamiliar terms: strange words, metaphors, unusual forms, but only in moderation. Action should rule the drama, not dialogue or spectacle. Special effects should be used sparingly. "Not every kind of pleasure should be required of a tragedy, but only its own proper pleasure" (1453b11). Action events (murder, sex, fights) distract from the plot and can be discussed but not shown. Everything should further and nothing should detract from taking in the complete action to maximize the pity and fear. "A likely impossibility is always preferable to an unconvincing possibility" (1460a26). The audience should not be distracted by thinking about the plot's construction. In fact, pushing the limit of the possible is one interest in stories. "The marvelous is a cause of pleasure, as shown by the fact that we all tell a story with additions, in the belief that we do our hearers a pleasure" (1460a18–19).

In applying these ideas, Aristotle warns, "There is not the same kind of correctness in poetry as in politics or indeed any other art." Even errors in poetry, failure of expression or of knowledge, can be used to serve the plot so long as they are plausible and not distracting. This forms the best criterion to judge such traditional "rules of Aristotle," as the unities of time, place, and action. That they be plausible and not distracting is more important than any quantitative restriction.

NICOMACHEAN ETHICS: A CLOSER READING

The *Nicomachean Ethics* is Aristotle's most widely read work. It is one of the more organized and finished of his lecture books and well illustrates his methods: to gather as much possible evidence (experiences, opinions, ideas), sort out the problems and possible solutions, then show which is the best. He finds the truth in each opinion, making it more coherent and consistent with other opinions. He hopes to avoid the corrosive effects of rhetoric by the mutual construction of language and exposure of its ambiguities. He continues the tension between prescriptive authority and mutual consensus present in Socrates and Plato, and the critical method urging the reader to reconstruct her own ideas. He remains close to the world of experience, and there is always more world to experience. Like the *Symposium's* lover seeking his other half, his erotic joy in classifying all the best fits between his ideas and the world helps heal his sense of incompletion. He continues Plato's vision that humans want the wholeness they lack and that the virtues (moral and intellectual) are the means to acquire this. "Happiness requires completeness in virtue as well as in a complete lifetime" (1100a4). Aristotle ardently loves both the world and reason.

Aristotle, like Plato, begins in the middle of things, with no axioms or revealed truth as a given starting place. The *Ethics* has a stuttering start, beginning in several places at once. He works toward more informed starting places giving new perspectives, as in the discussions of moral weakness and pleasure. "We must try to get at each of them [basic principles] in a way naturally appropriate to it, and . . . defin[e] it correctly, because it is of great importance for the subsequent course of the discussion. Surely, a good beginning is more than half of the whole, and as it comes to light, it sheds light on many problems" (1098b4–7).

Later editors divided the *Ethics* into ten books, each with a dozen or so chapters. We will carefully examine his method in Book 1 and then follow this through the rest of the work. It resembles Socrates' use of hypothesis in the *Phaedo*. Posit a likely explanation, consider why it won't work, resolve these issues, then use this with due caution in further inquiry. Like Plato's framing, the first pages set some parameters: language is a social construct, politics sets the context for inquiry, and ethics is not an exact science. Chapter 1 defines the good, using common usage and observation. "Every art and every inquiry, and likewise every action and choice, seem to aim at some good, and hence it has been beautifully said that the good is that at which all things aim" (Sachs 1094a1–2).[26] This gains agreement but invites questions if the good is the same for all. Like Plato in the *Republic,* good is more easily seen in the collective. In the polis (the soul writ large) we can observe ideas of good in debate and at work, as politics orders all activities for the best. "Since it legislates what people are to do and not to do, its end seems to embrace the ends of the other sciences. Thus . . . the end of politics is the good for man" (1094b5–8). "It determines which sciences ought to exist in states, what kind of sciences each group of citizens must learn, and what degree of proficiency" (1094a28–29). Social policies and practices affect where and how we seek the good. "Politics is to engender a certain character in the citizens and to make them good and disposed to perform noble actions" (1099b30–31). Through education, laws, customs, and language, a society defines its worldview. Deliberation cannot occur outside of a political context.

As ethics and politics are not strict natural sciences, so their inquiry is not exact, for example, the good seems to vary by place and time. "Problems of what is noble and just present so much variety and irregularity that some people believe that they exist only by convention and not by nature" (1094b14–16). With such irregular data, "we must be satisfied to indicate the truth with a rough and general sketch; when the subject and basis of a discussion consist of matters that hold good only as a general rule, but not always, the conclusions reached must be of the same order" (1094b 20–23). Maturity is needed to appreciate a general rule, while little experience or much emotion interferes. "Knowledge brings no benefit to this kind of person. . . . But those who regulate their desires and actions by a rational principle (*logos*) will greatly benefit from a knowledge of this subject" (1095a8–12). Experience enables us to account for what we do and why, which the Mean will later test.

Chapter 4 returns to the good. Most agree the highest good is happiness but disagree how this arises. Is it from doing an activity or having goods such as wealth, health, honors, knowledge? He finds three main goods: pleasure, politics, and contemplation. Ethics cannot demonstrate which is best but reviews the opinions and probabilities.

---

[26] "Sachs" is J. Sachs, *Nicomachean Ethics* (Newburyport, MA: Focus, 2002).
"All others are M. Ostwald, *Nichomachean Ethics* (New York: Bobbs-Merrill, 1962).

Meanings of pleasure and happiness evolve as we develop an appreciation of the life of contemplation; for example, the political life of honor fails because "[a] man might possibly possess it while asleep or while being inactive all his life and while in addition undergoing the greatest misfortune and suffering. Nobody would call the life of such a man happy" (1095b32–1096a2). He starts from common opinion, such as where most (wrongly) believe the life of (physical) pleasure is best. Like the *Phaedrus,* he requires knowing common opinion in order to begin educating it.

His next problem is that proclaimed wise men like Plato confuse the issues. Plato's Form of the Good is out of touch with both common opinion and experience (1096b32–350). Aristotle begins with the many common goods, arranged in ascending stability of pleasure and finally approaching something like Plato's completed Form. His inquiries often begin by describing Plato's views as nonsense in accord with our uneducated vision, but after we learn to see better, the value in Plato's ideas often becomes more clear. He criticizes the static Platonic Forms in popular opinion; he can (and did) live with a dynamic Plato.

Chapter 7 further defines the highest good as final (the goal of all activities) and self-sufficient (when gained it is adequate by itself), both qualities of happiness. He then digresses on man's "proper function," summarizing his *On the Soul* in thirty lines. Though at times sounding prescriptive, the functions described are always from observation and thus fallible. He finds three types of soul (life force): plants only eat and grow, animals also have sense perception, and humans alone have reason. Our rational soul has two parts, one ruling and the other ruled by reason. The active part "has the greater claim to be the function of man," as we can see activities but only infer potential. But activity alone is not enough. "[T]he full attainment of excellence must be added to the mere function" (1098a10). The complete activity is its true measure. So his "general sketch" or working definition of human good is "an activity of the soul in conformity with excellence... in a complete life" (1098a16–18). And now he is (more) ready to begin.

With the good clarified, he returns to happiness and reviews traditional and popular opinions about it. His dialectical method sifts language and opinions to find the best account. "Some of these views are expressed by many people and have come down from antiquity, some by a few men of high prestige, and it is not reasonable to assume that both groups are altogether wrong; the presumption is rather that they are right in at least one or even in most respects" (1098b26–29). All opinions hold some truth and so can be discussed and rehabilitated.

Book 7 further explains, "The proper procedure is the one followed in our treatment of other subjects: present phenomena [observed facts and beliefs of moral life] and, after first stating the problems inherent in these, demonstrate the validity of all the beliefs about these matters, and, if not, the validity of most of them or of the most authoritative. For if the difficulties are resolved and current beliefs are left intact, we shall have proved their validity sufficiently" (1145b2–7).

He argues from what is "natural" or "by nature," for example, "Men who love what is noble derive pleasure from what is naturally pleasant. Actions which conform to virtue are naturally pleasant" (1099a12–14). The noble is the full expression of being human and thus brings the fullest pleasure natural to humans.[27] It is the judicious person (*spoudaios*) who "loves the noble" and keeps high standards, the role model and hero in the *Ethics*.[28] "The chief distinction of [this] man is his ability to see the truth in each particular moral question, since he is, as it were, the standard and measure for such questions. The common men, however, are misled by pleasure" (1113a31–34). Anyone can develop this ability and find satisfaction in its full expression of his nature.

Happiness can always disappear in feelings of regret. Awareness of any lack negates our feeling of being complete. Happiness requires those external goods that enable action (money, friends, power) or those whose lack is painful (good birth, family, looks). The experience of loss, such as his own wife's death, leads us to unhappiness, unless we learn to live with less, which is one goal of the *Ethics*. Book 10 reveals a happiness complete in itself, beyond these lacks. As a progressive argument, no line can be taken as his last word. He begins trying to attract anyone interested in bettering her life and so is casting his net wide. Someone who recognizes the goodness of the *spoudaios* yet is still sorting out the necessities about external goods and their pleasures is a perfect candidate.

---

[27] "In the realm of nature things are naturally arranged in the best way possible.... If it is better that happiness is acquired in this way [by arete] rather than by chance, it is reasonable to assume that this is the way in which it is acquired" (1099b19–24). Nature is well ordered but, not conscious, does things for the best. Aristotle's nature, like Socrates at *Meno* 86, is relatively stable, can be described, and has a *logos*.

[28] *Spoudaios* is not easy to translate. "Serious" is overused, "earnest" Victorian, "high standards" too enforcing, and "good" misses the activity of the soul. "Judicious" has serious intent and weight without being inert.

Chapter 10 asks if one can be happy while still alive if happiness requires final completion. Troy's King Priam exemplified a good and happy man turned unhappy: his city destroyed, his fifty sons killed, and fifty daughters enslaved. "Frequent reverses can crush and mar supreme happiness.... Yet, nobility shines through even in such moments, when a man bears many great misfortunes with good grace not as insensitive to pain but as noble and high-minded" (1100b30–32). If new events limit the ability to act virtuously, then they compromise happiness. But "no function of man possesses as much stability as do activities in conformity with virtue: these seem even more durable than scientific knowledge.... Men who are supremely happy spend their time in these most intensely and continuously" (1100b12–17). This durable happiness can be recognized while one still lives. Aristotle reconciles the opposites by changing perspective, finding both motion and stability in the same event. Activities expressing one's virtuous nature seen from outside are many and various, but within this nature are all united in it. Contrary to Parmenides, he shows unity and motion can coexist.

Chapter 11 asks if happiness is affected by events after one's death. When is a complete life complete? Aristotle again uses his rhetorical skill to change the perspective, here whether the effect is significant if it happens at all or only in the degree to which it occurs. As many then felt the dead were affected by their progeny's actions, for example, fame, he agrees that there is some effect. But then he uses his stability-of-true-happiness thesis, saying that this effect is too slight to disrupt.

He next examines whether happiness deserves praise or honor; that is, is it measured by a standard (an athlete) or superior to any standard (a god)? We praise the high-measuring achievers, but those beyond the scale can only be acknowledged and honored. Virtue as the top of the scale deserves praise, while happiness, as beyond the scale, deserves honor. Happiness is "an *arche* (starting point), since for its sake we all do everything else. And the *arche* and cause of all good things we consider as worthy of honor and as divine" (1102a2–4). We have seen this use of popular religious talk before. The image of god as above the top of a scale does not mean any gods really exist. They only mark the limit.[29]

---

[29] Common language today continues this usage with the attribute "divine" in contexts that are hardly religious, for example, Bette Midler.

He then explains the role of the three-part soul in ethics. The soul has two irrational and two rational parts. The overlapping part with both qualities (conscious desires) is the entry to a serious and rational life. Desires are amenable to reason and education but do not of necessarily respond, as Cleitophon chooses not to talk in Plato's *Republic*. In the first half of the *Ethics*, the moral virtues persuade the desires to be rational; the second half examines the virtues of this reason. The work is progressive, with success in the first enabling success in the second.

We have now seen his methods in individual arguments, notably the difficulty to begin an inquiry with no special starting place. We now turn to his strategies in the progressive development of the work.[30]

Ethics examines virtuous activities that bring happiness. Developing (deliberately or otherwise) behavioral habits creates a "second nature." Habits define a person's character, predicting what one will do and where one will seek pleasure or avoid pain. The education of pleasure and pain, as in the *Republic,* is thus central to ethical training.[31] While most habits are repeated unthinkingly, virtuous habits are chosen as best. Making second-nature habits conform with the best of our basic nature is his strategy and leads to his exercise called the Mean.[32] Too much or little of a good thing can be bad, while the Mean is the right amount (consider Goldilocks). So a virtuous activity is neither too little nor too much. This is less about calculation than avoiding the extreme. "Moral virtue is concerned with emotions and actions [such as] fear, confidence, desire, anger, pity, and generally any kind of pleasure and pain. . . . To experience all of this at the right time, toward the right objects, toward the right people, for the right reason, and in the right manner—that is the median and the best course . . . the mark of virtue" (1106b18–23).

These multiple aspects of behavior define each moral situation as unique, needing its own response. "There are many ways of going wrong, but only one way which is right" (1106b28). The Mean

---

[30] The inquiry here includes the nature of Ethics itself, similar to Socrates' problems defining the art of politics or teaching virtue.

[31] Those gold stars in elementary school behavior modification programs directed us to feel pleasure toward the right things. *Clockwork Orange* (movie or book) examines the morality of educating pain.

[32] Again, capitalization of technical vocabulary here is for ease of reading, not to suggest higher states of being or any other qualification.

brings this right way into focus. The solution is in the situation, as form is in matter. One must consider all aspects, requiring general knowledge as well as the Mean. Knowledge verifies itself by rejecting all other possibilities (Aristophanes again). The Mean likewise sees what is too much and too little before selecting the middle. It is an ongoing mental exercise, demanding observation, information, and self-knowledge, as the Mean is relative to each person and must adjust to whatever affects our vision (prejudices, illness, expectations, and so on). He again unites the One and the Many. There is only one right response, but it is differently expressed or actualized by every person. Some behavior is never correct and lacks any mean: the emotions spite, shamelessness, and envy; and the actions adultery, theft, and murder. They can be disguised, as in war or abortion debates, and friends help us detect such self-serving usage.

The Mean is the key mental process for ethics; choice is its application. Choice requires a voluntary relation to an action. Involuntary acts are due to compulsion and should be avoided. If pushed, my fall is not voluntary, but if coerced, my resulting action is mixed. In a sense I agree to do a forced act, so it is not clearly excusable or not. Ignorance and passions are also problems. "Ignorance in moral choice does not make an act involuntary—it makes it wicked" (1110b31). Ignorance is forgivable if the agent regrets her action. Crimes of passion are inexcusable, as excessive passions, like errors in calculation, can be recognized and avoided. Choice results from deliberation, which we do about "things that are in our power and can be realized in action" (1112a32). "We deliberate not about ends but the means to attain them" (1112b12).

Wishes determine ends, but there are two competing opinions of them. Both are inadequate but with the proper distinctions can both be acceptable. That we "wish for the good" ignores that we can be mistaken or change. That we "wish for what seems good" loses the stable world amid appearances. Between too little or too much change, he finds a Mean in the "strict or unqualified sense of a word."[33] "In an unqualified sense and from the standpoint of truth the object of wish is the good, but that for each individual it is whatever seems good to him" (1113a22–23). He distinguishes the several meanings of a word while still seeing their connections. The

---

[33] Aristotle's "in the strict sense" move was common among Sophists like Thrasymachus in the *Republic*. The authority for this "strict sense" is convention and open to manipulation, as Aristotle was aware.

strict sense is the goal here, and what seems good can be used to educate us toward this goal. "What seems good to the judicious man is the true object of wish, while a worthless man wishes anything that strikes his fancy. It is the same with the human body; people whose constitution is good find those things wholesome that really are so" (1113a25–28). Healthy wishes, healthy mind.

With wish seeking the good and deliberation finding the means, we can become consciously moral beings (1114a10). We are what we wish for and do and are responsible for the habitual actions forming our character, even though without choice we learned and repeated them when young. We may not choose our early habits but do choose if we continue them. Our natural vision of the good developed by the Mean enables us to overcome encultured habits. We are responsible for what appears to us to be good. Just as some eyes are stronger, so some have better vision of one's natural good. "The aim we take for the end is not determined by the choice of the individual himself, but by a natural gift of vision, as it were, which enables him to make correct judgments and to choose what is truly good: to be well endowed by nature means to have this natural gift" (1114b6–8). Yet all can develop this vision adequately in our second nature by using the Mean, which instills and reinforces a habit every time we use it. "We control only the beginning of our characteristics: the particular steps in their development are imperceptible . . . yet since the power to behave or not in a given way was ours in the first place, our characteristics are voluntary" (1114b33–1115a3). The Mean develops the habit of using right reason.

The Mean then goes to work in the remainder of the *Ethics* finding twelve virtues here (three traditional and nine popular), plus wisdom. He includes fear of war, death or ill-fame, bodily pleasure, sharing, expressing wealth or self-esteem, ambition, temperament, social relations, presentation of self, amusing talk, and making and following rules and laws. Every human activity has a virtue, and whether this list tries to cover all of them is not clear. He asks how many virtues exist but does not argue that his list is complete. Piety is the only missing traditional virtue.[34] The eleven virtues in Books 3–4 prepare for the overall virtue of justice in Book 5, and all these for the completion of virtue as wisdom in the second half (compare to Plato's *Protagoras*). From the most common virtues of the mixed rational part of the soul, courage dealing

---

[34] Sometimes the list has four, with justice covering both divine and human relations. "Just and pious" were often said together as a pair.

with fear and self-control with pleasure, he ends with justice, the most rational and abstract, whose laws tell us how to act. The Mean applies less to justice and wisdom, so it makes sense to treat these last.

The complete expression of human potential in any activity is its virtue or excellence (*arete*). The complex Greek term *kalon* (noble or beautiful) enters here, often describing our role model, the judicious person.[35] *Noble* here means the best of humanity but can mislead with ideas of genealogy and aristocrats. Aristotle's point is "Be all you can be," as in the U.S. Army slogan. We need to see how success in each activity coalesces into the best human life. Each virtue contributes to this excellence of the whole and has less value when seen in separation, as Plato also discusses in the *Protagoras*. "Beautiful" suggests the aesthetic grasping of the whole, that everything needed is present and attractive. We are not pushed by something external (shame, social norms, and so on) to be virtuous but are pulled to virtue (like the stars to God) by seeing its beauty (completion). "But one ought not to be brave by compulsion, but because it is a beautiful thing" (Sachs1116b1–2). "Beauty" suggests a direct grasping that this is the best of its kind, that there is not too much or little (no need for Mean). Basic to his ethics is our ability to see complete human excellence and its attraction. Cultural "beauty" can be so manipulated that we do not trust what attracts us. Describing this whole as noble or beautiful requires an education.

The following chart shows each virtue with its realm of our emotional and active life and its mean and extremes. If one extreme is more opposed to the mean, it is in bold type. Aristotle did not find a name for some of his categories, and my names for these are in parentheses.

> Courage: concerns fear & confidence in areas of war, death, etc.
> > Over = reckless; Under = **cowardice**
> Self-control: desire for pleasure in physical pleasures
> > **Over** = self-indulgent; Under = (apathetic)
> Generosity: sharing material goods, both giving and receiving
> > Over = extravagance; **Under** = stinginess
> Magnificence: desire to share material goods, wealthy projects
> > Over = vulgarity; Under = petty, paltry

---

[35] Ostwald, Rackham in the Loeb, and Ross chose "noble"; a few such as Sachs chose "beautiful."

Greatness of soul: desire for honor by succeeding in life
    Over = vanity; **Under** = smallness of soul
(Ambition): desire for honor by succeeding in daily affairs
    Over = too ambitious; Under = not ambitious enough
Gentleness: temperament with regard to anger
    Over = short-tempered; Under = apathetic
(Friendliness): consideration for others in social relations
    Over = obsequious; Under = grouchy
(Truthfulness): consideration for self in social relations
    Over = boastfulness; Under = self-deprecation
Wittiness: consideration for humor in social relations
    Over = buffoonery; Under = boorishness
(Shame): fear of dispute (a pseudovirtue)
    Over = shame; Under = shamelessness
Justice: complete, concerns laws for all actions & all virtues;[36]
    partial, concerns fairness distributing goods (or evils)
    Extremes not present, only opposite is injustice

Each area of virtue as a resource contributes to a more stable and complete self. Responsibilities grow with these resources. Wealth, financial (magnificence) or experiential (great-soul), should be spent to display the best of being human. Resources permit more complete expression, contributing to both our own happiness and its social support in language, education, economics, and so on. We are always in the process of defining ourselves and our kind (compare to Socrates' self-exam)

Good has no extremes, so justice (complete virtue) here has no excess, deficiency, or will wisdom. The Mean paradigm does not explain these; it is a developmental rather than final explanatory tool. Justice concerns fairness in the distribution or restitution of goods. It considers proportional merit and portions that are too much or too little but not portions of itself. The Mean is an exercise for avoiding extreme behavior and reshaping our habits while practicing right reason. The forming of moral character gives the soul enough stability for the rest of the *Ethics,* the examination and practice of the intellectual virtues.

---

[36] "The laws make directives on every sphere of life, ... enjoining us to fulfill our function as brave men ... self-controlled ... gentle ... and similarly with the other kinds of virtue and wickedness" (1129b14–23).

"Let us make a fresh beginning (*arche*) and discuss these character-istics once again" (1139b13). He has helped us experience reason enough that we can begin examining it. Having clarified the moral virtues, we can do the same for the intellectual ones. There are five ways "by which the soul expresses truth: art (*techne*), science (*episteme*), practical judgment[37] (*phronesis*), theoretical wisdom (*sophia*), and intel-ligence (*nous*)"; respectively, production, demonstration, deliberation, contemplation, and intuition (1139b15—18). Book 6 describes these while Books 7–10 examine how practical judgment develops with moral strength and friendship into the wisdom of contemplation.

"Art is the characteristic of producing under the guidance of true reason" (1140a10). It concerns becoming instead of necessity, about things that are created by a producer, as they lack soul.

"What we know scientifically cannot be otherwise than it is … thus an object of scientific knowledge exists of necessity and is eternal" (1139b20–24). Science is based on demonstration from known starting points through logical premises to necessary conclusions.

Phronesis concerns things that change, how to "act in matters involv-ing what is good for man" (1140b21). "Virtue makes us aim at the right target; *phronesis* makes us use the right means" (1144a8–9). Action is about particulars and needs experience to know them. Age by itself does not bring wisdom. Without virtue as a guide, "street smarts" can be mere cleverness. "Wickedness distorts and causes us to be completely mistaken about the fundamental principles of action" (1144a35–6). Like children, one can be virtuous without reason, but this is unstable, ignorant of particulars, and doomed to fail. "Once he acquires intelligence … [it] will become that virtue in the full sense which it previously resembled. … As soon as he possesses this single virtue of *phronesis,* he will also possess all the rest [of the virtues]" (1144b12—14 and 1145a2). The deliberations in Books 1–5 are all *phronesis.*

Sophia involves "both *nous* and *episteme* [self-evident principles and demonstration]. It is science in its consummation, as it were, the science of the things valued most highly" (1141a19–21). "*Sophia* produces happiness, not as medicine produces health, but as health itself makes a person healthy. For since *sophia* is one portion of virtue in its entirety,

---

[37] "The translation 'practical judgment' is chosen here as the best way of conveying Aristotle's central understanding that ethical choices can never be deductions from any rules, principles, or general duties, but always require a weighing of particular circumstances and balancing of conflicting principles in a direct recognition of the mean" (Sachs 210).

possessing and actualizing it makes a man happy, as happiness consists in an activity of virtue" (1144a3—6). As justice culminates all the moral virtues, *sophia* culminates the intellectual virtues.

Intelligence (insight or induction) "apprehends fundamental principles," which are the foundations of science (1141a8). It grasps both the one in the many (universals) and the many in the one (particulars). "Intelligence apprehends the ultimates in both respects—since ultimate [facts] as well as primary definitions are grasped by intelligence and not by reason" (1143a35–1143b5, Loeb). Ross comments, "Induction is for him a process not of reasoning but of direct insight... after experience of a certain number of particular instances, the mind grasps a universal truth which then and afterward is seen to be self-evident."[38] This "self-evident" has the same function as recollection in Plato.

The hero of Books 1–5 is right reason as practical judgment and is often mistaken for the highest wisdom, just as the moral virtues are mistaken as superior to the intellectual ones. Right reason tames the bodily desires and emotions to choose the better course of action, while wisdom lies beyond such desire in the constant pleasure of habitual reason. To grasp and fulfill our nature is true wisdom and happiness. Attaining this is the plot of Books 6–10 with digressions on moral weakness and friendship. With no given *arche,* ethical inquiry proceeds by digressions to bring into focus the whole of human *arete* in the activity of *theoria* (contemplation), uniting desire and pleasure with reason.

In moral weakness (*akrasia*), one knows the right but does the wrong, claiming desire for bodily pleasures or emotions overcame reason. Right reason as guide seems to fail, but it is not desire defeating reason but a following of wrong reason. Appetite ruling reason is an immature condition like a child. The self-indulgent are deformed, choosing desire due to a lack of moral struggle or sense of regret in moral weakness. "The self-indulgent man feels no regret and as a result is incorrigible" (1150a21) and "thinks he ought to pursue desires, while the morally weak thinks he should not" (1152a6). Moral strength and self-control look similar, as "they both do nothing contrary to the dictates of reason under the influence of bodily pleasures" (1151–b35). The morally strong struggle with desire, but the self-controlled "find no pleasure in anything that violates the dictates of reason. A morally strong man... finds pleasure in such,

---

[38] David Ross, *Aristotle* (New York: Barnes and Noble, 1964), pp. 41 and 217.

but he is not driven by them" (1152a1–3). Thus, the morally weak or strong man is attracted by bodily pleasure, while the self-controlled knows true pleasure arises from fulfilling her nature with right reason, making physical pleasures secondary.

The morally weak person's problem is not a failure of knowledge but a compromise of it. Something prevents reason from working. "[Their] condition [is] similar to that of men who are asleep, mad, or drunk. That the words they utter spring from knowledge [of virtue] is no evidence to the contrary.... Beginning students can reel off the words they have heard, but they do not yet know the subject.... We must, therefore, assume that a man who displays moral weakness repeats the language in the same way as an actor speaks his lines" (1147a12–23).

The knowledge of the self-controlled person is the same as the morally strong/weak person in name only. "Moral weakness does not occur in the presence of knowledge in the strict sense, and it is sensory knowledge, not science, which is dragged about by emotion" (1147b15–16). Aristotle confirms both the Socratic maxim that to know the right is to do the right and the common opinion that people do what they think they should not do. In the strict sense, one only errs through ignorance, but in the popular sense, one can say, "I know smoking is bad for me, but I still do it." To know human nature in its wholeness is to respect this integrity, as a healthy person does not mutilate her body.

Moral weakness shows pleasure as the bridge from *phronesis* to *sophia*, distinguishing between physical and mental pleasures. "Even if some pleasures are bad, it does not mean that the highest good cannot be some kind of pleasure, just as the highest good may be some sort of knowledge, even though some kinds of knowledge are bad" (1153b8–9). Bodily pleasures involving appetite and pain are not always good, and their excesses define the self-indulgent person. "A self-controlled person avoids these pleasures. But there are pleasures even for the self-controlled" (1153a34–35). These are the pleasures of the mind. "Neither practical judgment nor any characteristic [virtue] is obstructed by the pleasure arising from it, but only by alien pleasures extraneous to it. The pleasures arising from study and learning will only intensify studying and learning, but not obstruct it" (1153a21–23). These pleasures do not end in pain or weariness or physical limitation. "Pleasant by nature are those things that produce the action of an unimpaired natural state" (1154b20). The exercise of virtue is the way to self-knowledge.

In Plato's *Phaedrus,* Socrates wonders if his soul is simple or complex and then says the true rhetorician knows all souls. Does he know all souls because he has incorporated their complexity or because he grasps his species nature shared by all humans? The same issue arises in this pivotal discussion of pleasure. Since our nature is not simple and complete, we change (actualize) during life. This changes what we find pleasant. If we were simple, the same action would always be most pleasant. "This is why god always enjoys one single and simple pleasure: for there is not only an activity of motion but also an activity of immobility, and pleasure rather consists in rest than in motion" (1154b26–27). If one action fulfilled our nature and could be done continually, then pleasure and happiness would be a way of life.

Philia (friendship) is our last preparation for *theoria*, twice as long as any other *Ethics* topic. Like politics, *philia* first seems relevant but not central. It is one of both the Boy Scouts' twelve laws and Aristotle's twelve virtues, the social concern for others. We are by nature social; our well-being requires associations. *Philia* is broad enough to include most face-to-face relations in a small community. Plato's Socrates calls his interlocutors "friends," which is also our usage. "*Philia* is best summed up in the Greek proverb 'friends hold in common what they have,' . . . (It holds) any association together: the family, the state, a club, a business partnership, or even the relation between a buyer and seller. It . . . gives different people something 'in common'" (Ostwald 214). Sachs adds it is "any association of people who spend time and do things together, share in pains and pleasures, and wish for each other's good. (It is) all love felt and practiced toward family members, fellow countrymen, and generally those like oneself" (Sachs 205).

Aristotle plays language and nature like an accordion, expanding the possible meanings or presences of each word or thing and then squeezing this down to its essence and elements. The Mean is such an essence within a range of behaviors. This approach determines dialectical or best-so-far descriptions, not fixed or absolute essences. Friendship is the drama of this method in our lives with respect to the good. As we mature, we can better see the good in most situations but also distinguish these from the essence of good as a whole. "Now in fact every man does not love what is really good for him, but what appears to him to be good" (1155b26). We need a means for critiquing apparent goods. Sharing goods among friends creates an interest in each other's welfare, like Socrates asking friends to join in his dialectical growth.

A life of virtue involves discovering and fulfilling one's essential nature to attain a life of stable happiness. Created objects get their nature from their creator, but humans were not created. We are an orderly part of an orderly nature and get our nature, our specification, from this participation. Interacting with friends is essential for this progressive discovery and completion of life. "Friends enhance our ability to think and act" (1155a16). His Mean helps identify our essential nature from the distracting extremes, such as brutishness, immaturity, godliness, physical pleasures, and so on. Seeing the extreme relies on much experience and sensitivity to the particulars in any situation. Our close friends are "like us" and, like the lovers in Plato's *Phaedrus,* mirror our condition, our habits, and character. We can see where we stand by observing their behavior and success, which reflect our own (1169b33). As we also more easily see our friends as wholes, we can observe their progress toward becoming a judicious person. As in *Phaedrus,* we are attracted by the good in our close friends and try to make it more explicit and stable. By identifying with them, we also see this good in us.

Friendships are defined by their types of affection: love of the good, the pleasant, or the useful. In the less exact sciences like ethics, we work from the pieces (often mistaken for the whole) to the whole, from opinions' partial truths to the synoptic view, placing these in a more rational structure. *Philia* is such a case. It unites all three in the strict sense, as the good is also pleasant and useful. *Philia* sharing only the pleasant or useful is defective, not sharing all things in common. These partial relations are *philia* only by analogy to the full and could evolve into full sharing of one's good. "Good men alone can be friends (based on) what they are, for bad people do not find joy in one another, unless they see some material advantage..." (1157a18–19).

Humans require *philia* to mature, to expand beyond the narrow self-interests of the desiring soul and find common interests in the activities of the rational. Here giving and receiving are the same, as the highest rational aspect is common to all, promoting growth toward wholeness. It responds to the issue of our nature in the *Republic's* Ring of Gyges, where invisibility leads to predatory behavior. "When people are friends on the basis of virtue, they are eager to do good to one another, since that is the mark of excellence as well as friendship.... If a person gives more than he receives, he will have no complaints against his friend, since he accomplishes what he set out to do; for each one desires what is good" (1162b6–13). This "big self" is shown by parents toward children. In sharing all things, giving and receiving merge.

Being a good friend helps us be a friend of the good, finding more in the soul than just appetites. Finding the good in us, we become lovable to ourselves. Self-love is the basis for friendship, containing all its elements. A good man has feelings of friendship toward himself; is consistent in judgment and desires; pursues what is good for the sake of his intellect, which "constitutes what each person really is"; enjoys his life and wants it to continue; enjoys spending time with himself; hides neither sorrows nor pleasures. "He knows no regrets" and treats his friend as himself "for his friend really is another self" (1166a10–30).

Good-less people have all the reverse and cannot be their own friend. The good is naturally in things; it is stable. "Intelligence always chooses what is best for itself, and a good man always obeys his intelligence" (1169a17). The bad person mistakes the good and is lost in a world of flux and frustrated hopes. What they desire and do constantly changes; they lack any basis to value their own life. Driven by desires, their "soul is divided against itself," feeling both sorrow and pleasure at the same time. They are full of regret (1166b5–24). They are haunted by memories and do not want to be alone. Not being lovable, they do not do good for themselves. "Good men neither go wrong themselves nor let their friends. Bad people . . . [lack] the element of constancy, for they do not remain similar even to themselves" (1159b6–8).

Friends want to live together, which is "the surest indication of friendship" (1171a2). Time spent with friends nourishes our best part, the rational soul.[39] "Living together means sharing each other's words and thoughts; it does not mean feeding in the same place as it does for cattle" (1170b12 and 14). Living together is sharing each other's company. "Some friends drink or play dice . . . go in for sports or hunt together, or join in the activity of philosophy; whatever each group of people loves most in life, they spend their days together doing" (1172a3–6). "Nothing characterizes friends as much as living in each other's company. [This is] wanted even by men who are supremely happy, for they are the least suited to live in isolation" (1157b19–22).

For a naturalist, one meaning of goodness is existence itself. If something is, it has something good about it. "Life is in itself good and pleasant. We can see this from the fact that everyone desires it, especially good and supremely happy men" (1170b26). "To perceive

---

[39] Again Plato's problem of how to nourish the soul in the *Phaedrus:* the gods get metaphysical true ideas, humans get friends and lovers.

that we are living is something pleasant in itself for existence is by nature good" (1170b1). If life is good, more life is better. The *spoudaios,* whose Goldilocks approach to life might seem timid, reveals himself to be an Achilles-like hero, for he "would rather choose to experience intense pleasure for a short time than mild pleasure for a long time; he would rather live nobly for one full year than lead an indifferent existence for many; and he would rather perform one great and beautiful act than many insignificant ones... He chooses nobility (beauty) at the cost of everything else"[40] (1169a22–25 and 32).

The *Ethics* ends as it opens, discussing the good, pleasure, happiness, and politics. Which goods provide the best pleasures leading to lasting happiness, and what educational and social preparation gives us access to this knowledge? First he reexamines pleasure. "There is no pleasure without activity, and every activity is completed by pleasure" (1175a20). Pleasure arises from full actualization, as "a completeness that superimposes itself upon it, like the bloom of youth in those who are in their prime" (1174b33–34). An experienced guide helps. "In all matters of this sort we consider that to be real that seems so to a *spoudaios*... If virtue and the good man, insofar as he is good, are the measure of each thing, then what seems to him to be pleasures are pleasures and what he enjoys is pleasant.[41] ... Those pleasures that complete the activity of a perfect or complete and supremely happy man can be called in the true sense the pleasures proper to man" (1176a16–26).

True pleasure is the completion experienced in the peak performing of the most rational human activity, *theoria,* a sight term like *oida* (know/see, root of idea/form) that unites physical and mental vision. "Contemplation" is the usual translation, a mental vision able to go on endlessly, even in the dreams of the judicious. Pleasure requires continuous peaking, but in most situations we tire and "are incapable of continuous activity" (1175a4). *Theoria* is "self-sufficiency, leisure, and as much freedom from fatigue as a human being can have" (1177b22). Here alone rational activity is fully active. It knows the *archai* and demonstrations in the sciences, sees the whole of all

---

[40] Achilles chooses a short but brilliant career in *Iliad* IX 410–416 but changes his mind in Hades, preferring a slave's life. *Ody.,* XI 488–91.

[41] Here he is responding to Protagoras's "man is the measure of all things." Humans do measure all things in deliberating and making choices. The judicious person is the whole measure; some lives are better than others.

things and how each is related to the other, and becomes completely satisfied. It has no desire toward this vision, even for it to continue, as sense of space and time diminish and we enter a divine-like condition. "We assume the gods are in the highest degree blessed and happy. But what kind of actions are we to attribute to them?" Ordinary human action is "petty and unworthy of the gods" (1178b9–10 and 17). "Deprived of acting, and still more of making anything, what remains except contemplation?" (Sachs 1178b20–21). "Thus the gods' activity which surpasses all others in bliss must be contemplation, and the human activity most akin to it is therefore most conducive to happiness" (1178b22–23).[42]

He needs to give multiple arguments for the superiority of *theoria* because a demonstration is not possible. He is not optimistic about the results of his effort. "*Logoi* evidently do have a power to encourage and stimulate young men of generous mind, . . . well-born and truly enamored of what is noble to be possessed by virtue; they [cannot] turn the common run of people to goodness and nobility, [as] drawing fine distinctions is not the strong point of most people" (1179b6–11 and 1172b4). On Meno's query if virtue arises from breeding, teaching or habit, Aristotle finds breeding is out of our power, teaching works only if "the soul of the listener [is] first conditioned by habits" (1179b25), and forming habits is the goal of the law and politics. "A man who wants to make others better [must] learn something about legislation" (1180b23). Ethics needs politics to organize the development of reason, enabling effective choice and a stable society where reason can be applied. "The law does have the power to compel, being the rule of reason derived from some sort of practical judgment and intelligence" (1180a21–22).

John Dewey said major problems are not so much resolved as dissolved. We have seen Aristotle in the *Ethics* work through an issue until it disappears in a larger perspective or becomes an ongoing problem in a larger context. With each new view, he announces that now we can again begin. It is only fitting that he ends the *Ethics* ready to further the inquiry in a new start, "So let us begin our discussion" (1181a23).

---

[42] Aristotle's gods exist to inspire the celestial bodies to move in their circles. We desire to be divine to gain their happiness; thus, offering a divine life is a strong rhetorical strategy. They operate here like an ideal, the highest human conception of a thing, whether it exists or not.

AN ARISTOTLE SURVIVAL KIT:
TEN THINGS TO KEEP IN MIND
WHEN READING

1. He is a **rhetorical** master. He spent his life studying and practicing both sides of arguments. He uses language precisely but also for persuasion. Dialectic carries the argument within a science, but rhetoric informs his many discussions about the sciences and arts. He exposes the equivocal aspects of language to reduce its instability.

2. He is a **systematic** thinker, which does not mean knowing the final system. "If later and lesser thinkers, by attributing to his doctrines a finality which they did not deserve, hindered rather than helped the advance of knowledge, it is surely unfair to hold Aristotle himself responsible."[43] Humans are by nature rational and systematizers. We seek order to make our lives more stable. Limited in time and space, we cannot experience directly the order of the universe or our own natures. He promotes inquiry and discourse by organizing observations, experiences, and ideas and by regularizing vocabulary. He believes the world is orderly but doubts we can comprehend it. His knowledge resembles Socrates' hypotheses: the best current idea but always fallible. While the bodiless gods express their wholeness doing eternal logic problems, we find satisfaction in inquiry, in being systematic.

3. Aristotle is **thinking** in his writing, not merely elaborating the ultimate truth. Responding like Plato to Socrates' claim that philosophy cannot be written, he develops a living, thinking writing. He works through problems, involving us in the array of issues and alternate solutions. He wrote dialogues for many years and continues this drama of ideas in his treatises, moving from presumed knowledge to criticism to revision, and so on. What he criticizes from one view, he may later support from another, as with a common sense versus an educated view.

4. Thinking is a potential we actualize both over our lifetime and within an argument. As it becomes more comprehensive, we need to review what was inadequately viewed before. This

---

[43] W. S. Hett, *Aristotle*, vol. VIII in Loeb (Cambridge, MA: Harvard University Press, 1975), p. 393.

reviewing proceeds from the new understanding, the *arche* or **starting point** that initiated the inquiry. Because Aristotle begins in the middle of things, he often requires a series of new *archai* before he achieves the adequacy he desires. An earlier *arche* may be less complete than a later one.

5. Aristotle is a **naturalist**, committed to examining the things of the world as they are and taking these as a standard. His perspective of nature is from within each object or science, just as the forms that define a thing are within it and do not exist separately. Whatever is, is explicable in the present environment. "Nature never makes anything in vain" means there is an account for the way things are—but not a prescription. He personifies Nature as a godlike force, suggesting supernatural knowledge, but this is only the mediating religious imagery seen previously.

6. He often uses **historical material** not for the purposes of history but to orient us for understanding his argument. He needs to address the assumptions of his audience about these previous events, thinkers, and ideas. This is a rhetorical situation, and he shapes the debate toward his solutions. He is more factual in discussing historical events, as in the *Politics,* than with the philosophical ideas of his predecessors.

7. **Every experience and opinion contains some truth**. Popular opinions, beliefs of common sense, and constructions in language or political constitutions or ideas of goodness, all can serve as starting points of inquiry. In inquiry, truth advances from faint sketches to firmer outlines but rarely attains a complete portrait.

8. The genius of inquiry is to see how things compare—the similarities and differences. The genius of sophistry is to manipulate these. **Making proper distinctions** is the heart of Aristotle's systematizing. One must follow carefully what is being differentiated and how. He teaches us to ask, "According to what?" Things differ if seen as actual or potential, part or whole. Justice "in the strict sense" is all of virtue but in common sense is the specific virtue of due proportion. He can make opposites similar, differing only in degree of a quality, or oppose similar things by revealing their essential difference.

9. "*Men ... de*" means "on the one hand ... and on the other," meaning that there are two ways to view something and both

must be considered. Aristotle spent his life making and criticizing arguments on **both sides of an issue**. He often uses this to reveal complexity where previous thinkers found simplicity and to find a distinction to serve his purposes. Looking at both sides can either minimize or maximize differences. It pleases the audience by giving a feeling of comprehensiveness.

10. Finally, Aristotle continues Plato's **antidualism.** Earlier thinkers organized experience using opposites, as Pythagoras's table of opposites. Plato and Aristotle believed these were only in our thinking and not in the world. Aristotle resolved dualisms in two main ways: moderation pulling them back into the Mean and mediation showing they are really inseparable, as in ethics and politics, form and matter, soul and body, theory and practice. For extremes of vice or of oligarchy and democracy, each has a Mean that resolves the opposition.

Epilogue

Greek Philosophy after Aristotle

"From the first Stoic to the last Neoplatonist, there is no essentially new principle added to philosophy . . . (inquiry turns inward and this) subjectivism ends naturally in skepticism, the denial of all knowledge and the rejection of all philosophy."[1] Many share Stace's opinion that later Greek philosophy becomes defensive and seems to lose its creative impulse in the dogmatic schools of the Stoics and Epicureans and their Skeptic critics. Inquiry seems to stagnate in the Hellenistic world created by Alexander's conquests and continued after the Roman conquests two centuries later. The Greeks lost their political independence, but their language and culture dominated the eastern Mediterranean and captivated the later Romans. Indeed, three Romans give us the most complete Hellenistic texts, the Stoics Marcus Aurelius and Epictetus, and the Epicurean Lucretius. Yet for all the influence these schools had in Roman culture, they seem self-absorbed and narrow compared with the grand visions of Plato and Aristotle, visions helpfully supported by the survival of their texts. The apparent move from outer dialogue to inner dogmatism in these schools is also reflected in the increasingly prominent Mystery

---

[1] W. Stace, *A Critical History of Greek Philosophy* (New York: St Martin's Press, 1962), p. 343.

religions, culminating in Christianity. Reason as a guide to living well seems to be in trouble.

Evaluating Hellenistic philosophy is difficult, as few original documents survive and testimony is clouded by polemics both ancient and modern, like Stace's facile dismissal. After the bright lights and big pictures of Plato and Aristotle, these schools seem very modest, yet they had a strong influence for over three centuries and continued working until their "pagan" ideas were closed down by the Emperor Justinian in AD 529. In these last few pages I will give a summary of their main ideas and some suggestions for how inquiry continues, especially in their critiques of each other. It is helpful to read critics who try to reconstruct their reasoning, like Long and Sedley or Irwin, explaining how they could believe things that seem so strange today.

Socrates' intentions in his inquiry is the issue over which the schools divided. Were his daily discussions seeking confirmation or revelation, or were they more of a fitness exercise. As Meno asked about virtue arising from birth, exercise, or learning, was Socrates most concerned with discovering his own nature, exercising his reason, or developing a new view of the world? The Skeptics discover that nature, including ours, is unknowable; the Stoics practice that our preferences are ultimately irrelevant; and the Epicureans learn that all things are transient clusters of atoms. Each leads to the same goal: peace of mind by a calming of fears, hopes, and desires, specifically the desire to know, the hope of personal success, and the fear of death. For Plato and Aristotle (P&A),[2] Socrates equally desired excellence and knowledge while being conscious of his mortal limits. The tension of this unity creates the possibility of inquiry in their work, being both dynamic and orderly, progressively systematizing but not dogmatic, expressed in their uniting such potential dualisms as form–matter, body–soul, human–divine, and so on.

Other contemporary Socratic progeny carried forward a very different lesson, an anti-intellectualism that brought them closer to the Sophists, even to the point of charging for their classes. "Teaching, discussion, and demonstration gave way to suggestion, persuasion through rhetoric and reliance on direct, personal impression."[3] Our knowledge of these teachers is sketchy, but their opposition to P&A is

---

[2] The use of such initials is pleasing neither to the sense nor the mind but does save space, which is here a necessity.

[3] E. Brehier, *The Hellenistic and Roman Age* (Chicago: U. Chicago Press, 1965), p. 2.

clear and shows the Athenian philosophic community as more diverse than we sometimes think. There were three main but short-lived mid-fourth-century schools: Megarians, Cyreniacs, and Cynics. All reduced the field for discussion. Megarians argued against the ability of an idea or ideal to represent a thing, logical distinctions such as degrees of difference, and the principle of noncontradiction. Like Socrates in the *Phaedo,* they reject nature study to better study man. Thus, the practical study of rhetoric is preferred to the never-ending discussions of philosophy. Their students avoided science, math, and music. The Cyreniacs focused on basic sensory facts instead of rational constructs and on happiness as the flow of pleasure (Gr. *hedone*) rather than the fixity of ideas. As feeling pleasure is their only good, so impressions are the basis of knowledge, denying any shared experience.

The Cynics (*Kunos* = dog) were the most colorful and famous of this group, the anarchists and Taoists who promoted self-sufficiency (*autarkeia*), cosmopolitanism, and asceticism, along with a deep distrust of social convention, intellectual learning, and physical comfort. They may have been called dogs either for their naturalist opposition to convention or for their adamancy in guarding wisdom.[4] They rejected both the Sophists' political scheming and philosophers' use of reason to organize experience. Reason is good only for rejecting false opinions, not making true ones. The first Cynic, Diogenes of Sinope, came to Athens at age 60 and taught for thirty years during the death of the *polis* and between the deaths of P&A. He was known for going without shelter or much clothing or food. His use of reason only to reject itself resembles the Parmenidean freezing of logic into the One. He opposed all order: political, moral, or logical. These deconstructionist tendencies did not lend themselves to a well-defined school, yet their activities continued up to the sixth-century-AD closing of the schools.

Socrates was a hero for these other Socratic schools, not for his omnivorous inquiry but as a wise man seeking the best way to live. The post-Aristotelians (PA) continued this pursuit of Socrates as sage, like Aristotle's *spoudaios* man of virtue, or as quietist, like Plato's *sophos* in the *Republic* seeking shelter from political storms. They still profess an interest in logic and nature but subordinate both to ethics, which

---

[4] "The medieval Dominicans punned similarly on their name calling themselves the 'watchdogs of the Lord.'" J. Owens, *History of Ancient Western Philosophy* (Englewood Cliffs, NJ: Prentice-Hall, 1959), p. 366.

now comes to mean for Cynics, Skeptics, Stoics, and Epicureans, respectively, a life without illusions, mistakes, disturbances, or pains.

The PAs continue the earlier Socratics' anti-intellectual elements but in a context of intense argument and intellectual creativity. All seek to free us from the troubles of independent thinking and examine nature and logic only to get beyond them. Epicureans are interested in the atomic structure of nature only to validate sense experience and deny any permanent constructs, like an immortal soul. These sense experiences then guide us to a life of quietism in our effort to avoid pain. Stoics seek to reveal divine reason in nature and then merge into this order of the universe and away from frustrating personal preferences. The Skeptic's experience of (and insistence upon) all arguments having two sides prepares him for accepting indifference toward all argument and belief. All of these goals find peace of mind by thinking one's self out of thinking. P&A seek moments of *theoria* arising out of the practice of dialectic, while the PAs want to be impassive, undisturbed, self-sufficient (but no Self), and indifferent (*apathia, ataraxia, autarkia, adiaphoros*). They lack the *eros* of the spirited youth that Socrates says is a prerequisite for pursuing philosophy. Some like Vlastos and Nussbaum have observed that Socrates' *eros* also can be cool and ironic, using the young men but not really needing them.[5] This Socrates is the model for the Stoic sage, a man of pure reason and beyond all desire. P&A think philosophy can only exist through the desire to know, while the PAs believe the end of philosophy must be beyond all desire.

The Skeptics, while less eristic than Cynics, also believed that knowledge was impossible.[6] Pyrrho (365–275) was their founding sage. Like Socrates, he wrote nothing and lived an exemplary moral life.

He thought the basic instability of nature made our opinions and ideas irrelevant—neither true or false. If there is no difference between true and false, then we should let go of making judgments (Gk. *epoche*) and find peace from their disagreements. His followers were not concerned with physics or logic and criticized the Stoics and Epicureans for the weakness of their arguments in these areas.

---

[5] M. Nussbaum, "The Chill of Virtue," Review of G. Vlastos, *Socrates, Ironist & Moral Philosopher* (New Republic, 9–16 and 23, 1991), pp. 34–40.

[6] The Skeptic (examine) name was not used until the mid-first century AD. Earlier they were called aporetics (impasse), ephetics (epoche—suspension of judgment), or zetetics (seekers—of the truth).

Skeptics had the fewest assumptions and broadest criticism. Under Arcesilaus in the third century and Carneades in the second century, Plato's Academy returned to its aporetic roots and became a center of skeptic activity, leading the fight against the Stoics. Cicero and Sextus Empiricus were later Roman Skeptics.

Epicureans are the less complex of the two main schools. Epicurus defined most of the main principles, leaving little for followers to develop. He borrowed Democritean atomism for his physics and from this derived his "all sense impressions are true" epistemology. Illusions, such as a stick looking bent in water, are due to judgment, not sight. Intuition (noninvalidation) convinces us about nonsensory reality, like atoms. As there are only atoms and void, all that is (including ideas) are merely temporary joinings of atoms. Atoms join when they spontaneously swerve, not due to any necessity. There are an infinitude of atoms, thus an infinitude of joinings, including many universes both like and unlike ours. As sensation dies with the body, there can be no experience of death or after-death. Thus, death is nothing to fear. Since all of our experience is based on sensation, good sensations will make a good life. Thus, he seeks pleasure (*hedone*), or more exactly, he avoids pain, and virtues are behaviors that help him accomplish this. Gods, being completely happy, cannot be in any way involved with the world.

The Stoics are more complex both in length and depth: more thinkers on more topics. Epicureans tried to negate the illusions that arise due to not understanding the atomic structure of reality, while the Stoic orientation was engagement in the world (facts) in order to better understand and thus become one with its reason. Theirs is a way of affirmation with reason (reality, god, Zeus) present in all things at all times. Thus, all facts lead to Reason. Facts just are and must be, yet we assent to them in order to practice reason and train our free will. Stoics are in the world but not of it, desiring the whole of which any moment is just a reflection. Thus, they accumulate but not to possess. Their logic is inductive, their physics a divine materialism (*logos*), and their ethics a selfless rationalism. Virtue alone is good, and reason alone is virtuous. As rational, this is the best of all possible worlds, with no evil in it.[7] Thus, Stoics value stability and often the status quo. Active matter (*pneuma,* breath) penetrates all matter and rationalizes it. All events (including thought) are

---

[7] The counterarguments anticipate Voltaire's *Candide*.

determined by reason and recur exactly in an endless cycle. They take the religious image from Heraclitus that from fire come all things, which then return to fire. Human life is insignificant except as part of this process.

A significant question to face is this: Why do we consider Plato and Aristotle to be the Greek philosophers most worth discussing instead of the Stoics and Epicureans who held center stage for over five centuries? It seems only a few historical accidents keep us from still being caught up in the three-way polemics in which the Stoics and Epicureans each tried to show their superiority, while the Skeptics showed why neither of them were. The fall of pluralistic Rome, which enjoyed the debates, and the rise of Christianity with its need for a more sophisticated theology that it borrowed from Neoplatonism (and much later added Aristotle when his writings returned to Europe via Arabic scholars), pushed the PAs out of the mainstream. Their weak notion of the gods as immanent or impotent, the simple materialism of their physics, their willingness to live with paradox and rhetoric, and most of all, their later sclerosis, the loss of the ability to adjust their arguments to their opponents and circumstances, finally caught up to them. They had a long run, and their appeal continues to instruct us.

Further Reading

Collections of the original writings:

Barnes, J., ed., *The Complete Works of Aristotle*, Princeton, NJ: Princeton University Press, 1984.

Cooper, J., ed., *Plato Complete Works*, Indianapolis, IN: Hackett, 1997.

Kirk, G. S., Raven, J. E., and Schofield, S., eds., *The Presocratic Philosophers*, 2nd ed., Cambridge, England: Cambridge University Press, 1983.

Loeb Classical Library, Greek and English bilingual editions of all Greek texts, Harvard University Press.

Long, A. A., and Sedley, D. N., eds., *The Hellenistic Philosophers*, Cambridge, England: Cambridge University Press, 1987.

The Cambridge University Press "Companion to" Series has both a variety of essays and an extensive bibliography in each volume:

Cambridge History of Hellenistic Philosophy, Algra et al., eds., 2005.

To Aristotle, J. Barnes, ed., 1995.

To Early Greek Philosophy, A.A. Long, ed., 1999.

To Greek and Roman Philosophy, D. Sedley, ed., 2003—general.

To Plato, R. Kraut, ed., 1992, with Socrates and culture bibliography.

To Stoics, B. Inwood, ed., 2003.

Understanding a thinker is always open to revision, so it is best to get several points of view among critics. Much can be learned from people we disagree with. Plato often says Socrates stirs up (Gk. *kinew*) others, and the following are some favorite movers and shakers on the Greeks:

Benson, H., *Essays on the Philosophy of Socrates*, Oxford, England: Oxford University Press, 1992.

Cherniss, H., *The Riddle of the Early Academy*, New York: Garland, 1980.

Dodds, E. R., *The Greeks and the Irrational*, Berkeley: University of California, 1951.

Friedlander, P., *Plato: An Introduction*, New York: Harper & Row, 1958.

Irwin, T., *Classical Thought*, Oxford, England: Oxford University Press, 1989.

Kerford, G. B., *The Sophistic Movement*, Cambridge, England: Cambridge University Press, 1981.

Nietzsche, F., *Philosophy in the Tragic Age of the Greeks*, Chicago: Gateway, 1962.

Randall, J. H., *Aristotle*, New York: Columbia University Press, 1960.

Randall, J. H., *Plato: Dramatist of the Life of Reason*, New York: Columbia University Press, 1970.

Roochnik, D., *The Tragedy of Reason*, New York: Routledge, 1990.

Solmsen, F., *Intellectual Experiments of the Greek Enlightenment*, Princeton, NJ: Princeton University Press, 1975.

Index

INDEX

Thucydides, 21
Timaeus, 155
Tredennick, H., 156, 158
Trojan War, 10

Universe
basic stuff of, 25
composition, 2

Versenyi, 99
Vestusta Placita, 5
Vlastos, Gregory, 100
Voltaire, 26

water, 28, 32
Wisdom, 102
Works and Days, 24

Xenophanes, 2, 16, 33–36
irony works, 36
on divine and all beings, basic
nature, 33
on skepticism, 35
on stuff of god, 33–34
Xenophon, 5
memoirs of Socrates, 90,
93–94

Zeno, 62–64
on dialectics, 62
on space and time, 63–64
paradoxes of motion, 63
infinity, 63
Parmenidean logic of, 63
Zeus, 14